D1553595

Massachusetts

Patricia Harris, David Lyon, Anna Mundow, Lisa Oppenheimer
Photography by James Marshall

COMPASS AMERICAN GUIDES
An imprint of Fodor's Travel Publications

Compass American Guides: Massachusetts

Editor: Paula Consolo
Designer: Tina Malaney
Compass Editorial Director: Daniel Mangin
Editorial Production: David Downing
Photo Editor: Jolie Novak
Archival Research: Melanie Marin
Map Design: Mark Stroud, Moon Street Cartography

Cover photo, James Marshall: Colonel Ashley House, Berkshire County

First Edition
ISBN 0-676-90493-9
ISSN 1542–3441

Compass American Guides
1745 Broadway, New York, NY 10019

PRINTED IN SINGAPORE

10 9 8 7 6 5 4 3 2 1

If you could only see
I know you would agree
There ain't nowhere else to be
But Massachusetts.

Arlo Guthrie

C O N T E N T S

Maps

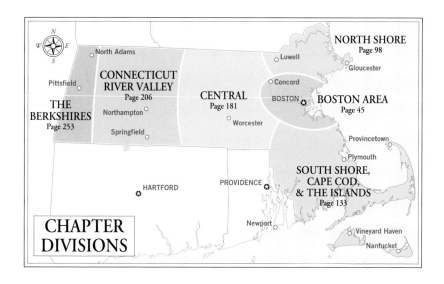

NORTH SHORE
Page 98

Gloucester

CONNECTICUT
RIVER VALLEY
Page 206

CENTRAL
Page 181

BOSTON

BOSTON AREA
Page 45

THE
BERKSHIRES
Page 253

Northampton

Springfield

Worcester

Provincetown

Plymouth

SOUTH SHORE,
CAPE COD,
& THE ISLANDS
Page 133

HARTFORD

PROVIDENCE

Newport

Vineyard Haven

Nantucket

North Adams

Pittsfield

Lowell

Concord

**CHAPTER
DIVISIONS**

Literary Extracts

Topical Essays and Sidebars

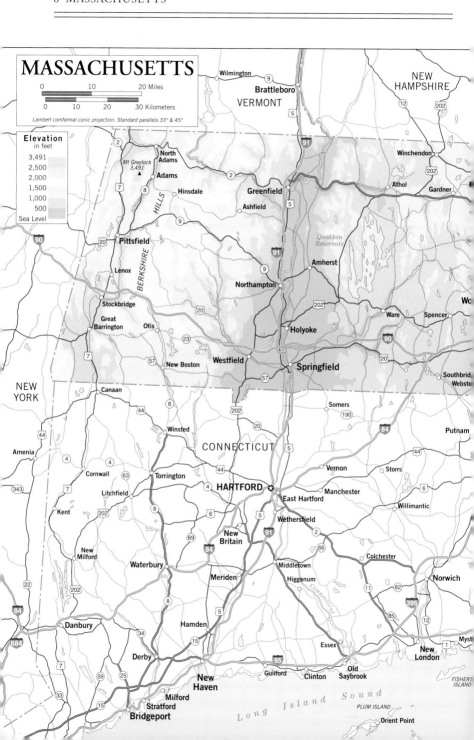

MASSACHUSETTS

0   10   20 Miles

0   10   20   30 Kilometers

Lambert comformal conic projection. Standard parallels 33° & 45°

Elevation
in feet

3,491
2,500
2,000
1,500
1,000
500
Sea Level

Mt Greylock
3,491
▲

MASSACHUSETTS FACTS

Nicknames: Bay State, Puritan State, Pilgrim State
Capital: Boston
State motto: "By the sword we seek peace, but peace only under liberty."
State flower: Mayflower
State tree: American elm
State dog: Boston terrier
State cat: Tabby
State bird: Chickadee
State drink: Cranberry juice
State song: "All Hail to Massachusetts," by Arthur J. Marsh
Entered the Union: February 6, 1788 (the sixth state to do so)
Miles of highway: 34,725

■ POPULATION 6,349,097 (2000 U.S. CENSUS)

FIVE LARGEST CITIES BY POPULATION

Boston:	589,141
Worcester:	172,648
Springfield:	152,082
Lowell:	105,167
Cambridge:	101,355

■ GEOGRAPHY AND CLIMATE

With 10,555 square miles of land and water, Massachusetts is the 45th-largest state.
Highest point: Mount Greylock, 3,491 feet
Lowest point: Atlantic coastline, sea level
Water: The state has 4,230 miles of rivers and more than 1,100 lakes and ponds.
Highest recorded temperature: 107° F, recorded at Chester on August 2, 1975
Lowest recorded temperature: −35 ° F, recorded at Chester on January 12, 1981
Key Industries: Biotechnology, computer software development, electronics, education and research, environmental technology, financial services, health services, medical technology, telecommunications, textiles, tourism

A cranberry harvest in the Plymouth area.

■ Interesting Facts

- Massachusetts has 65 public and private colleges and universities, including Harvard, the Massachusetts Institute of Technology (MIT), Tufts University, Boston University, Boston College, Smith College, Williams College, and the University of Massachusetts.
- The median age in Massachusetts is 36.
- More than half of the state's population lives in the greater Boston area.
- More than 25,000 residents work in state-based biotechnology firms.
- The sports of basketball and volleyball (first known as "mintonette") were invented in Massachusetts in the 1890s.
- Bay Staters over age 25 with a bachelor's degree or higher: 33.2%
- Home ownership rate in 2000: 61.7%
- Norfolk County, which includes Boston, is the birthplace of four U.S. presidents: John Adams, John Quincy Adams, John F. Kennedy, and George Herbert Walker Bush.

INTRODUCTION

High atop Beacon Hill in Boston, the golden dome of the State House catches the sun's first rays. When the physician and author Oliver Wendell Holmes declared in 1858 that the building was the hub of the solar system, the garrulous "Autocrat of the Breakfast Table" was indulging in his usual hyperbole. But Bostonians had a habit of such non-Copernican thinking, placing themselves at the center of everything—first in history, first in education, first in innovation.

Not having won a World Series for the better part of a century, modern Bostonians are a tad more humble about their place in the universe, if just as proud of their city. Wind through the Colonial alleyways of the North End to visit Old North Church, and you're likely to encounter a neighborhood resident who will tell you to stop at Bova's Bakery because the bread just came out of the oven, or steer you down to the Langone playground for a lively game of bocce. Window-shop along the broad boulevards of Back Bay, and someone might point to the New England Life building, where dioramas show Back Bay when it really was a bay. Wander the glass canyons of the Financial District and you could find yourself having lunch with a stockbroker under the pergola at Post Office Square Park, surrounded by monumental art deco skyscrapers.

The State House might not be the center of the solar system, but it is undeniably the hub of the Massachusetts roadways—Mile Zero, from which the calculus of Bay State cartography inevitably commences. Many roads radiate from the Hub, and each quickly becomes its own path. Massachusetts, as it turns out, is a state of coexisting possibilities, or, as the constitution calls it, a true commonwealth.

Follow the maritime route through the Pilgrim towns of the South Shore down to the long arm of Cape Cod with its come-hither finger of Provincetown. At the Homeric rosy-fingered dawn, weary Portuguese fishermen haul their nets into Virgin-Mary-blue fishing boats just offshore while the last "P'town" revelers stumble toward bed. Around to the east, on the Cape's forearm, surf pounds relentlessly on the long sandy strands of the Cape Cod National Seashore.

If you head west down the trail of Revolutionary War skirmishes and through the fevered transcendental woods of Emerson and Thoreau, you will suddenly enter the open hilltops of apple country, where America's first fruit bowl gave birth

The Ayer Mill in Lawrence was one of New England's largest textile mills.

to Johnny Appleseed, and Colonial-era orchards still produce the lion's share of the Bay State apple crop. Tripping through the little postindustrial towns of central Massachusetts, you'll discover yourself on one of America's first "scenic highways," the old Indian trade route known as the Mohawk Trail. You can almost picture families creeping along through the foliage in Nash Ramblers as the little ones ask, "Are we there yet?" You're not—until you spin through the aptly named Hairpin Turn and down into North Adams, an erstwhile 19th-century mill town busily reinventing itself as a post-millennial hotbed of hipster art. Turn south through long vistas of dairy pasture and suddenly you will be transported into the Berkshires, where the spreading lawns of Tanglewood huddle in the valley at Lenox and dancers soar at mountaintop Jacob's Pillow in Becket.

Drive northwest from Boston, straight as the old industrial canal, to Lowell, first of the mechanized miracles on the Merrimack River. Here farmers' daughters were transformed into factory laborers until they had the audacity—nearly a century later and farther downstream—to launch the American labor movement. Follow the footsteps of Jack Kerouac through Lowell's haunted canals and beat streets, remembering Jack's childhood dreams of Dr. Sax's dark music amid the mills. Leave a token on his grave at Edson Cemetery. When hunger strikes, you can eat with the newest generation of immigrants in a little shop making spicy bowls of Vietnamese *pho* (noodle soup) or plates of wide rice noodles with scallions, egg, and shrimp.

Creep north along the coast to the granite jaw of Cape Ann, thrust defiantly into the dark Atlantic. The huge trawlers are drawn up for repair at Gloucester Marine Railway, a reminder that even though the sea has claimed 10,000 Cape Ann fishermen, they still venture out to the Grand Banks and outer shoals to haul their lines. At Gloucester's Rocky Neck and north in Rockport harbor, men and women in paint-daubed smocks wax eloquent about the light, coaxing you into their geranium-festooned galleries to share a vision still wet on the canvas. It's true: Cape Ann seems lit with an internal glow, luminous as sunset clouds, glinting as distant whitecaps. Follow the road around to the fertile green marshes of Ipswich, where "Chubby" Woodman first breaded and fried a clam in 1916 and where his descendants still cook the fried clams by which all others are judged. Keep winding north, with the sea on your right, into foursquare Newburyport, where the downtown is as quaint and civil as the village's name, the outskirts as wild and windswept as the Plum Island dunes, where piping plovers nest and ospreys wheel and dive against a mackerel sky.

Steer your way along the Connecticut Valley's River Road, where the fields shout "harvest!" from 10,000 years of topsoil and the weathered tobacco barns spread their brown-board wings like a dragonfly emerging from its chrysalis. Wave to the tractor driver when he pulls over to let you by. Pausing in Northampton, sip a cafe latte (organic milk and fair-traded coffee, of course) served by a sardonic waiter with a thing for Kierkegaard and one semester to go for his doctorate at UMass. Whir through Kerouac's "Great American Night" to the clean, well-lighted space of a Worcester diner, where the waitress with tragic eyes demands to know how you want your eggs, hon', and is that milk or cream with the coffee?

Back in 1937, anonymous scribes of the Federal Writers Project penned the landmark overview of the state, *Massachusetts: A Guide to Its Places and People,* offering what one wag entitled "Enough of its History to Explain its People." Perhaps it is worth turning the idea on its head. See the state—from its bumpy western mountains to its looming Cape Cod dunes—and stop to chat with the characters who inhabit the landscape. It's a truism that Massachusetts has forgotten more history than most states can claim, but somehow the past means more in present tense. Use this book as a guide to the state, and do not hesitate to look at monuments and Federal homes, sailing ships and Pilgrim gristmills. But stop, too, to converse with whomever you encounter, aiming to get from Massachusetts enough of its people to explain its past.

—Patricia Harris and David Lyon

From the beach, the lighthouse at Truro appears to peek over the Cape Cod dunes.

H I S T O R Y

Long before Massachusetts became the Cradle of Liberty, the state was a forested territory coveted for its proximity to water. Its natural resources were appreciated by native peoples and by the European settlers, who founded communities along what are now Cape Cod, Boston Harbor, and the North Shore. Over the years, inland areas have undergone a population explosion, and acres of Colonial forest have been transformed into rambling suburban developments. At the same time, forests that had been clear-cut two centuries ago to create farms have been allowed to regenerate, resulting in a patchwork of woodland divided by old stone walls.

The profile of the Commonwealth has changed as dramatically as the landscape itself. That Massachusetts was once a bastion of Puritan rule might seem paradoxical given the state's current reputation for liberal-minded thinking, but the area has long courted the independent-minded. It was, after all, the Pilgrims escaping British rule who defied the crown to the point that their charter was revoked. And it was here that similarly enlightened patriots began heating up the brew that would turn into the Revolution. Years later, entrepreneurs such as Francis Cabot Lowell sparked a revolution of an industrial sort, and people such as Henry Lloyd Garrison, Ralph Waldo Emerson, Julia Ward Howe, Henry David Thoreau, and Isabella Stewart Gardner started or became involved in movements that included abolitionism, transcendentalism, women's rights, environmentalism, and the arts and culture. Meanwhile, the activities of those aforementioned patriots have generated a thriving tourism industry. That the state's residents continue to reconceive their physical and psychic worlds was never more evident then in the mid-to-late 20th century, when New England's industrial base unraveled. The transition from manufacturing to technology was hardly seamless, but the citizenry exhibited the same sort of pluck their patriotic forebears had.

Some things, of course, have remained unchanged. Massachusetts's status as an intellectual center has been enhanced in the modern era by the presence of some of the world's finest institutions of higher education. Politics has remained in the forefront, most notably through the legacy of the late President John Fitzgerald Kennedy. And current residents continue to appreciate their natural environment, though the perspective these days centers more on recreation than industry.

Stone walls are all that is left of farms that have returned to forest in formerly clear-cut areas.

History Time Line

8000 B.C. Paleo-Indians arrive in region.

A.D. 1500 Native peoples of the Algonquian language group, including the Massachusett, Nauset, Wampanoag, Pocumtuck, and other tribes, inhabit the territory of present-day Massachusetts.

1602 Capt. Bartholomew Gosnold, the first Englishman to land in New England, anchors the *Concord* off New Bedford, names Cape Cod.

1614 Capt. John Smith maps New England coast.

1616 Smallpox epidemic ravages New England's native population.

1620 On September 20, English Pilgrims aboard the *Mayflower* sail for America; on November 11, anchored off Provincetown, they sign the Mayflower Compact, binding them to a democratic form of government; on December 21, they disembark at Plymouth.

1621 Pilgrims and Wampanoag Indians, led by Massasoit, sign peace pact, first such treaty between European settlers and American Indians. First Thanksgiving celebrated.

1623 English merchants found fishing colony at Gloucester on Cape Ann.

1626 Colonists from Cape Ann establish Naumkeag, later called Salem.

1629 Massachusetts Bay Company receives royal charter; John Winthrop elected first governor of the soon-to-be Massachusetts Bay Colony.

1630 The *Arabella* sails from Southampton, England, carrying John Winthrop and 700 Puritans to the New World, where they first land at Salem, but later move to Charlestown and then to what is now Boston.

1636 Harvard College, first American college, founded in Newtowne, later known as Cambridge.

1644 Massachusetts general court passes law promoting conversion of Indians to Christianity. Two years later, heresy is made punishable by death.

1660 Mary Dyer hanged for her Quaker beliefs in Boston.

1675 In retaliation for the execution of three Indians by Plymouth colonists, the leader of the Wampanoags, Metacom (also known as King Philip), attacks Swansea, setting off King Philip's War.

1676 King Philip is killed in Rhode Island, ending the war in southern New England, though Indians in Maine and New Hampshire continue to fight.

1692 Witchcraft hysteria grips Salem; between June and October, 20 people, including 14 women, are executed.

1704 The *Boston News-Letter,* the first regularly published newspaper in the colonies, begins publication; comes out weekly until 1776.

1711 Great fire burns roughly one-third of Boston.

1764 In response to British effort to raise revenue from its colonies via the Sugar Act and later the Stamp Act, Boston merchants boycott British goods.

1770 Angry mob, protesting the stationing of British troops in Boston, confronts patrolling soldiers, who fire on the crowd and kill five; engraver Paul Revere issues color prints of the event, known as the Boston Massacre.

1773 In opposition to a newly imposed tax on tea and the refusal of the British to return a shipload of tea to England, patriot activists launch the Boston Tea Party, dumping the tea into Boston Harbor.

1774 British close Boston Harbor to shipping until Boston Tea Party damages are reimbursed. Massachusetts sends delegates to the first Continental Congress in Philadelphia, where 54 representatives from every colony except Georgia meet to discuss how to respond to new British demands.

1775 The first battles of the Revolutionary War take place in Lexington and Concord, and a yearlong siege of British troops in Boston begins. British win Battle of Bunker Hill, but suffer many casualties.

1776 Colonial troops drive British forces from Boston, ending siege.

1780 State constitution adopted with bill of rights extending to black slaves; it is the oldest written constitution in the world still in effect. John Hancock elected state's first governor.

1786 Post-war economic depression causes hardship, especially for those in the western counties. Revolutionary veteran Daniel Shays leads armed insurgents in revolt known as Shays's Rebellion.

1787 Daniel Shays leads march of 1,200 men on the Springfield Arsenal in January, but the insurgents are stopped by an act of the national government; newly free American colonists realize need for a strong federal constitution.

1797   John Adams, born in the Massachusetts Bay Colony in 1735, becomes second president of the United States. His wife, the former Abigail Smith of Weymouth, becomes First Lady. In 1800, they become the first presidential couple to occupy the newly constructed White House.

1812   Massachusetts governor Caleb Strong declares a statewide fast in opposition to War of 1812 against Great Britain; 44-gun USS *Constitution* defeats 38-gun British frigate *Java,* earning nickname "Old Ironsides."

1814   Francis Cabot Lowell opens Boston Manufacturing Company in Waltham. This was the first textile plant to integrate spinning and weaving under one roof, first to employ a predominantly female workforce, first to offer company-sponsored housing, and, in 1821 (four years after Lowell's death), site of nation's first industrial labor strike.

1825   John Quincy Adams, of Braintree, son of John Adams, becomes sixth president of the United States.

1826   First American railroad built. The track runs 3 miles, from Quincy to the Neponsit River.

1831   William Lloyd Garrison publishes first issue of *The Liberator,* an abolitionist newspaper demanding immediate freedom for slaves; the next year he helps to found the New England Anti-Slavery Society, the first such group in the United States.

1836   Ralph Waldo Emerson's essay "Nature" is published, setting forth principles of the philosophical, religious, and literary movement known as transcendentalism.

1837   Massachusetts Board of Education established; in 12 years as its first secretary, Horace Mann develops a school system that becomes a model for public education in the United States.

1845   Henry David Thoreau builds cabin on Walden Pond, where he lives for two years writing a journal that will be the basis for his most famous book, *Walden, Life in the Woods,* published in 1854.

1850   *The Scarlet Letter,* a novel written by Salem-born Nathaniel Hawthorne and set in Puritan Massachusetts, is published.

1851   Herman Melville's novel *Moby-Dick,* set aboard a whaler that ships out of 19th-century Nantucket, is published.

1896 In Springfield, Brothers Charles and Frank Duryea found the Duryea Motor Wagon Company, the first manufacturer of gasoline-powered cars in the United States.

1897 First subway in the United States opens in Boston.

1904 Strike of 25,000 Massachusetts textile workers begins in Fall River on July 25, shutting 85 mills for six months.

1912 Two-month strike of workers protesting wage cuts and sweatshop conditions closes all the mills in Lawrence.

1920 Italian immigrant radicals Nicola Sacco and Bartolomeo Vanzetti are arrested for the murder of two men during a robbery in South Braintree; their trial is highly sensationalized; despite a lack of evidence, they are found guilty, setting off worldwide protest; they are executed in 1927.

1957 Re-creating voyage of its namesake, the *Mayflower II* docks in Plymouth, Massachusetts, on June 13, after 54-day sail from Plymouth, England.

1961 John Fitzgerald Kennedy, born in Brookline, becomes 35th president of the United States.

1966 Edward W. Brooke, Massachusetts attorney general, becomes first African-American elected to the U.S. Senate by popular vote.

1974 Racial violence erupts at South Boston High School over a court-ordered busing plan to desegregate city schools.

1990 Thirteen works of art, valued at more than $200 million, stolen from Isabella Stewart Gardner Museum in Boston; called the largest art theft in history.

1991 Boston's Big Dig begins. The Central Artery/Tunnel Project to replace six-lane elevated highway with 7.8 miles of 8- to 10-lane underground expressway is described by some engineers as a challenge on the scale of building the Panama Canal or the English Channel Tunnel because it is taking place in the middle of a major city.

2001 On April 10, Jane Swift, pregnant with twins, becomes the first woman governor of Massachusetts and the first pregnant governor in U.S. history.

On October 31, Massachusetts Senate and House of Representatives retroactively exonerate five of the witches hanged in Salem in 1692.

Colonists dump tea in this 1789 engraving of the Boston Tea Party. (Library of Congress)

■ MASSACHUSETTS ERAS AND LEADERS

■ NATIVES AND PILGRIMS

Legend has it that Nordic explorers ventured along the American coast hundreds of years before Columbus. It is certain the locals, having seen foreign faces from as far back as the 11th century, were not surprised by the European arrival, but the fact that the 17th-century visitors decided to stay required diplomacy on all sides. Two of the early players were an Indian negotiator and the second governor of Plymouth Colony.

SQUANTO (TISQUANTUM) (UNKNOWN–1622)
Native American interpreter and negotiator
b. Probably near Plymouth, Massachusetts

In the 17th century, the great Wampanoag Chief Massasoit was largely considered the Native American leader, but it was the Pataxet tribe member Squanto who wielded the most influence. Kidnapped in 1614 by Englishman Thomas Hunt, Squanto was nearly sold into slavery in Spain before monks intervened on his behalf. Years later, he returned home to find that most of his people had succumbed to a plague, and he took up residence with the tribe of Massasoit.

Having lived for half a decade among Europeans, Squanto was schooled in the language of English, making him indispensable as an interpreter between the native people and the settlers. In 1621, he negotiated a peace treaty between the two.

Although history recalls Squanto as a benevolent friend to the Pilgrims, guiding them in the fine arts of living off the land, not all of his motives were selfless. As the most proficient English speaker in his tribe, Squanto manipulated circumstances to serve his own interests. At one point, he courted gifts from his fellow tribesmen in exchange for persuading the settlers not to unleash a great "plague" on the natives. Such maneuverings nearly caused war between the two peoples and eventually led to Massasoit's cry for Squanto's head. Protected by the settlers, Squanto succumbed instead to illness in 1622.

WILLIAM BRADFORD (1590–1657)
Second governor of Plymouth Colony
b. Austerfield, Yorkshire, England

Leading the charge of the Pilgrims was practical-minded William Bradford. Like many who sailed with him, Bradford crossed the Atlantic in a quest for religious peace. Growing up in Yorkshire, the Englishman had become disenchanted with the Church of England early in life, and by age 17 he had joined an unaffiliated congregation in a nearby town. But such unauthorized churches were staunchly outlawed in 17th-century England, leading religious separatists like Bradford to seek refuge elsewhere.

After more than 10 unfruitful years in the Netherlands, Bradford and his compatriots began to look for greener pastures, and plans for the *Mayflower* journey were hatched. Bradford, whose meticulously kept records and journals indicate a steadfast individual, was a driving force behind the crossing. He busied himself with the task of organizing and financing the impending journey.

Such leadership skills would serve Bradford and the Plymouth colonists well. That first, harsh winter claimed more than half of the Pilgrims, including the colony's first governor, John Carver. Bradford seemed the natural successor and was subsequently elected. In later years, the task of governing grew increasingly daunting, as additional ships brought new colonists and settlers fanned out to form towns outside the colony's original boundaries. Despite the challenges, however, Bradford rose to the task. He remained at his post for more than three decades, until shortly before his death in 1657.

■ PURITAN RULE

The early decades of Massachusetts were years of marked growth. In 1635, the Massachusetts Bay Colony saw the formation of its first school, the Latin School, where such luminaries as Benjamin Franklin and John Hancock were educated. The nation's first college, Harvard, was founded in what is now Cambridge just a year later. Though numerous adventurers arrived in search of religious freedom, those who did not abide by the Puritan faith would find little more tolerance here than they did at home in England. Such intolerance would climax with the Salem Witch Trials near the end of the 18th century.

JOHN WINTHROP (1588–1649)
First governor of Massachusetts Bay Colony
b. Suffolk, England

Among the colonists who came after William Bradford was John Winthrop, a deeply religious man. Winthrop wholeheartedly embraced the Puritan movement, aimed at "purifying" the Church of England. Not only was the church not to Winthrop's liking, but he also believed that the social climate of increasingly bawdy London threatened the moral well-being of his family.

A man of means, Winthrop had been schooled as an attorney, making him a natural choice to lead the fledgling Massachusetts Bay Company on its venture in creating a colony in the New World. With Winthrop as their governor, the group of 700 colonists arrived in Salem in 1630 and later resettled on the more hospitable terrain around what is now Boston Harbor.

A devoted governor, Winthrop is said to have agonized over the fate of his charges, roughly 200 of whom were lost the first winter. He went as far as to dig into his own pockets to keep the colony afloat, but his "City Upon a Hill" (a term coined in a famous address made during the transcontinental voyage) was not impervious to outside influences. Not everyone embraced the Puritan philosophy, and Winthrop, the colony's sporadic governor until 1649, fielded challenges on political and religious fronts. Notable foes included Anne Hutchinson, who was exiled for her Quaker-like antinomian beliefs. Hutchinson's banishment was one of a series of religion-related events that colored the Winthrop legacy in both heroic and villainous lights.

John Winthrop, the first governor of the Massachusetts Bay Colony.
(American Antiquarian Society)

OBSERVATIONS

As well *Historical* as *Theological*, upon the NATURE, the NUMBER, and the OPERATIONS of the

DEVILS.

Accompany'd with,

I. Some Accounts of the Grievous Molestations, by DÆMONS and WITCHCRAFTS, which have lately annoy'd the Countrey; and the Trials of some eminent *Malefactors* Executed upon occasion thereof: with several Remarkable *Curiosities* therein occurring.

II. Some Counsils, Directing a due Improvement of the terrible things, lately done, by the Unusual & Amazing Range of EVIL SPIRITS, in Our Neighbourhood : & the methods to prevent the *Wrongs* which those *Evil Angels* may intend against all sorts of people among us ; especially in Accusations of the Innocent.

III. Some Conjectures upon the great EVENTS, likely to befall, the WORLD in General, and NEW-ENGLAND in Particular ; as also upon the Advances of the TIME, when we shall see BETTER DAYES.

IV A short Narrative of a late Outrage committed by a knot of WITCHES in *Swedeland*, very much Resembling, and so far Explaining, *That* under which our parts of *America* have laboured !

V. THE DEVIL DISCOVERED : In a Brief Discourse upon those TEMPTATIONS, which are the more Ordinary *Devices* of the Wicked One.

By **Cotton Mather.**

Boston Printed by *Benj. Harris* for *Sam. Phillips.* 1693.

Mary Dyer (circa 1611–1660)
Quaker activist
b. London, England

Anne Hutchinson's supporters included the determined Mary Dyer, who with her husband, William, first came to Massachusetts in the 1630s. Dissatisfied with the church, she espoused Hutchinson's ideas about religion and was shunned as a heretic. By the end of the decade, the Dyers were forced to move to Rhode Island.

During a visit to England in the 1650s Mary discovered the Quaker faith, and she became increasingly defiant of the Puritan rule. Under the governorship of John Endecott, Massachusetts laws were enacted not only to punish the Quakers themselves, but also to impose hefty fines (as much as 100 pounds) on any ship that brought Quakers into the colony.

Although she had been exiled from Massachusetts, Dyer defiantly returned to Boston. There she enraged officials by railing against the increasing hostility toward Quakers, who were routinely imprisoned, whipped, or worse for their faith. Dyer found herself repeatedly jailed and ultimately sentenced to death. Although once granted a last-minute reprieve (so last-minute that the noose had already been placed around her neck), Dyer tempted the fates once too often and was finally hanged in 1660.

Mary Easty (circa 1634–1692)
Last "witch" to be hung in Salem
b. Probably Yarmouth, Massachusetts

By the late 17th century, the age of religious intolerance had reached a feverish pitch. Up in Salem, the rallying cry against "the devil" achieved notorious heights when 20 men and women were executed as purveyors of witchcraft. At the peak of the frenzy, roughly 150 locals were behind bars.

Among the so-called witches was Mary Easty. In her 50s, Easty was a respected woman of means, married and living well with her husband and seven children on a valuable farm. Such good fortune, say historians, may have made her the subject of envy and a target to those who would levy accusations of witchcraft. When local

Cotton Mather, the author of The Wonders of the Invisible World, *initially supported the witchcraft hysteria of 1692 but later helped to dispel it. (Massachusetts Historical Society)*

girls began feigning "fits," during which they claimed visions of menacing appari-
tions, Easty was accused, as were her two sisters, Rebecca Nurse and Sarah Cloyse.

Sent to prison in August 1692, Easty seemed to win a reprieve and was at one
point released. But persistent accusers returned her to jail, where she fashioned an
impassioned plea on behalf of all of the accused: "I Petition to your honours not
for my own life for I know I must die and my appointed time is sett but the Lord
he knowes it is that if it be possible no more Innocent blood may be shed."

Easty lost her bid for pardon and was hanged on September 22, 1692, but her
words were not lost on the colonists, and her death marked the beginning of a turn
against the witch hunt. Wrote Bernard Rosenthal in *The Salem Story,* "At another
time, Mary Easty's appeal would have had minimal influence at best; but with the
acceleration of confessions, what she urged publicly must surely have been discussed
privately. The spectacle of so many people rushing to proclaim their witchcraft rein-
forced the trepidations of those dismayed by the proceedings." The court was dis-
banded in 1692, making Easty's day at the gallows the last of the Salem executions.

■ SEEDS OF REBELLION

Pilgrims had come to the New World to escape religious restrictions, but their
brazen independence was ill tolerated by the crown. In 1684, the Massachusetts
Bay Charter was revoked and the Massachusetts Bay Colony was reorganized to
include Plymouth and Maine. It would take nearly another century before the new
generation of colonists would make their position of independence perfectly clear.

SAMUEL ADAMS (1722–1803)

Statesman and Revolutionary patriot; "Father of the American Revolution"
b. Boston, Massachusetts

Exactly 30 years after Mary Easty's demise came the birth of Samuel Adams. A
cousin to the nation's second president, Adams was schooled at Harvard but was an
unfortunate businessman who saw early failures in his life as a merchant. He nevertheless discovered a penchant for politics and is considered by many to be the
"Father of the American Revolution."

A vocal opponent of British rule, Adams watched his father's wealth succumb to
the effects of the monarchy. Some say such misfortunes drove both his distaste for
the English government as well as his yearning for independence. Regardless of
motive, Adams lobbied heavily for his cause, pressing ahead when others were

ready to give up. Says Andrew Alexander, assistant director of the Paul Revere House, "Adams was the guy in the back of the smoke-filled room who was coming up with all these ideas for keeping things going. He liked the manipulation and agitation. He was good at that. He was not about to let it die."

The journalistic essays and articles he penned furthered Adams's fame as a rising patriot and made his voice among the loudest in the cry against "taxation without representation." Rallying the Sons of Liberty against the tea tax, he achieved particular notoriety for leading the Boston Tea Party on December 16, 1773. Membership in the first Continental Congress helped Adams bring his message of independence colony-wide. That he put his name at the bottom of the Declaration of Independence no doubt fulfilled one of his greatest desires. "If I have a wish dearer to my soul than that my ashes may be mingled with those of a Warren and Montgomery, it is that these American States may never cease to be free and independent," he told a gathering at the Philadelphia State House in August 1776.

After the revolution, Adams held numerous political offices, including governor of Massachusetts. He died in 1803.

PAUL REVERE (1735–1818)
Patriot, artisan, and businessman; subject of famed Longfellow poem
b. Boston, Massachusetts

Unlike some of his contemporaries, Paul Revere was not groomed as a budding statesman or politician; nevertheless, his exploits in the Revolutionary arena left a lasting impression on the country.

An artisan by birth and later a shop owner, Revere had several occupations during his 83 years, including silversmith (a trade he inherited from his father), coppersmith, and even dentist (contrary to legend, curators at the Paul Revere House assure visitors, Revere had no hand in George Washington's famed false teeth).

Although his handiwork in silver and copper was accomplished enough to have preserved his name, it was the words of Henry Wadsworth Longfellow that ensured Revere's stature as a legend. Acquainted with local activists through community groups, Revere spent time on Samuel Adams's Committee on Safety and milled about Boston by night to gather information about loyalist activities. On April 18, 1775, dispatched by Dr. Joseph Warren, Revere rode to Lexington where he was told to warn Adams and John Hancock that the British regulars were coming to arrest them. That Revere had two riders with him on that famous night is largely unknown to the general public, perhaps because neither William Dawes nor Samuel Prescott appeared in the Longfellow poem.

A twice-married family man with 16 children, Revere remained active until shortly before his death in 1818. After the war he held offices in several local lodges, but his primary successes came as a businessman. Revere earned his living with, among other things, an iron and brass foundry, a hardware store, and a silver business that produced more than 5,000 objects.

Paul Revere heads for Lexington on his famous midnight ride. (Concord Free Public Library)

JOHN HANCOCK (1737–1793)
Statesman and Revolutionary patriot; signer of Declaration of Independence
b. Boston, Massachusetts

If Samuel Adams was the heated voice behind the revolution, John Hancock was the man in front. Born in Boston in 1737, Hancock was never lauded for his intellect. Rather, his influence has largely been credited to his riches—garnered from a wealthy uncle who left his young nephew a fortune in business and cash. Such wealth made Hancock visible as the patriots' wealthiest advocate and perhaps their most flamboyantly attired.

"The manners and habits of Mr. Hancock had, not a little, contributed to countenance the malicious imputations. His fortune was princely. His mansion displayed the magnificence of a courtier, rather than the simplicity of a republican. Gold and silver embroidery adorned his garments and on public occasions, his carriage and horses, and servants. Livery emulated the splendour of the English nobility. The eye of envy saw not this magnificence with indifference," wrote the Reverend Charles A. Goodrich in his 1829 book, *Lives of the Signers of the Declaration of Independence.*

Nevertheless, Hancock was largely respected, most notably for his efforts in stirring the revolution. Railing against the British government, he earned his place alongside Adams as an enemy of the crown and was secreted in Concord with Adams the night Paul Revere arrived bearing his warnings.

In his 56 years, Hancock held numerous prominent positions, including that of president of the Continental Congress and the first governor of the state of Massachusetts. Still, perhaps his most renowned legacy remains his bold and fittingly showy signature at the bottom of the Declaration of Independence.

■ **INDUSTRIALISTS AND INTELLECTUALS**

The road to independence brought the burgeoning nation one set of perils; the task of maintaining the nation brought yet another. Conflicts after the Revolutionary War included the War of 1812 against Great Britain, in which Americans hoped to reverse a series of British and French rulings that had stifled the country's maritime trade. Massachusetts leaders opposed the war and, along with representatives of four other New England states, talked seriously about secession. The War of 1812 ended with nothing gained and the business of trade still threatened. It was industrial progress that eventually brought the state out of the doldrums, and the emergence of intellectual luminaries—the so-called thinkers, such as Ralph Waldo Emerson and Henry David Thoreau—that engaged the region with transcendentalism and talk of abolition.

CHARLES BULFINCH (1763–1844)
Architect
b. Boston, Massachusetts

Without Charles Bulfinch, nothing about Boston would look the same. The architect, who forever left his mark on the Boston skyline, was born in 1763 to a prominent Boston family. Although he earned a degree from Harvard, it was Bulfinch's extensive travels through Europe that provided much of his education. For three years in the 1780s the eager student traveled the classic cities in England, France, and Italy, and he returned to Boston with a flair for neoclassical style. In the decades that followed, Bulfinch reinvented his home city, transforming it from a stalwart of Colonial drab into a hub of Federalist elegance.

Influential throughout the city, Bulfinch also worked in the political arena. He held several government jobs, including a stint on the Board of Selectmen. Still, the man who is known as the country's first native-born professional architect is best remembered for his buildings, roughly 40 of them, in Boston as well as its surrounds. Much of his influence can be found on Beacon Hill, where numerous residences bear the architect's unmistakable imprint. Standing here is one of his most noteworthy contributions: the golden-domed State House, completed in 1798, which solidified John Winthrop's vision of a "City on the Hill."

Bulfinch later was tapped by President James Monroe to be the architect of the United States Capitol. Surprisingly, such esteemed exploits made Bulfinch happy but never wealthy. He died in 1844.

Francis Cabot Lowell (1775–1817)
Industrialist
b. Newburyport, Massachusetts

Born in 1775 in the heat of the nation's struggle for independence, Francis Cabot Lowell went on to stage another revolution: In the early 19th century, he started the Boston Manufacturing Company and changed forever the way America did business.

At the turn of the 18th century, trade still ranked as the country's prized industry, but events leading up to the War of 1812 damaged many trade routes and profits began to plunge. Lowell saw manufacturing as the wave of the future. He knew that the nation would need adequate technology to compete with Britain, where an industrial revolution had already taken hold. The entrepreneur traveled to England to examine the widely used power looms, which had replaced the hand looms still being used in the states. Returning home with the technology lodged in his memory, Lowell recruited the talents of engineer Paul Moody, with whom he constructed the nation's first power loom. At Lowell's Waltham-based Boston Manufacturing Company, for the first time cotton was spun and woven under one roof. The country's first textile mill with a power loom, it set the stage for the industrialization of the north.

The advent of Lowell's factory had social implications as well. For the first time, women were welcomed into the workplace, and 15- to 30-year-olds routinely were courted into the ranks of what would become known as the Mill Girls. Lowell himself, for whom the city of Lowell would eventually be named, was respected for being a caring employer, but other owners were not as well regarded.

In 1821, just four years after Francis Cabot Lowell's death, the Mill Girls responded to issues surrounding wages by staging a walkout. According to the Charles River Museum of Industry, the event would go down in history as the nation's first industrial strike.

FRANCIS CABOT LOWELL

HORACE MANN (1796–1859)
"Father of public education"
b. Franklin, Massachusetts

It's no surprise that so many schools bear the name of Horace Mann, who devoted his life to the state's public school system and is widely known as the "father of public education." Born into an impoverished family in Franklin, Massachusetts, Mann was allowed to study in a classroom only a few weeks a year. The rest of his childhood days were spent working the family farm. Dedicated to learning all that he could, the industrious student read and studied on his own, furthering his education enough to gain acceptance into Brown University and later into law school.

A practicing attorney, Mann occupied several political positions before he accepted the role as the state Board of Education's first secretary. Believing that quality education was an antidote to rising poverty, the new secretary attended to his task with vigor. "Education then, beyond all other devices of human origin, is a great equalizer of the conditions of men—the balance wheel of the social machinery. I do not here mean that it so elevates the moral nature as to make men disdain and abhor the oppression of their fellow men. This idea pertains to another of its attributes. But I mean that it gives each man the independence and the means by which he can resist the selfishness of other men," he wrote in his 12th annual report of the department.

Although colonists had long ago recognized the importance of public education—the nation's first public school opened in 1635—there were no standards to keep all schools above par, and teacher education was virtually nonexistent. During more than a decade as secretary, Mann successfully overhauled the state's schools. He crusaded for teacher training schools (the first such so-called normal school was established in 1839), increased financing, and free libraries.

Mann left his seat on the board and headed for Congress in 1848. In 1854, he was named head of Antioch College in Ohio, where he remained until shortly before his death in 1859.

HENRY DAVID THOREAU (1817–1862)
Writer and environmentalist
b. Concord, Massachusetts

Born in 1817 to humble beginnings, Henry David Thoreau is known as the nation's first environmentalist, but he was perhaps as much an enigma as a man of influence. Son of a pencil-factory owner, Thoreau attended Harvard before joining his father for a time in the family business. Perhaps surprisingly, he took to the task with vigor, tinkering with the graphite/wood arrangement and, according to John H. Leinhard, a professor of mechanical engineering and the host of the radio show *The Engines of Our Ingenuity*, actually concocting a better pencil.

The achievement did not occupy Thoreau for long. Wrote his friend Ralph Waldo Emerson in *Atlantic Monthly*, "His friends congratulated him that he had now opened his way to fortune. But he replied that he should never make another pencil. 'Why should I? I would not do again what I have done once.'"

From 1845 to 1847 Thoreau retreated to Emerson's cabin alongside the splendor of Walden Pond. It was here that he wrote journal entries for what would become his most famous work—*Walden, Life in the Woods.* This book earned him a following that remains strong today. It is most evident in a large, celebrity-backed movement—whose members include the rock singer-songwriter Don Henley—to protect the natural splendor of Walden Pond from a proposed development of office buildings and condominiums.

An abolitionist, Thoreau was arrested in 1846 for not paying taxes to support the Mexican War, a conflict he railed against. His action merited him status as the first American proponent of passive resistance. "I do not hesitate to say, that those who call themselves Abolitionists should at once effectually withdraw their support, both in person and property, from the government of Massachusetts, and not wait till they constitute a majority of one, before they suffer the right to prevail through them," he implored in his essay "On the Duty of Civil Disobedience." Thoreau died of tuberculosis in 1862.

JULIA WARD HOWE (1819–1910)
Suffragist and writer
b. New York City

Born to a prominent New York family in 1819, Julia Ward Howe grew up the quintessential socialite. Schooled in music, history, and multiple languages, she thrived in the literary world and kept good company with such New England royalty as Ralph Waldo Emerson and Henry Wadsworth Longfellow.

Married in 1843, the former Ms. Ward relocated to Boston to join her husband, Samuel Howe, a physician and director of the Perkins Institute for the Blind. The couple's worldwide travels inspired Mrs. Howe's literary gifts, and she published numerous poems and plays.

It was in the wee hours of a visit to Washington during the Civil War, after hearing soldiers intone the marching song "John Brown's Body," that Mrs. Howe penned the now famous words to the "Battle Hymn of the Republic." "She lay perfectly still. Line by line, stanza by stanza, the words came sweeping on with the rhythm of marching feet, pauseless, resistless. She saw the long lines swinging into place before her eyes, heard the voice of the nation speaking through her lips. She waited till the voice was silent, till the last line was ended; then sprang from bed, and groping for pen and paper, scrawled in the gray twilight the 'Battle Hymn of the Republic,'" wrote her daughters Laura E. Richards and Maud Howe Elliott in the book *Julia Ward Howe, 1819–1910*.

In later years, Howe honed her interests in philosophy, religion, and world events. In co-founding the New England Women's Club in 1868, she found an avenue for pursuing causes near to her heart, such as world peace. As leader of the Massachusetts Suffrage Association, Howe became influential in the quest for a woman's right to vote. She died in 1910 at the age of 91.

ISABELLA STEWART GARDNER (1840–1924)
Arts patron
b. New York City

Founder of the eponymous museum, Isabella Stewart Gardner was a New Yorker by birth, the daughter of a wealthy Irish immigrant father who, upon his death, left a fortune even by today's standards—nearly $2 million.

Wealth aside, the former Ms. Stewart was a curious sort for her day, as fond of the high arts as she was of a good boxing match. Following her marriage to John Lowell Gardner Jr., she relocated to Boston, and in the years that followed, she became a source of local fascination as much for her arts patronage as for her purportedly scandalous lifestyle, which included betting on the horses.

Mr. and Mrs. Gardner's extensive worldwide travels ultimately became art-collecting expeditions, during which Isabella amassed enough works to fill a Venetian palace. As it happens, that's precisely what she built: an elegant structure in the Fenway designed to house her carefully gathered artworks. The Isabella Stewart Gardner Museum opened in 1903. Today, the esteemed institution is unique for a collection that, eclectic in nature, characterizes not only the artists, but also the collector herself.

Isabella Stewart Gardner *(1888), by John Singer Sargent. (© Isabella Stewart Gardner Museum)*

■ THE MODERN ERA

Massachusetts's legacy as an intellectual center continued in the 20th century with the proliferation of universities and with the state's evolution into a high-tech center. On the political front, several local politicians graduated to the national scene. The state also found its future in its past, mining its historic riches to lure tourists from around the world.

TIP O'NEILL (1912–1994)
Speaker of the U.S. House of Representatives
b. Cambridge, Massachusetts

Thomas P. "Tip" O'Neill was a man of modest beginnings. The grandson of Irish immigrants, the colorful politician came of age in a working-class North Cambridge neighborhood within sight of the Harvard campus. The disparity between the privilege of the "haves" and the poverty of the "have-nots" was not lost on O'Neill, and this realization laid the foundation for his future career, which spanned half a century.

"Someday, I vowed, I would work to make sure my own people could go to places like Harvard, where they could avail themselves of the same opportunities

that these young college men took for granted," he wrote in his 1987 autobiography, *Man of the House.*

A self-described politician from a young age—"Even as a youngster, I knew everybody in our neighborhood," he mused in his book— O'Neill was still in high school when he began immersing himself in politics, working for Alfred E. Smith's 1928 presidential campaign. His own first bid for public office, which he lost, was made while still a senior at Boston College.

In the years that followed, he served in the Massachusetts State House, where he worked energetically

John F. Kennedy (left) with his parents and most of his siblings. (JFK Library)

to change the dominant party from Republican to Democrat. O'Neill succeeded, went on to represent Massachusetts in the United States House of Representatives and rose to the position of Speaker of the House. The larger-than-life politician is amply remembered in his home state through exhibits at his alma mater as well as the Thomas P. O'Neill federal building. O'Neill retired from public office in 1986; he died eight years later.

JOHN F. KENNEDY (1917–1963)
35th President of the United States
b. Brookline, Massachusetts

The Kennedy clan had already risen to prominence in the early 20th century, but it took John to turn the dynasty into royalty. The second of nine children, Kennedy hardly seemed preordained for a great life in politics. The man who would grow up to be president began life in Brookline as a somewhat sickly child for whom schooling seemed to come second to social life. A 1930 report card held by the Kennedy Museum and Library shows a student for whom "effort and application" was only in the "good-to-poor" range. It was elder brother Joe who seemed destined for a life in politics. But with Joe's death in World War II, John, now a war hero himself, shelved his plans for teaching and, at his father's urging, took the Kennedys into the spotlight.

"The first time I met Jack Kennedy, I couldn't believe this skinny, pasty-looking kid was a candidate for anything," wrote Tip O'Neill in *Man of the House.* But all that would change. "In all my life, I never saw anybody grow the way Jack did; he turned into a great personality and a beautiful talker."

As a candidate for president, the 43-year-old Kennedy made unprecedented use of the media, employing youth, good looks, and a picture-perfect family to his expert advantage. Although history may remember the election as a landslide, it was surprisingly evenly divided, with Kennedy claiming victory over Richard Nixon by a mere 118,000 votes.

During his years in office, Kennedy continued to use the media, holding an unprecedented 63 press conferences and thus greatly increasing the American public's access to the presidency. The Kennedy administration was marked by such events as the Cuban missile crisis and NASA's first Mercury space flights. It came to an end on November 22, 1963, when President Kennedy, riding in a motorcade with his wife, Jacqueline, at his side, was assassinated in Dallas, Texas.

EDWARD BROOKE (1919–)
United States senator
b. Washington, D.C.

The first African-American to win a seat in the U.S. Senate by popular vote, Edward Brooke made a lasting mark on both the Bay State and the nation's capital. Schooled at Howard University, Brooke, a World War II veteran, arrived in Boston to earn his law degree from Boston University. He established himself as an attorney and made several unsuccessful attempts for state office before being elected Attorney General in 1962.

Although he was already renowned for his efforts in uncovering political corruption, Brooke made history in 1966 when he was elected to the U.S. Senate. In a state with few black voters, the moderate Republican became the first African-American since the Reconstruction era to hold a seat in the Senate and the first ever to win by popular vote. (The nation's first two African-American senators were elected during the 1870s by their state legislators.)

Senator Brooke's charisma and political instincts took him far in Washington. He emerged as "a champion of a host of liberal programs on behalf of the poor, including Medicare, Social Security, and housing legislation," wrote Sally Jacobs in a 2000 profile in the *Boston Globe.* "Eloquent and engaging, imbued with an old-school sense of privatism and manners, his suit invariably pressed even after brutal stretches on the road, Brooke was likened by many to Jack Kennedy," she continued. "And in Washington, especially during the early years, he was in hot demand at the dinner table."

Particularly ardent on the subject of affordable housing, Brooke was instrumental in the passing of an amendment limiting the percentage of income that tenants of officially sanctioned affordable housing must pay for rent. His successes continued until 1978, when questions relating to his personal finances led to a failed bid for reelection. After leaving the Senate, he returned to the law and was named chairman emeritus of the board of the National Low Income Housing Coalition, a position he still holds.

SEIJI OZAWA (1935–)
Classical music conductor
b. Shenyang, China

Long before he came to Massachusetts, Seiji Ozawa was already making his mark on the classical music scene. Ozawa made early career appearances in France and Germany in the 1950s and in the 1960s worked alongside classical greats such as Leonard Bernstein, who hired Ozawa as an assistant conductor at the New York Philharmonic. A 1962 performance in San Francisco marked Ozawa's first professional appearance in this country and the beginning of a lengthy North American career.

The legendary Seiji Ozawa, the conductor who had it all: "energy, fire, excitement," plus a bit of glamour to boot.

Early photos of the young Ozawa, his hair closely cropped, appearing in Boston and elsewhere in the 1960s seem to belie the spirit he engendered later on. He first guest-conducted in Boston in 1964, but by the time he had taken the reins as musical director of the Boston Symphony Orchestra in 1973, Ozawa's image had morphed into his trademark look, a visage punctuated by a longish coif—described as everything from shaggy to floppy—that was a decided departure from the buttoned-down look of the classically trained. Still, while his unique energy and appearance made him unusual in the music world, it also made him a landmark in Boston and the Berkshires and an instantly recognizable celebrity elsewhere. "He had energy, fire, excitement. And if I dare bring up this controversial category: glamour," the music critic Michael Steinberg told National Public Radio in 2002.

Wielding his baton in Boston for nearly 30 years, Ozawa outlasted five governors, countless trends in music, and six presidential administrations. Summer 2002 marked his final appearances with the Boston Symphony. He now holds the post of music director for the Vienna State Opera.

LARRY BIRD (1956–)
Basketball player
b. West Baden, Indiana

Although basketball is not one of Massachusetts's classical mediums, few in the state would argue that Larry Bird's accomplishments were anything less than art. Born in 1956, the famed cager got his start on the basketball courts of a small Indiana town. During Bird's high school years, local games would routinely attract thousands of spectators. In later years there were more fans, according to the National Basketball Association, than the town had residents. Bird's star rose yet higher at Indiana State University, where he helped the once lagging team find a place in the NCAA finals.

In 1979, Bird began to work his magic for the NBA's Boston Celtics in the old Boston Garden. A once glorious franchise that had floundered during the 1970s

suddenly sprinted to a winning season, and during the 1980s, with help from two other Boston Celtic greats—Robert Parrish and Kevin McHale—the Bird's team won numerous titles. His moves on the court became the stuff of legend, and he is remembered at the NBA Hall of Fame as an "unflappable" player whose pivots and steals turned the tide of a game.

Bird retired from the Celtics before the 1992–93 season. In 897 games with the team, he scored 21,791 points and had 8,974 rebounds and 5,695 assists. To great fanfare, his number (33) was retired on February 4, 1993. He coached the Indiana Pacers until resigning for health reasons, but diehard Celtics fans hold out hope that he'll return to the team in a front-office capacity.

B O S T O N A R E A

John Collins Bossidy, in his famous toast at the 1910 Holy Cross alumni dinner, called Boston the "Home of the Bean and the Cod," referring to the city's culinary standouts—baked beans and fried cod—as well as its relationship with the fishing industry. Since then, the moniker Beantown has stuck, no doubt to the chagrin of the Boston Brahmins. Still, the city's claims to fame are as varied as the people you might ask about them.

Students of history, for example, laud Boston's place in our developing nation, and they are in esteemed company. "I do not speak with any fondness but the language of coolest history, when I say that Boston commands attention as the town which was appointed in the destiny of nations to lead the civilization of North America," wrote Ralph Waldo Emerson in *The Natural History of Intellect* (1893). Scattered throughout downtown Boston and its outlying suburbs are relics of the region's role in freeing the nation from British rule.

Educators point to the city as a bastion of thinkers, with Emerson, Thoreau, and Hawthorne leading a long line of Boston luminaries. Few would argue that Boston doesn't have more than its share of champion intellectuals, drawn to the area by its myriad universities, which include Harvard and the Massachusetts Institute of Technology.

Politically, Boston will be forever aligned with Camelot and the legacy of the Kennedys, no matter that less liberal politicians have since made inroads. The physician and writer Oliver Wendell Holmes referred to the State House as the "hub of the solar system," a description that was later upgraded to the "hub of the universe" and attributed to the entire city. A plaque at Washington and Summer Streets even declares that Filene's is the "Hub of the Universe," though it will come as no surprise that the statement was made by the department store's founder.

These days the city is striving to live up to its reputation as a "European" city in its art, shopping, and nightlife. That the city's streets are so narrow and walkable certainly makes it feel European, but the origin of this layout is reportedly attributable to 18th-century bovines rather than Old World aristocrats (the roads are said to have started out as cow paths).

Touring the Charles River by dragon boat.

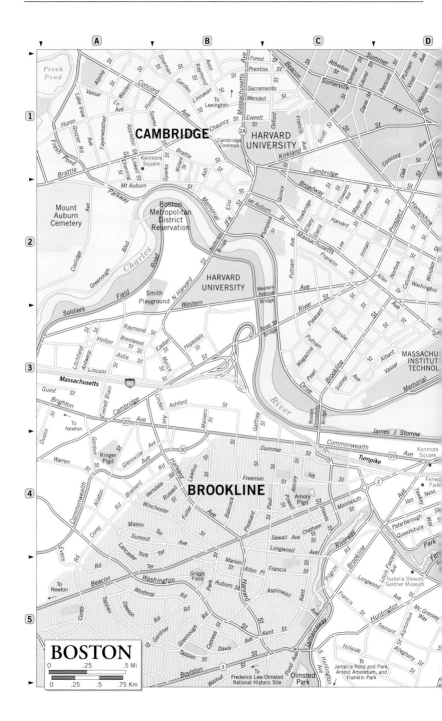

BOSTON

0   .25   .5 Mi

0   .25   .5   .75 Km

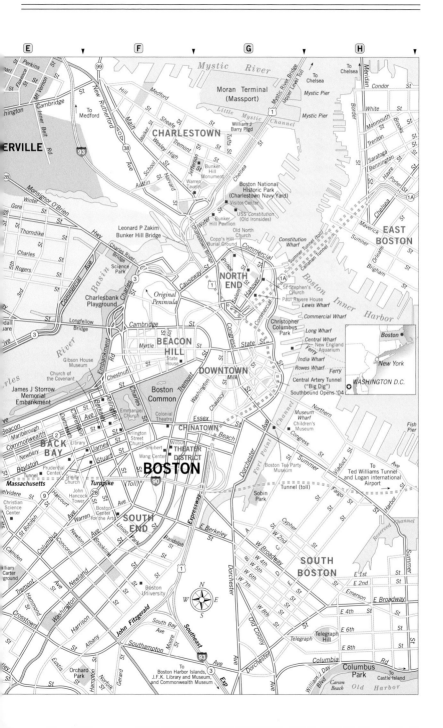

Boston is all it purports to be: historic, academic, literary, politically liberal, self-consciously stodgy, and lovable at heart—in no small part because it is full of surprises. Just when you conclude that the pale, thin man sitting opposite you on the T—the one in the bow tie who got on at Harvard Square—is a direct *Mayflower* descendant, he greets a friend in his native Russian. You might never guess that the true *Mayflower* descendant is the girl with the pin through her nose.

■ HISTORY

In *The Flowering of New England,* the literary critic Van Wyck Brooks noted that there were books in Boston "when the wolves still howled on the summit."

"Learning was endemic in the Boston mind as befitted a town whose first inhabitant, the Cambridge Scholar Blaxton, who had built his thatched cottage with a garden and spring on the site of Louisburg Square, had brought his library with him," wrote Brooks.

William Blaxton was joined in 1630 by John Winthrop's colonists, who had quit marshy Charlestown and named their hillside Trimountaine (the origin of Tremont Street), and later Boston, after a Lincolnshire town. It was an unimposing site: 783 acres of glacial bumps connected to the mainland by a narrow causeway, with good fishing and unpredictable weather. Even today—after centuries of leveling, land reclamation, and expansion—the city covers just over 48 square miles.

Boston's early survival and later prosperity depended on the sea, a fact that is recognized in the representation of the "Sacred Cod" that still hangs in the State House. The settlement's destiny, in the view of Winthrop and those who governed after him, hinged on its ability to rule itself. When England twice attempted to revoke the colony's charter in the 17th century, Bostonians armed themselves to defend it. A royal governor was appointed in 1691, but Boston merchants enjoyed virtual free trade until 1764, when punitive tariffs were enforced and at first covertly, then violently, opposed.

■ REVOLUTION IN THE AIR

In 1768, rioting forced the British to dispatch troops to patrol the city's crooked streets, and in 1770 a brawl that became known as the Boston Massacre resulted in the deaths of five colonists on King Street, now State Street. Three years later, tax protesters dumped three shiploads of tea into the harbor. By turning Boston into

Civil War woodcarver John Haley Bellamy cut the most famous warship figureheads of his day.

their military stronghold, the British ensured that the city would also become the epicenter of the American Revolution.

In April 1775, news of the British advance on Lexington and Concord was semaphored to Paul Revere by lamplight from the Old North Church, and Bunker Hill in nearby Charlestown became one of the war's early battle sites. When George Washington seized Dorchester Heights overnight, the British were faced with defeat and evacuated Boston on March 17, 1776.

Following a brief postwar depression, Boston's prosperity was reactivated by the China trade in silks, spices, and porcelain, and East Boston became a center for shipbuilding in the early 1830s. Wooden clipper ships built here dominated the trade routes in the 1850s, but when shipyards refused to build steam-powered iron ships in the next decade, the harbor went into decline.

■ "THINKING CENTER"

Boston officially became a city in 1822, and between 1824 and 1858 the peninsula was enlarged by leveling the hills and filling in Back Bay and the coves. The causeway, or Neck, was also raised and widened. From 1830 onward, the railroads hastened urban development, and as Boston's industrial empire expanded, so did its attitudes. Beacon Hill, home to the magnates of the Industrial Revolution, also became the headquarters of free-thinking and social reform.

"All I claim for Boston," Oliver Wendell Holmes declared, "is that it is the thinking center of the continent, and therefore of the planet." Residing in the city or the surrounding areas were the country's leading 19th-century intellectuals, among them the abolitionist William Lloyd Garrison (1805–1879), the psychologist William James (1842–1910), and the philosopher George Santayana (1863–1952). Edgar Allan Poe was born here in 1809, Ralph Waldo Emerson gave Walt Whitman literary advice on Boston Common, and William Dean Howells experimented with literary realism at the *Atlantic Monthly,* where he served as editor.

■ IDEALISTS AND IMMIGRANTS

The Boston Draft Riots of 1863, an uprising by prospective conscripts, reflected local opposition to participation in the Civil War, but the Beacon Hill aristocrat Robert Gould Shaw embraced another attitude. An abolitionist, he commanded

A bird's-eye view of Boston, ca. 1877. (Library of Congress)

the Union Army's famous black 54th Massachusetts Regiment—half of which fell, along with Shaw, outside Charleston, South Carolina, in 1863. Shaw's sister later wrote of her 26-year-old brother's departure: "His face was as the face of an angel, and I felt perfectly sure he would never come back."

The post–Civil War era was one of tremendous industrial and commercial growth. In 1898, the first subway in America opened at Tremont Street, and in 1901, ships leaving Boston Harbor carried goods valued at $143 million while imports amounted to just $80 million. Meanwhile, Irish immigrants, who first flooded the city in 1846, the year of Ireland's potato blight, had increased their numbers and their power sufficiently to dominate Boston's politics. Yankee political ascendancy ended in 1914 with the election of mayor James Michael Curley, and the consolidation of Boston Irish power would culminate in the 1960 presidential victory of John Fitzgerald Kennedy.

■ Progress and Urban Renewal

When the city created the 2.5-mile Freedom Trail in 1958, it used the 16 historic sites on the trail to celebrate Boston's notable past, but it continued to move forward. Urban renewal—a policy or an abomination, depending on your preservationist views—began in the 1960s with accelerated construction of highways, the brutalist Government Center buildings and parking garages, and the Prudential Center. The financial district was further expanded in the 1970s and 1980s, and buildings along the waterfront were converted to house the Children's Museum and other institutions.

The latest blot on the landscape is the seemingly endless shoveling of the Big Dig, a project that involves putting underground one of the city's busiest thoroughfares, to create more lanes for the estimated quarter-million cars that pass through each day. The multibillion-dollar project (history's costliest roadwork, its price tag stood at $14.1 billion through 2002) is nothing if not vintage street theater. Viewing hours: anytime, especially when you're stuck in traffic. Admission: free or $10.4 billion-plus, depending on residence.

Despite what seems like constant changes, Boston remains a walkable city—more walkable than drivable these days. The relatively low skyline is owed both to the city's geography (city blocks are not big enough to accommodate the huge base required for skyscrapers) and strict zoning laws on height. A one-mile stroll in any direction takes you through 300 years of architecture.

■ **BOSTON WATERFRONT** *map pages 46–47, G/H-2/3*

For many Bostonians, the waterfront *is* Boston. The sea, or at least its inlets, touches most of the city, and though today's harbor activity may be more recreational than seafaring, the record-breaking pollution of the 1980s has apparently been reversed and derelict wharves revitalized. Boston continues to reclaim its shore, and today, neighborhoods from Charlestown down to South Boston can take advantage of the lapping water. The Harborwalk, nearly two-thirds complete, will eventually allow for an uninterrupted shoreline stroll of more than 40 miles.

The Downtown Waterfront might be characterized as the nucleus of both the city's birth and its renewal. Original 1710 structures at **Long Wharf,** including the Chart House restaurant, abut the 1989 Long Wharf Pavilion and Park. The Long Wharf Marriott (296 State Street), modern in every detail, is designed to look like a ship, although some complain that it seems to be upside down.

The area's tourist appeal increased exponentially in 1970 with the addition of the **New England Aquarium,** whose three-story ocean tank displays 2,000 species of exotic fish, sharks, sea turtles, and eels. There are also strutting penguins and exhibits on aquatic environments from the Amazon rain forest to the Antarctic. Those who want a chance to view sea creatures in the wild join a naturalist-guided whale watch—though the whale population can seem plentiful or paltry, depending on the day. For a larger-than-life experience, the aquarium has an IMAX theater, for which tickets are sold separately. *On Central Wharf; 617-973-5200.*

You know you're at the **Children's Museum** when you see the humongous milk bottle that guards the entrance. The renovated warehouse, a wonder of giant LEGO structures, enormous soap bubbles, and interactive exhibits, also provides the ultimate in climbing, sliding, swinging, and dressing-up opportunities. *Museum Wharf, between the Congress Street and North Avenue Bridges; 617-426-6500.*

The **Boston Tea Party Museum** resides near Museum Wharf in a replica of the brig *Beaver,* the smallest of the three ships assailed by rebellious colonists on a fateful night in December 1773. The museum stages reenactments of the meetings inspiring the event and of the actual dumping of the tea. The kitschy yet charming attraction was damaged by a fire in 2001 and will remain closed until at least early 2004. *Midway across the Congress Street Bridge; 617-269-7150.*

Lunch alfresco on Commercial Wharf.

The unmistakable entrance to the Children's Museum.

Though a shadow of its former fishing-heyday self, the waterfront remains a working port at **Fish Pier.** Built in 1912, Fish Pier, or Pier 6, is the focal point of the city's seafood industry, although the possibility of commercial development here is always on the horizon. The live catch, a fraction of what it was when the dock hosted hundreds of boats, is auctioned off to vendors at 6 every morning. Only the leftovers are made available to "civilian" buyers. The quality of nearby fish restaurants ranges from mediocre to superb. In the latter category is the No Name (617-423-2705), where fishermen ate their meals well into the 20th century. *Pier 6, Northern Avenue, just past the World Trade Center.*

■ BOSTON HARBOR ISLANDS

More than 30 islands link Boston's inner and outer harbors in an archipelago embracing 1,200 land acres over 50 square miles. All but the outermost rocks share a common origin: they are glacial drumlins, heaps of glacial debris shaped like the back of a teaspoon. Ranging in size from less than an acre to 214 acres, the harbor islands have a long history. Some were summer fishing camps for Native Americans, and at least one was regularly planted in corn. Colonists farmed some of the islands into the early 1800s, a few became retreats for the yachting rich, and fishermen continued to use others into the 20th century. Over the years, the nearest islands were annexed by a land-hungry population, while the others became places to dump such unsightly or unsavory facilities as prisons, reform schools, poorhouses, hospitals, quarantine centers, prisoner-of-war camps, police shooting ranges, missile bases, garbage dumps, and sewage treatment facilities.

Since the 1950s, however, most of the islands have been abandoned, although a few summer cottages persisted on Peddocks Island. In 1970, the state began to acquire the remaining privately held islands (municipalities own many of them) to create a park. In 1996, Congress designated the islands as a National Recreation Area, to be administered by the National Park Service in cooperation with local governments. Boston Harbor Islands National Recreation Area now comprises more than three dozen islands, but only six are open to the public: George's, Peddocks, Lovell, Grape, Bumpkin, and Gallops.

To observe the islands, ocean, and waterfront at their blushing best, take one of the myriad **Boston Harbor cruises.** *From Rowe's Wharf: Massachusetts Bay Lines; 617-542-8000. From Long Wharf: Boston Harbor Cruises; 617-227-4321. Liberty Fleet (schooner); 617-742-0333.*

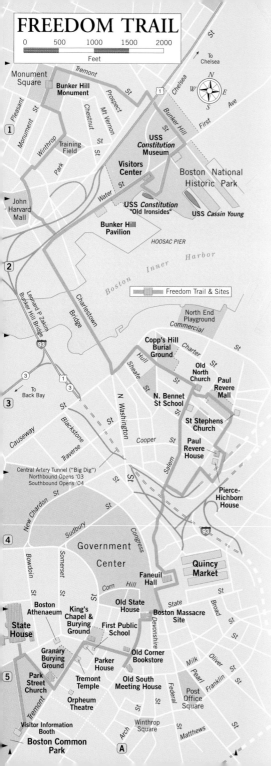

FREEDOM TRAIL

| 0 | 500 | 1000 | 1500 | 2000 |
Feet

To Chelsea

Monument Square

Bunker Hill Monument

Monument St

Prospect St

Chestnut St

Mt Vernon St

Training Field

Chelsea St

Bunker Hill St

First Ave

USS Constitution Museum

Visitors Center

Boston National Historic Park

Pleasant St

Winthrop St

Park

Water St

John Harvard Mall

USS Constitution "Old Ironsides"

USS Cassin Young

Bunker Hill Pavilion

HOOSAC PIER

Boston Inner Harbor

Leonard P Zakim Bunker Hill Bridge

Charlestown Bridge

Freedom Trail & Sites

North End Playground

Commercial St

Copp's Hill Burial Ground

Charter St

Hull St

Sheafe St

Old North Church

Paul Revere Mall

N. Bennet St School

St Stephens Church

Paul Revere House

To Back Bay

N Washington St

Blackstone St

Cooper St

Salem St

Pierce-Hichborn House

Traverse St

Central Artery Tunnel ("Big Dig")
Northbound Opens '03
Southbound Opens '04

New Chardon St

Sudbury St

Government Center

Congress St

Quincy Market

Faneuil Hall

Somerset St

Bowdoin St

Corn Hill

Old State House

State St

Broad St

Boston Massacre Site

Boston Athenaeum

King's Chapel & Burying Ground

First Public School

Devonshire St

State House

Granary Burying Ground

Parker House

Old Corner Bookstore

Milk St

Oliver St

Pearl St

Franklin St

Park Street Church

Tremont Temple

Old South Meeting House

Federal St

Post Office Square

Orpheum Theatre

Tremont St

Winthrop Square

Arch St

Matthews St

Visitor Information Booth

Boston Common Park

■ FREEDOM TRAIL

map this page

The past and present converge on Boston's Freedom Trail, a 2.5-mile path—marked with red paint and bricks—that connects 16 sites relating to the early history of America. The Freedom Trail forms a perfect introduction to the central core of Boston, where the city and the nation began. No other city, except perhaps Philadelphia, can lay claim to so many sites directly related to the American Revolution.

Because the trail traces a Colonial city embedded in the midst of a modern one, it isn't always as easy to follow as a sanitized theme-park version might be. The Freedom Trail is a walk through nearly four centuries of Boston, warts and all. If your trek leaves you too tired to make the return trip from Charlestown on foot, you can always board a water shuttle. Among the extra benefits are the great city views.

The sites on the next page are listed in order of their location on the Freedom Trail, beginning with the State House on Beacon Hill and heading north.

Downtown and Market District

Park Street Church. *See page 58 for more details.* Built in 1809. Open from Tuesday through Saturday in summer; Sunday services held year-round. *Tremont and Park Streets; 617-523-3383.*

Granary Burying Ground. *Page 58.* Laid out in 1660; open daily. *Tremont Street near Park Street Church; 617-635-4505.*

King's Chapel. *Page 58.* Built between 1748 and 1754; call for days open. *58 Tremont Street; 617-227-2155.*

King's Chapel Burying Ground. *Page 58.* Oldest part laid out in 1631; open daily. *Tremont and School Streets; 617-635-4505.*

Old Corner Bookstore (Boston Globe Store). *Page 58.* Built in 1712; open daily. *1 School Street, at Washington Street; 617-367-4000.*

Old South Meeting House. *Page 58.* Built in 1729; open daily. *310 Washington Street, at Milk Street; 617-482-6439.*

Old State House. *Page 61.* Built in 1713; open every day. *206 Washington Street; 617-720-3290.*

Boston Massacre Site. *Page 61.* Just east of Old State House. *State Street near Devonshire Street.*

Faneuil Hall. *Page 62.* Built in 1742; open daily. *Dock Square; 617-242-5642.*

Beacon Hill

State House. *Page 69.* Built between 1795 and 1798; open weekdays. *Beacon and Park Streets; 617-727-3676.*

Boston Common. *Page 72.* First settled in the 1620s. *Bounded by Park, Tremont, Boylston, and Charles Streets.*

North End and Charlestown

Paul Revere House. *Page 82.* Built in 1677; open daily (closed on Mondays from January through March). *19 North Square; 617-523-2338.*

Old North Church. *Page 83.* Built in 1723, the church is open daily. *193 Salem Street; 617-523-6676.*

Copp's Hill Burial Ground. *Page 85.* The oldest part was laid out in 1660; open daily. *Hull and Snowhill Streets; 617-635-4505.*

Bunker Hill Monument. *Page 85.* Erected in 1825; open daily. *Monument Square, Boston National Historical Park, Charlestown Navy Yard; 617-242-5641.*

USS *Constitution*. *Page 85.* Launched in 1797; open daily. *Charlestown Navy Yard; 617-242-5670.*

■ **DOWNTOWN BOSTON** *map opposite page*

Boston's downtown streets date from the late 17th century and still define the city's scale. The towering slabs of the financial and government districts may cast a shadow over the old labyrinth, but in most places, pedestrians and motorists alike must submit to the city's original curves. The **Freedom Trail** of historic, Colonial, and post-Revolutionary sites winds through this area.

Park Street runs along the north side of the Boston Common. The main landmark here is the 1809 **Park Street Church,** which replaced a huge granary previously on the site. Next door is the **Granary Burying Ground,** established in 1660 and named for that earlier building. Its 1,600 or so graves include those of Paul Revere, Samuel Adams, John Hancock, and victims of the Boston Massacre.

At 88 Tremont Street is **Tremont Temple,** America's first racially integrated church, and at 60 School Street (at the intersection with Tremont) is the **Parker House,** now the Omni Parker House, in operation as a hotel since 1856. The Saturday Club of 19th-century intellectuals met here with such visitors as Charles Dickens, and mementos are exhibited in the foyer.

The **King's Chapel and Burying Ground** occupy the corner opposite the Parker House. Originally Anglican, the church was founded in 1688 and became Unitarian after the Revolution; the present structure was built between 1749 and 1754. The British monarchs William and Mary presented the altar table in 1696, and Paul Revere cast the bell in 1816. The 1631 Burying Ground, the city's oldest cemetery, contains the graves of the first colonists as well as that of Elizabeth Pain, buried in 1704, who was branded with the letter "A" (for "adulteress") and may have been the model for Hester Prynne in Nathaniel Hawthorne's *The Scarlet Letter.*

Past one early site of Boston Latin, the nation's first public school (founded in 1635 and attended by Benjamin Franklin), and the 1865 Old City Hall is the **Old Corner Bookstore.** Now named the Boston Globe Store, this may be the oldest brick structure in the city. It was built for the apothecary of Thomas Crease on the site of the heretic Anne Hutchinson's house after it was destroyed by the fire of 1711, which burned roughly a third of the city. From 1845 to 1865, it was the office of Ticknor and Fields, the publisher of Nathaniel Hawthorne, Ralph Waldo Emerson, Henry Thoreau, Henry Wadsworth Longfellow, and Harriet Beecher Stowe. *1 School Street, at Washington Street; 617-367-4000.*

Old South Meeting House, the shrine of American independence, stands at the corner of Washington and Milk Streets. Built in 1729 as a house of worship,

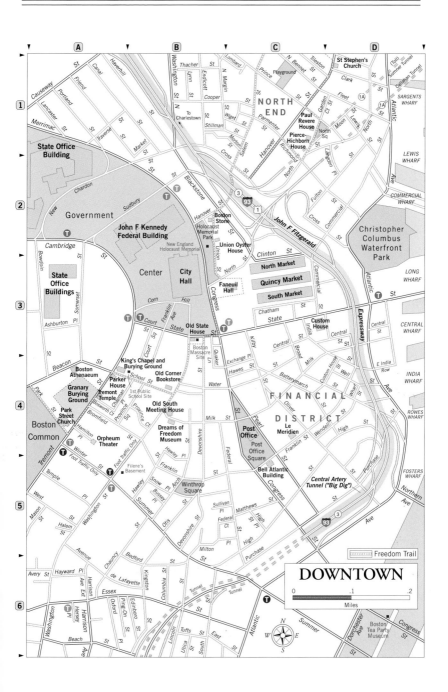

DOWNTOWN

0   .1   .2
Miles

------- Freedom Trail

FRANKLIN

the red brick church later gained notoriety as a meeting place for rabble-rousing patriots. "Who knows how tea will mingle with salt water?" Samuel Adams shouted to the 5,000 tea-tax protesters who assembled here on December 16, 1773, launching the Boston Tea Party. The British, perhaps in spite, assigned the church as an indoor riding arena for British soldiers, who ripped out the pews to use for firewood. Plans to demolish Old South in 1876 were blocked by Ralph Waldo Emerson and others. *310 Washington Street; 617-482-6439.*

Vying for the role of most important building in Boston, the **Old State House** looks fragile beside its modern, multistory neighbors, but in its day it showed muscle. Boston's oldest public building, it was built in 1713 to replace Boston's first Town House, which served, among other things, as town hall and burned in 1711. The Old State House was the epicenter of rebel activity. A cobblestone circle about 10 feet east of the Old State House marks the **site of the Boston Massacre,** and on July 18, 1776, the Declaration of Independence was read from the balcony. The government outgrew the building in 1798 and moved to its current digs on Beacon Hill. Having fallen into disrepair, the Old State House was in danger of being packed off and shipped to Chicago when, in 1881, the Bostonian Society stepped in to preserve it as a museum. The Old State House Museum traces Boston's history, with an emphasis on colonial times and early statehood. The building also houses the Boston National Historical Park Visitors Center. The well-informed park rangers can help you plan your tour of Boston's historic sites, and you can make use of the restrooms and other amenities provided. *206 Washington Street; 617-720-3290 (museum); 617-242-5642 (visitors center).*

Boston's residents didn't all come over on the *Mayflower.* The city is second only to New York as a port of entry for immigrants, having welcomed more than 100,000 newcomers per year to American soil in the early part of the 20th century. Benjamin Franklin, not surprisingly, was the son of English immigrants, and though he is associated more with Philadelphia than Boston, he was born here. The house where Franklin was born burned, but the site is now occupied by the **Dreams of Freedom Museum,** which salutes the city's immigrants and celebrates their contributions. In this high-tech facility, a holographic Benjamin Franklin serves as guide, and a film laden with special effects provides the grand finale to a visit. *1 Milk Street; 617-338-6022.*

Benjamin Franklin's parents are among those interred at the Granary Burying Ground.

■ FINANCIAL DISTRICT *map page 59, C/D-4/5*

Close to State Street is Boston's financial district, where the generally dull architecture is redeemed by the inspiring art deco **John W. McCormack Post Office and Court House** (5 Post Office Square, at Congress Street); the 360-degree mural of telephone workers and the phone-related exhibits in the **Bell Atlantic Building** (185 Franklin Street), which is open on weekdays during business hours; and the N. C. Wyeth paintings in the Julien Bar of the **Le Meridien** (250 Franklin Street). **Government Center,** an 11-acre 1960s concrete wind tunnel between Cambridge and Congress Streets, has no such redeeming features, although its garage has the notoriety of having once been condemned.

The original patriots who gathered at **Faneuil Hall Marketplace** doubtless never envisioned visitors throwing back beers named in their honor. This complex has earned itself landmark status on many levels—if not for its historical significance than for its shops, entertainment, and restaurants. Such blatant commercialism isn't for everyone; some locals won't set foot in the place. Still, many find it accommodating to their social lives, if not their wallets. Though the entity is collectively referred to as either Faneuil Hall or Quincy Market, neither moniker is entirely correct, as the two are technically separate.

Faneuil Hall is named for Peter Faneuil, who created it in 1742 as a marketplace, not much different from its current incarnation. The hall acquired the nickname Cradle of Liberty after hosting numerous meetings of irate colonists speaking out against the British. The nearby **Quincy Market,** named for Boston Mayor Josiah Quincy, was added in the 19th century. By the 1970s, the two spaces had fallen into disrepair, but developers updated the marketplace mix and sparked a trend that has been repeated in such places as Manhattan's South Street Seaport.

To those lapping up an ice-cream cone, Faneuil Hall's history may seem beside the point. But the top floor houses the Ancient and Honorable Artillery Company of Massachusetts, America's oldest military group, founded in 1638, and park rangers give daily 15-minute talks in the Great Hall itself. *Opposite Congress Street, near the intersection of State Street; 617-635-3105.*

Those who wish to dine amid history can take a table at **Union Oyster House.** Opened in 1826, the country's oldest continuously operating restaurant served Daniel Webster and claims to have offered the first toothpick. With all that history, the food could have been an afterthought, but it is actually quite good, albeit pricey, and the oyster bar is legendary. *41 Union Street; 617-227-2750.*

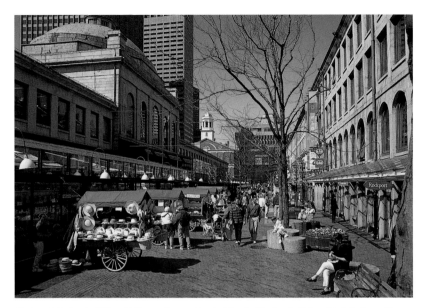

Quincy Market building (left) stands opposite the North Market building (right); Faneuil Hall can be seen in the background.

■ THEATER DISTRICT *map page 46–47, F-4*

Boston's Theater District centers on Tremont and Boylston Streets. Theater did not exist in the city until 1792, thanks to the legacy of the Puritan ban, but stage entertainment flourished in the 19th century. Censorship—or even the threat of censorship—unwittingly aided this expansion, as "Banned in Boston" often guaranteed box-office success.

At one point more than 40 venues operated here. Several of the survivors have been beautifully restored, some of them still used solely for theatrical productions, and others now multipurpose facilities. The oldest of venues is the 1900 **Colonial Theatre** (106 Boylston Street), followed by the 1903 **Majestic Theatre** (219 Tremont Street), the 1910 **Shubert** (265 Tremont Street), the 1914 **Wilbur** (246 Tremont Street), and the 1925 Metropolitan, which these days goes by the name of the **Wang Center for the Performing Arts** (268 Tremont Street).

The building housing the **Charles Playhouse** (74 Warrenton Street) was a church erected in 1839. It served as a Prohibition-era speakeasy and a fashionable nightclub before becoming a theater in 1958.

For years, the neighborhood abutting the Theater District was known as the **Combat Zone.** But that stretch of strip joints and other questionable enterprises has largely been eradicated. Early in the new millennium only one "adult entertainment" venue was still in business, and even its future was in doubt. The area remains grittier than most in downtown Boston, but a metamorphosis has begun. Backers hope the Combat Zone and the Theater District will be transformed into a larger arts district that will include some still-to-be-restored movie palaces on Washington Street. One sign that things are on the move is the new **Millennium Place** (Avery Street, near Tremont Street), with its spiffy Ritz-Carlton and entertainment complex.

■ CHINATOWN *map pages 46–47, F-3*

Adjacent to the Theater District is small but lively Chinatown, comprising Beach, Oxford, Tyler, and Hudson Streets. This area, originally called South Cove, began attracting Chinese residents when railroad jobs dried up during the late 19th century and immigrants moved east in search of work. A strike by workers at a North Adams shoe factory provided temporary jobs, but when it was settled, the Chinese, uprooted again, moved here. The enclave slowly grew from a population of a few hundred in the early 20th century into today's community of more than 5,000 people from all over southeast Asia. The emerging pan-Asian restaurant scene is attracting the downtown office crowd for lunch.

(above) Chinatown Boy Scouts pose for a photograph in the 1930s. (Boston Public Library)
(opposite) The beaux-arts Majestic Theatre turned a century old in 2003.

■ BEACON HILL *map opposite page*

When you come upon brick-lined roads and gaslit street lamps, you know you've wandered into Beacon Hill. For two centuries Boston's most prestigious address, this preserved 19th-century district is one of America's finest architectural treasures—a neighborhood that legally enforces good taste. Including part of the Boston Common and roughly outlined by Bowdoin Street, Cambridge Street, and Storrow Drive, the hill feels like a self-contained village. The elegant row houses are protected by strict development regulations, but residents enjoy the convenience of having fine food, antiques, and everyday supplies just steps away in the quaint (and expensive) shops and restaurants on Charles and Cambridge Streets. Home to the original Boston Brahmins, the hill comprises just one square mile of Boston, but its residents no doubt hold a good chunk of the city's wealth.

Designed by the renowned architect Charles Bulfinch, the **Harrison Gray Otis House** is the birthplace of Beacon Hill high society and is the prototype for the Federal-style residences that characterize the area. Mr. Otis, who capped off a career in politics as the third Mayor of Boston, left his mark on the city by helping to develop the tony Beacon Hill enclave. He and merchant Jonathan Mason were among a group of people who formed the Mount Vernon Proprietors, collectively known as the fathers of Beacon Hill. Built in 1796, the Otis residence had several incarnations, including a 19th-century stint as a boardinghouse. Despite its one-time state of disrepair, the house has been meticulously restored as a museum by the **Society for the Preservation of New England Antiquities,** which offers tours. One of the glorious residence's many surprises is the exuberance of the Colonial and early Federal decoration. *141 Cambridge Street; 617-227-3956.*

Also on Cambridge, practically next door to the Otis House, is the 1806 **Old West Church,** which replaced a 1737 wood-frame structure. Recitals are staged on the church's Fisk tracker-action pipe organ. *131 Cambridge Street; 617-227-5088.*

Narrow thoroughfares like **Holmes Alley** are typical of the North Slope's 17th- and 18th-century streets, while nearby **Rollins Place** presents a 19th-century architectural tease: a false portico concealing a 20-foot fall to Phillips Street. Pinckney Street once divided white from black, rich from poor. The 1797 **George Middleton House** (5–7 Pinckney Street) is thought to be the oldest extant house built by African-Americans; it was shared by Middleton, a livery man, and Louis Glapion, a hairdresser.

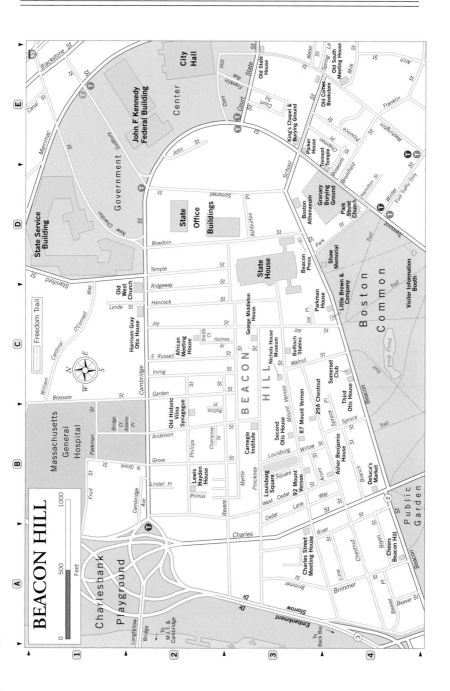

BEACON HILL

Built in 1806, the **African Meeting House** is now part of the Museum of Afro-American History. The New England Anti-Slavery Society was founded here in 1832, and Boston's first black school was started in the basement. *8 Smith Court; 617-725-0022.*

Beacon Hill's streets share a pedigree, but many have managed to cultivate their own unique personalities—whether by design or by chance. The famed purple windows of **Chestnut Street** were originally considered a defect, but the oddly shaded glass now adds character to the street. **No. 29A** is the area's oldest house, as its rippled 1820 window glass attests. Richard Henry Dana lived at No. 43 before choosing the sea over Harvard and describing his experiences in *Two Years Before the Mast.* The historian Francis Parkman lived at 50 Chestnut from 1863 to 1895, during which time he completed *The Discovery of the Great West* and other books.

Acorn Street supplies undiluted Beacon Hill charm. With original cobblestones and a slight overabundance of window boxes, it is one of the most photographed streets on the hill. Its smaller residences attest to the street's long-ago history as housing for "the help."

(above) Green grass grows between cobblestones in early summer on Acorn Street.
(following spread) Beacon Hill, as seen from the Charles River.

Visitors who long to get a glimpse inside a Beacon Hill residence should head to harmonious **Mount Vernon Street,** where the **Nichols House Museum** is open for tours. The four-story town house, designed by Charles Bulfinch, was home until 1960 to Rose Standish Nichols, a writer and landscape architect notable for her books on gardening. As stipulated by her will, the Federal-style row house is preserved with many of Nichols's belongings. *55 Mount Vernon Street; 617-227-6993.*

The novelist Henry James lived on Mount Vernon Street for a brief time and finished the novel *Daisy Miller* at No. 131. From 1817 to 1819, the statesman Daniel Webster lived at 57 Mount Vernon Street.

Louisburg Square, purported to be the city's wealthiest block, runs between Mount Vernon and Pinckney Streets. The Greek Revival section, built between 1834 and 1847, faces onto a handkerchief of greenery that hardly deserves the term "park," but it is private—and therefore coveted—real estate. Louisa May Alcott lived at No. 10 from 1885 to 1887, suffering from the poisonous effects of mercury ingested while nursing in the Civil War. Jenny Lind, the "Swedish Nightingale," was married in No. 20, and more recent residents include Senators Edward Kennedy and John Kerry.

Charles Street is downhill but hardly down-market. Originally the neighborhood's shoreline, the pretty thoroughfare is lined with restaurants and antiques shops. A couple of grocery stores and a hardware store keep terminal cuteness at bay. The **Charles Street Meeting House** (Mount Vernon and Charles Streets), erected in 1807, was a center of abolitionism.

Across Embankment Road are the **Charles River Esplanade** and the **Hatch Memorial Shell,** which hosts performances by the Boston Pops Orchestra as well as Fourth of July fireworks and other extravaganzas.

On the opposite end of Beacon Hill, the golden-domed **State House** presides over Boston Common, its cornerstone laid in 1795 by the revolutionaries Samuel Adams and Paul Revere. Built on land once owned by John Hancock, the state's first governor, the building took shape over more than a hundred years. It began with the redbrick neoclassical centerpiece designed by Charles Bulfinch. A large Italian Renaissance extension—roughly five times the size of the original structure—was added in 1895. Two white marble wings were completed in 1917, and the glass dome–topped Great Hall behind the east wing was added in 1990.

A double staircase from the magnificent Doric Hall leads to the chamber of the House of Representatives, where the 1784 Sacred Cod—a huge wood codfish presented by Boston merchant Jonathan Rowe as a reminder of the importance of the

fishing industry—still hangs as the House's unofficial mascot and good-luck charm. The upstairs library houses some articles of interest, but many of the oldest objects and documents are now on view at the Commonwealth Museum on Morrissey Boulevard. *Beacon Street between Bowdoin and Joy; 617-727-3676.*

Boston Common is the country's oldest public park, originally used as a common grazing ground for the cows of local farms. The still unspoiled acreage was first settled by William Blaxton, who built a cabin here in 1624 and later sold the 48 acres to John Winthrop's Puritans. Criminals, Quakers, adulterers, and witches were pilloried and hanged here throughout the 17th century. As recently as the 18th century, Back Bay's waves still broke on the Common, and boats launched from these banks carried British soldiers to march on Lexington and Concord and to attack Bunker Hill. Over the years, the park became a notable rallying point: This is where patriot Samuel Adams railed against British interference, Martin Luther King Jr. drew vast crowds, and Pope John Paul II celebrated Mass. Numerous monuments and plaques—including the Boston Massacre Memorial, created in 1888 by Robert Kraus—pay homage to the city's noble past. *Bordered by Beacon, Charles, and Tremont Streets.*

On the Common, across from the State House, is the **Shaw Memorial,** an arresting bas relief by Augustus Saint-Gaudens, commemorating Col. Robert Gould Shaw and the all-black 54th Massachusetts Regiment. A young white officer born to a prominent Boston family, Shaw volunteered to command the 54th and led it in the 1863 Civil War attack on Fort Wagner in Charleston, South Carolina. Many men of the regiment died in that action, including Shaw. Their names are inscribed on the memorial.

Today, the Common serves as a place for recreation. Visitors can throw a ball, glide along the frozen Frog Pond in winter, or simply take a stroll. The city's **Visitor Information Booth** is on the Common at Tremont Street, near the Park Street subway station, a National Historic Landmark. From here it is an easy walk to the residences of Beacon Hill, the retail euphoria of Newbury Street, or the crooked streets of the city's origin.

You can walk through the first two floors of the **Boston Athenaeum,** which was established in 1807 as "a retreat for those who enjoy the humanity of books" and which is still splendidly hushed and humane. A renovation of the building—it's on the outskirts of Beacon Hill just east of the State House—was completed in 2002. *10½ Beacon Street; 617-227-0270.*

Cheers Beacon Hill, a neighborhood bar on the northwestern edge of the Common, was for years known as the Bull & Finch Pub, but it became so popular after becoming the inspiration for the television sitcom *Cheers* that its owners changed the name so fans of the show wouldn't be confused. The bar is in the basement of the Hampshire House hotel, which occupies the former Thayer mansion, built in 1910 in the Georgian Revival style. *84 Beacon Street; 617-227-9605.*

■ **BACK BAY** *map pages 46–47, E/F-3/4*

Graceful Back Bay and the airy parks that circle it are the expression of a confident, optimistic city. In 1857, Boston embarked on the 30-year project of converting 450 acres of tidal slime into a model of residential planning and civic amenity. To the inhabitants of a cramped 19th-century city, the vision of space and symmetry must have been heady. For a pedestrian enjoying the broad sweep of Commonwealth Avenue today, it still is.

Commonwealth Avenue, Back Bay's seam, is a 240-foot-wide boulevard with central mall, modeled on Baron Haussmann's Parisian boulevards. Marlborough, Beacon, Newbury, and Boylston Streets run parallel to it, while the cross streets occur in alphabetical order, from Arlington to Hereford, beginning at the Public Garden. Statues of Alexander Hamilton, Leif Eriksson, and the historian Samuel Eliot Morison punctuate the boulevard, along with a handful of closely monitored American elms. Cherubs, gargoyles, and other creatures enliven the harmonious facades of the buildings lining the avenue. The normally slow pace of Boylston Street picks up considerably one Monday each April when the Boston Marathon sets up its finish line. Look for the race on Patriots' Day, when the Commonwealth celebrates the road to revolution.

The **Gibson House Museum** on Beacon Street provides a glimpse of the good life in late-19th-century Boston. The five-story Victorian row house was built for the first Gibson in 1859, and among its residents was poet Charles Hammond Gibson Jr., who was perhaps better known for his purported eccentric behavior than his poetry. Three generations of Gibsons left their mark on the decor, which has been called everything from eclectic to hodgepodge. The house is adorned with ornate wallpaper, original woodwork, and various beautiful and downright odd relics from the Gibson family. As one visitor remarked, "It looks like they just walked out the door." *137 Beacon Street; 617-267-6338.*

Newbury and Boylston Streets may be the district's fashionable shopping destinations, but this is Boston, and even on these perfumed streets, theology gives commerce a run for its money. **Arlington Street Church, Emmanuel Church, Church of the Covenant,** and **New Old South Church** are all graceful structures, though **Trinity Church,** on the Clarendon side of Copley Square, is the district's gem. In an essay on his 1877 creation, architect Henry Hobson Richardson described it as a "free rendering of the French Romanesque," a modest summation of a sublime achievement. It remains today the place where brides vie to say their nuptials—reserving their spot, so the quip goes, before they've found the groom.

More secular inspiration is supplied by the **Boston Public Library,** its oldest section completed in 1895 according to the design of Charles McKim, of New York City's McKim, Mead & White architectural firm. The most regal portion of this pseudo-Renaissance palazzo faces Trinity Church. Constructed largely by Italian artisans, the library has an imposing marble entrance hall, massive bronze doors decorated with reliefs by Daniel Chester French (best known for the Lincoln Memorial in Washington, D.C.), and many suitably ennobling murals. The Italian theme is echoed in the library's charming interior courtyard. A more modern addition, designed by Philip Johnson and completed in 1971, is on Boylston Street. *666 Boylston Street; 617-536-5400, ext. 216.*

The architectural firm headed by I. M. Pei was responsible for the 60-story **John Hancock Tower,** a gleaming edifice whose mirror-like facade literally reflects its surroundings. Completed in 1976, the building has a quirky history that includes having had its windows fall out onto the streets below (a problem since repaired). With any luck, the rooftop observation area, closed in 2001, will offer its bird's-eye views to visitors sometime soon. *200 Clarendon Street.*

The 50th-floor deck of the nearby **Prudential Center** is still open to visitors and offers a 360-degree view of the city. The building is largely considered one of the major blots on the city's skyline, but, nonetheless, you know you're looking at Boston when you see it. *800 Boylston Street; 617-859-0648.*

The vast **Christian Science Center,** which the founder of the sect, Mary Baker Eddy, referred to as "our prayer in stone," dominates the intersection of Huntington and Massachusetts Avenues. The center's Mapparium, a spectacular three-story stained-glass globe, was built in 1935 to a scale of 22 miles to an inch. *200 Massachusetts Avenue; 888-222-3711.*

Trinity Church and Copley Square.

Kenmore Square, with its confused street crossings (Commonwealth Avenue, Beacon Street, and Brookline Avenue all intersect here), has the frenetic feel of a miniature Times Square. The area is marked by a gleaming Citgo sign, a beloved icon that is a far cry from the quaint historic structures most often associated with Boston. Erected in 1965, the red triangle is as much an emblem of the area as the baseball stadium down the street. In 1983 residents proved their devotion by rallying to save the sign from being dismantled. Still, there's more to Kenmore Square than neon. The social—if not the financial—structure of the area is dominated by **Boston University.** Restaurants and chain stores cater to the thousands of students that call the mammoth campus home.

Fenway Park, meanwhile, turns out students of delayed gratification: Boston Red Sox fans, whose baseball team last won the World Series in 1918. The team sold Babe Ruth to the New York Yankees in 1920 and has tested its followers by snatching defeat from the mitt of victory ever since. Dating from 1912, intimate Fenway is major-league baseball's oldest park still in use. Tours are given, but they're best taken sooner rather than later, because redevelopment of the park is always under consideration. *4 Yawkey Way, off Brookline Avenue; 617-236-6666.*

Atlantic Fish Co. is famous for its myriad preparations of fresh seafood.

■ EMERALD NECKLACE AND THE FENS *map pages 46–47*

It took a group of visionary planners to turn Back Bay swamp into an elegant, symmetrical neighborhood, and it took Frederick Law Olmsted, considered the founder of American landscape architecture, to make the area a pleasant place to live. Arriving in Boston in the late 19th century, Olmsted was already well known for his work on New York City's Central Park. His mandate in Boston was to create a continuous series of showpiece parks that would provide crowded city dwellers with the health benefits of green acres and clean air.

Olmsted had a hand in only six of the nine resulting parks, but the Emerald Necklace project is among his greatest achievements. Today's Necklace stretches from the serene Public Garden in Boston proper to the lovely shady walks of the Arnold Arboretum. Lovers of the outdoors can also choose from Boston Common, Commonwealth Avenue Mall, Back Bay Fens, the Riverway, Olmsted Park, Jamaica Pond, and Franklin Park. Such open spaces attract numerous weekend warriors; Olmsted himself, however, would have frowned on anything so strenuous and would have expelled the joggers and athletes who currently pound his turf.

The **Back Bay Fens** area is comprised of North Basin, a marshy bird haven, and South Basin, with its rose garden, baseball diamonds, and cinder track. **Muddy River, the Riverway,** and **Olmsted Park** meander gracefully and offer an interesting selection of native and exotic trees. Fifty-foot-deep springs feed the 120-acre **Jamaica Pond,** whose natural terrain Olmsted admired so much he left it more or less as he found it.

About a 10-minute walk from Jamaica Pond is Fairsted, which the National Park Service operates as the **Frederick Law Olmsted National Historic Site.** The landscape architect's home and office—he moved here in 1883—contains more than a million design records, including documents and drawings from his Boston parks projects, Central Park, and the White House. After his retirement in 1895, his son, Frederick Law Olmsted Jr., and stepson, John Charles Olmsted, continued their father's work, changing the firm's name to Olmsted Brothers and, as their staff grew, adding additional structures to Fairsted, which not surprisingly, has well-landscaped grounds. The Olmsted site is open for touring only on Fridays and weekends. *99 Warren Street, Brookline; 617-566-1689.*

A joint project of Harvard University and the city of Boston, the **Arnold Arboretum** is the park system's showpiece, with more than 15,000 specimens on 265 acres in Jamaica Plain. *125 Arborway; 617-524-1718.*

Olmsted considered **Franklin Park,** east of the arboretum, among his greatest accomplishments. Years of neglect have damaged the original design, and the park is slowly going to seed, despite being home to the Franklin Park Zoo and its fine African Tropical Forest. *Zoo: 1 Franklin Park Road, off Route 28; 617-541-5466.*

■ ■ ■

Close to the Back Bay Fens are the Museum of Fine Arts and the Isabella Stewart Gardner Museum. Founded in 1870 and established on its present site in 1909, the **Museum of Fine Arts, Boston** (MFA) is one of the country's largest art museums, remarkable not just for its size (a permanent stock of more than a million objects) but also for the range of its collection. The Asian art holdings, for example, are unrivaled in the Western Hemisphere. Thanks to a 30-year collaboration with Harvard University on archaeological digs in Egypt and the Sudan, the museum's Nubian and Old Kingdom collection is surpassed only by that of the Cairo Museum. The MFA also has extensive impressionist and post-impressionist galleries and a fine cross-section of American paintings, sculpture, furniture, and the decorative arts. *465 Huntington Avenue, just south of the Fenway; 617-267-9300.*

Comparisons become irrelevant when you reach the **Isabella Stewart Gardner Museum.** There is simply nothing like it—anywhere. The exquisite Venetian palazzo was completed in 1901 to house Mrs. Gardner's astonishing art collection of nearly 2,500 objects from 30 centuries. She began collecting while traveling in Europe to recover from the death of her only child, and her keen eye was assisted by shrewd advice from Renaissance connoisseur Bernard Berenson, among others. The result is a fine collection of Italian Renaissance works; French, German, and Dutch masterpieces; modern paintings that include works by Degas and Matisse; and paintings by Gardner's friends James McNeill Whistler and John Singer Sargent. *280 The Fenway; 617-566-1401.*

(opposite) The Gardner's sculpture courtyard. (© Isabella Stewart Gardner Museum)
(above) Maya plate, Guatemala, A.D. 700–800. (Museum of Fine Arts, Boston)

BOSTON WITH KIDS

With all of its efforts to be perceived as a "Big" city (at least in the philosophical sense), Boston hasn't forgotten its little people. Lots of attractions are kid friendly. Freedom Trail activity books, available at in-town visitors centers, turn learning history into a badge-hunting mission. Many of the sites come to life with living history actors in season, and tours can be tailored to appeal to any age group. Of course, kids don't need or want every activity to be a designated tourist attraction. Train lovers are often entertained simply by riding the T, particularly when the trains move out of the underground tunnels and into sunlight. Although locals might dispute the Big Dig's allure as "entertainment," kids are enthralled with the huge beams and construction equipment.

A sampling of more traditional attractions:

On the littlest kid front, nobody does it better than the **Children's Museum.** This happy little enterprise was a trailblazer in its time, the first of its kind to create exhibits marked with the revolutionary term, "Please Touch." Today's Children's Museum is a far cry from the little building in Jamaica Plain. Staples like Science Playground, Grandparents' House, Hall of Toys, and PlaySpace have been entertaining kids 10 and under for years. *300 Congress Street; 617-426-6500.*

The idea of taking a vehicle from the roadway into the river may seem to define the term "accident," but the folks at **Boston Duck Tours** have made a cottage industry out of doing it on purpose—and with a flawless safety record to boot. Easily recognized by their tanklike demeanor and plastic curtains, 17 retired World War II amphibious vehicles (their name a convoluted wartime acronym that technically spells DUKW) tool around Boston on a historical land-based voyage before splashing down for a paddle across the Charles River. Kids love the company's approach to history, and

Playing is learning at the science museum.

Swan boats in the Public Garden—nearly always a hit with kids.

most come away with a few facts. Overall silliness prevails, with con-duck-tors gamely encouraging those on board to quack at designated moments. But it's all in good fun, and even the most stoic adults will be hard pressed to suppress a smile (or a terrified grimace) as the "ducks" hit the drink. *790 Boylston Street; 617-723-3825.*

What playgrounds do for the body, the **Museum of Science** does for the mind. This vast institution is a utopia of tinkering, where Science in the Park takes that playground concept and turns it into a lesson in physics. Kids and grownups will find it hard to tear themselves away from the 3-D Virtual Fish Tank, where some computer-generated fish are unleashed to terrorize other computer-generated fish. And what would an institution of this caliber be without a T-Rex or two? The Mugar Omni Theater, which plays IMAX and other films, and the Charles Hayden Planetarium complete the experience. *Science Park, Route 28 and Memorial Drive; 617-723-2500.*

The fact that Boston is easily walkable doesn't mean that kids will necessarily want to walk it. **Old Town Trolley Tours** is a healthy compromise. Faux trolleys take in all the important sites. Historical narrative is provided, and there are unlimited opportunities to hop on and off along the way. Kids who prefer the dark side of fun can hop aboard the playfully ominous Ghosts and Gravestones tour. Pickup is at any of 16 stops, including the New England Aquarium, on Central Wharf. *617-269-7010.*

—Lisa Oppenheimer

■ OTHER NEIGHBORHOODS

■ **SOUTH END** *map pages 46–47, F-4*

Before it runs into Massachusetts Avenue, Tremont Street bisects the 500-acre South End, the nation's largest National Historic District. This neighborhood of fine 19th-century row houses, tiny parks, and expansive avenues should not be confused with heavily Irish South Boston. The South End has housed each immigrant group, from the Irish to the more recent Puerto Ricans. Gentrification is slow but detectable, particularly in Union Park, near the **Boston Center for the Arts** (539 Tremont Street; 617-426-5000). The BCA's fanciful Cyclorama, opened in 1884 for the exhibition of the 400-foot-long *Battle of Gettysburg* painting, has served many uses. The boxer and South End native John L. Sullivan, the "Last of the Bare-Fisted Sluggers," fought here in the mid-1890s, and it was here that Albert Champion invented the spark plug in 1907.

■ **NORTH END** *map pages 46–47, G-2*

It is not just the Central Artery (and current "Big Dig") that cuts the North End off from downtown: it's a state of mind. This village of narrow, winding 17th-century streets and minute squares is antique, Italian, and blessedly unself-conscious. In summer Italian "feasts" are held for the pleasure of residents, not tourists, although everybody is welcome. These street festivals are named to honor saints, but the food is worshiped too.

Chichi restaurants have made their way into the neighborhood, but some of the best food here is served without frills in restaurants smaller than your kitchen. Nevertheless, weekend nights find diners ambling from restaurant to restaurant in search of that hard-won empty table. Waiting times of an hour or more are not unheard of, so make reservations when you can.

The **Paul Revere House** is Boston's oldest dwelling, the only 17th-century structure occupying its original site. Built in 1680, it was bought in 1770 by Revere, who lived here until 1800. The house was a tenement in the 19th century but was saved from demolition in 1902 and became a museum several years later. The exterior is typical of the 17th century, and the interior is restored to reflect that century as well as Revere's life and time. On guided tours only (call ahead for a schedule), you can visit the adjacent Pierce-Hichborn House, built about 1711 and later owned by Revere's cousin, a boat-builder. *19 North Square; 617-523-2338.*

Paul Revere's house in the North End is Boston's oldest dwelling.

Hanover Street is dominated by the tower of **St. Stephen's Church.** The church was built in 1714, but Charles Bulfinch transformed it into its current glory in 1804. The only Bulfinch-designed church still standing in Boston, it contains a bell cast by Paul Revere. *401 Hanover Street.*

The nearby Paul Revere Mall leads to **Old North Church,** which was erected in 1723. Old North Church—officially Christ Church—is Boston's oldest and most famous house of worship, known for that April 18 night in 1775 when two lanterns suspended from the steeple warned the patriots in Charlestown that the British were coming to Concord by boat, not on foot. On June 17, Britain's Gen. Thomas Gage watched from atop the church as his officers and men were mowed down by American fire on Bunker Hill. Today's steeple is a 1955 reproduction, both previous versions having been toppled by hurricanes (in 1804 and 1954). The crypts, where many of the church's original members are interred, are viewable during the summer, when the "Behind the Scenes" tours are running. The 300-year-old property still houses an active Episcopalian congregation, and there is an hour-long peal of bells each Sunday at noon. The peal is the oldest in America. *193 Salem Street, at Hull Street; 617-523-6676.*

Copp's Hill Burial Ground dates from 1659 and includes the graves of ministers Cotton and Samuel Mather, Capt. Thomas Lake ("peridiously [sic] slain by ye Indians in 1676"), and Mr. Prince Hall, Revolutionary soldier and head of the Black Masons. During the Battle of Bunker Hill, the British launched artillery assaults from the cemetery, and Gen. John Burgoyne noted "we threw a parcel of shells, and the whole town was instantly in flames." The Great Molasses Flood of 1919 occurred at Copp's Hill Terrace, across from the burial ground, when a 2.5-million-gallon molasses tank burst, and a molasses wave demolished several houses, killing 21 people. *Hull and Snowhill Streets; 617-635-4505.*

■ **CHARLESTOWN** *map pages 46–47, F/G-1*
Charlestown was settled in January of 1629 by Salem colonists, most of whom died of starvation and exposure. John Winthrop and his group found the site equally unwelcoming in 1630 and soon decamped to Boston. Virtually leveled by British artillery during the Battle of Bunker Hill, Charlestown was largely rebuilt in the 19th century, and gentrification is currently homogenizing this traditionally working-class area.

The **Bunker Hill Monument** is perched on Breed's Hill, where the famed Revolutionary War battle was actually fought. This battle signaled victory for the American Colonial forces, even though they were technically defeated. "Nothing could be more shocking than the carnage that followed," one British officer later wrote of the waves of assault that ended in hand-to-hand fighting. The victorious British suffered heavy casualties, and their besieged position in Boston was further weakened. "I wish this cursed place was burned," General Gage wrote in his report to London. Forty veterans of the battle attended the laying of the obelisk's cornerstone in 1825, and Daniel Webster delivered the oration. The nearly 300 stairs to the top may leave you winded but happily rewarded with stellar views.

The Charlestown Navy Yard, which was established in 1800 and remained active until 1974, is the home of the **USS *Constitution*** and the heart of the historic waterfront. Nicknamed "Old Ironsides," the *Constitution* was the first of America's superfrigates when launched in 1797. Winning 42 battles, losing none, capturing 20 vessels and never having been forcefully boarded, the *Constitution* scored its final victory in 1815, when it captured two British ships off Madeira.

There's dancing in the streets on Bunker Hill Day.

Twice consigned to the breaker's yard but rescued by popular demand and refurbished (less than 10 percent of its timbers are original), the *Constitution* now gets one outing a year, on the Fourth of July, when it is turned around in Boston Harbor. *Boston National Historical Park, Charlestown Navy Yard; 617-242-5601.*

The Navy Yard complex also holds the **USS *Constitution* Museum** (617-426-1812), which displays some of the famous hull along with nautical equipment and other artifacts, and the **Bunker Hill Pavilion** (617-241-7575), where *Whites of Their Eyes,* a multimedia re-creation of the battle, plays throughout the day. Also at the pavilion is the **Charlestown Navy Yard Visitor Center** (617-242-5601).

■ SOUTH BOSTON AND BEYOND *map pages 46–47, G/H-4/5*
On a peninsula once known as the Dorchester Neck, "Southie," as South Boston is affectionately called by locals, became a district separate from Boston proper shortly after the Revolution. Back then, the sparsely populated peninsula was inhabited primarily by well-to-do Yankees and became what historian and author Thomas O'Connor has called "the nation's first suburb." The swell of the area's Irish immigrant population during the Potato Famine of the late 1840s changed Southie from one of the city's most diverse communities into the predominantly Irish enclave that it is today, though small but active communities of Italians, Poles, and Armenians also live here.

The 35th U.S. president receives a grand salute in the imposing glass atrium of the **John Fitzgerald Kennedy Library and Museum,** designed by I. M. Pei. On 10 acres overlooking Boston Harbor, the facility has a serene, almost eerie quality, punctuated by JFK's long-abandoned sloop bobbing in the water outside. Exhibits here tell the story of Kennedy's days in politics, from his rise in the Senate to the waning days of the period that became known as "Camelot," after the fantasy court of King Arthur. Although the galleries sometimes feel like a theme park, they are in keeping with a presidency characterized as much by photogenic charisma as by political brilliance. (Kennedy gave a record 63 press conferences while in office, and these remain stirring.) Millions of pages of documents and manuscripts on the building's fourth floor are accessible to students of history. Original pages by the author Ernest Hemingway were donated to the library by his widow, Mary. They are housed in the fifth-floor Hemingway Room, decorated in a style the writer would have preferred, complete with an antelope head from his 1933 safari. *Columbia Point, off Morrissey Boulevard; 617-929-4500.*

Outdoor café on Harvard Square.

■ CAMBRIDGE *map page 88*

Separated from Boston by the Charles River and bisected by Massachusetts Avenue, the city of Cambridge is dominated by Harvard University and swayed by each fresh intellectual breeze. The minds that inhabit the Massachusetts Institute of Technology also play a major role in the city's life.

Cambridge was founded in 1630 on the site of a marketplace that is now Harvard Square. The original Puritan settlers called their home Newtowne, but the name was changed to Cambridge in 1637 to honor the alma mater of many of the colony's leaders. Commerce is still the main activity of Harvard Square, although the merchandise has changed. Emerging from the Red Line T stop, you will find national and international newspapers at **Out of Town News,** one of the city's best-stocked news agents. The **Harvard Coop** (rhymes with "soup"), directly opposite, sells textbooks, souvenir coffee mugs, and T-shirts. The narrow streets radiating at oblique angles from the Square are lined with an eclectic variety of bookstores, boutiques, cafés, and restaurants.

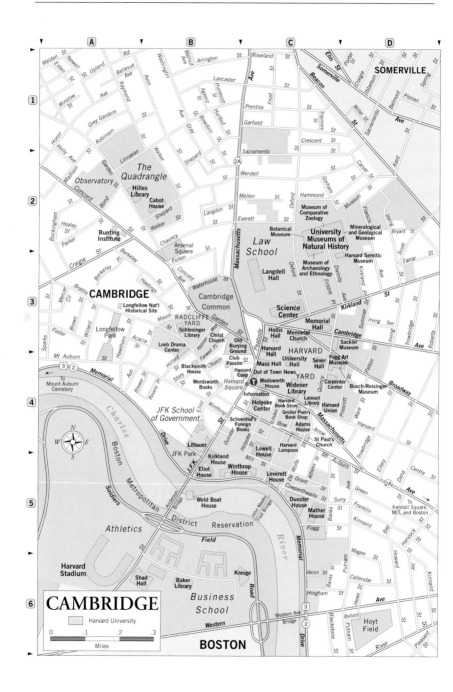

The elm-shaded **Cambridge Common** (Garden Street and Massachusetts Avenue), north of Harvard Square and circled today by ceaseless traffic, is surely the city's most pleasing and historic park. Set aside in 1631, it was reduced to its current 16 acres in 1724 and now tolerates baseball games, tai chi, courting couples, and impudent pigeons. Here George Washington took command of the Continental Army on July 3, 1775. Local lore has it that the precise spot was marked by an elm that was toppled in 1923; the site is now marked by a plaque. The **Old Burying Ground** and **Christ Church,** opposite the Common and bounded by Farwell Place and Church Street, also have Revolutionary connections.

Brattle Street is an architectural delight. Surrounded by long, green lawns and Georgian gardens, its stately mansions—models of proportion and order—sit far back from the broad, tree-lined street. Two of them are open to the public. The 1688 **Hooper-Lee-Nichols House** (159 Brattle Street; 617-547-4252) is one of Cambridge's oldest houses. Henry Wadsworth Longfellow lived from 1837 to 1882 at what's now the **Longfellow National Historical Site** (105 Brattle Street; 617-876-4491), a yellow clapboard house dating from 1759. Long before the poet took up residence, George Washington slept here—from July 1775 through April 1776, during the siege of Boston. The site is open from mid-May to October.

Within walking distance is the lovely **Mount Auburn Cemetery,** the country's oldest garden cemetery. Longfellow, Isabella Stewart Gardner, Mary Baker Eddy, and the statesman Charles Sumner are buried here. *580 Mount Auburn Street.*

■ HARVARD UNIVERSITY *map opposite page*

Harvard University, which has a student population of about 18,000 in its two colleges and 10 schools, owns almost 400 acres of land and 400 buildings in the Cambridge-Boston area. The Massachusetts Bay Colony established a college here in 1636 "to advance Learning and perpetuate it to Posterity; dreading to leave an illiterate Ministry to the Churches, when our present Ministers shall lie in the Dust," according to a 17th-century account. In 1638 young cleric John Harvard died in Charlestown, leaving half his fortune and all his books to the college. In recognition, the Great and General Court called the school Harvard College. The Puritan school imposed a monastic code, limiting tobacco use and forbidding a student to "buy, sell, or exchange anything above the value of a sixpence." Today, however, the institution's accumulated wealth—architectural, archaeological, artistic, literary, and historic—makes a brief tour of its campus and museums impossible. Allow several hours, days, or years. *For general information: 617-495-1000.*

Calm, shady **Harvard Yard** contains the university's historic buildings, Massachusetts Hall (1720) being the oldest. Dating from 1815, University Hall, with its statue of John Harvard, is the demarcation point between the Old Yard, which contains five 18th-century buildings, and the New Yard, whose 18th- and 19th-century buildings include **Widener Library**—the largest university library in the world and third-largest library in the country. It is named for Henry Elkins Widener (class of 1907), whose books were donated, along with funds to house them, when Widener died in 1912 on the RMS *Titanic*. Even if you don't have a Harvard library card, you can enter the lobby and view the historical dioramas and John Singer Sargent murals.

The **Harvard Museum of Natural History** comprises three separate but related museums, with one admission. Thousands of glass flowers, created as educational tools in the late 19th century, are on display at the **Botanical Museum.** These fabulous re-creations were crafted in minute detail, right down to the insects on them, by the father-son team of Leopold and Rudolf Flaschka. Mother nature's baubles are in abundance at the **Mineralogical and Geological Museum,** where you will also find space debris that has fallen to earth. The fascinating, although at times creepy, **Museum of Comparative Zoology** has, among other things, a taxidermic zoo. *26 Oxford Street; 617-495-3045.*

Adjoining the Museum of Natural History is the equally fascinating **Peabody Museum of Archaeology and Ethnology.** The Peabody, founded in 1866, contains Maya objects from Copán and Chichen Itza, gold figures from Panama, findings from predynastic Egypt, and materials from the Lewis and Clark expedition. *11 Divinity; 617-496-1027.*

Harvard has three art museums that together house one of the world's finest university art collections. Oldest of the three, the **Fogg Art Museum** (32 Quincy Street; 617-495-9400) displays European and American prints, sculptures, drawings, and paintings dating from the Middle Ages to the present. Because of the Fogg's refreshingly modest size, the medieval pieces, French 19th-century landscapes, pre-Raphaelite creations, and American paintings of the 18th and 19th centuries can be viewed without exhaustion. Grafted onto the Fogg in 1991, Werner Otto Hall houses the Germanic art of the **Busch-Reisinger Museum** (Prescott Street; 617-495-9400), which is entered through the Fogg's second floor.

Harvard's Memorial Church.

The holdings include major works by such 20th-century masters as Max Beckmann, Paul Klee, and Franz Marc. Ancient Asian, Islamic, and Indian art are found in the **Arthur M. Sackler Museum** (485 Broadway; 617-495-9400), which has one of the finest collections of archaic Chinese bronzes and jades in the West.

■ **KENDALL SQUARE** *map pages 46–47, E-3*

Kendall Square, east of Harvard on Route 2A, is a center of the biotechnology industry. Casting a long shadow here is the area's other great educational institution, the **Massachusetts Institute of Technology** (77 Massachusetts Avenue; 617-253-1000). This school's small, quirky **MIT Museum** (265 Massachusetts Avenue; 617-253-4444) includes exhibits on the history of the slide rule and beautiful holographic art. The **Hart Nautical Museum** (55 Massachusetts Avenue), part of the MIT Museum, has a fine collection of ship models.

■ **LEXINGTON** *map pages 8–9*

Although the official beginning of the Revolutionary War is said to have occurred at the North Bridge in Concord, it was in Lexington on April 19, 1775, that the minutemen first encountered British troops. Cozy, sedate Lexington, an affluent suburb of Boston, looks nothing like a battlefield today, but once a year, at dawn on April 19, it is again overrun by redcoats and patriots. Re-enacting the town's most heroic moment and providing a chilling glimpse of the battle, implacable British soldiers and agitated militiamen once again face each other on the Lexington Green. It all seems entertainingly quaint until Major Pitcairn shouts "Lay down your arms, you damned rebels, and disperse!" The first shot is fired, and the British soldiers, exhausted and jumpy after a night's marching, fire volley after volley, then level their bayonets to charge the men standing just feet from them. Eighteen Americans fall (eight died), and the effect, even on camcorder-wielding spectators, is palpable.

Lexington looks much as it did when the British set out from Boston to seize a rebel military supply at Concord, and Paul Revere, along with William Dawes and Samuel Prescott, set out to alert the countryside. The houses surrounding the green are original, as is the late-17th-century **Buckman Tavern** (1 Bedford Street, on the Lexington Green; 781-862-5598), where more than six dozen minutemen waited through the night for the British troops. Samuel Adams and John Hancock were staying at the **Hancock-Clarke House** (36 Hancock Street; 781-861-0928), now a museum, when Revere rode out to warn of the British intentions.

History still resonates in the 900-acre **Minute Man National Historical Park,** which runs from Lexington through Lincoln to Meriam's Corner in Concord, along the route of Battle Road. Minute Man park also includes the area around the North Bridge in Concord, where the "shot heard 'round the world" was fired. This is where the opening chapters of the Revolutionary War unfolded.

Today, you can retrace the soldiers' course on the **Battle Road Trail,** a 5-mile path for pedestrians, bicycles, wheelchairs, and baby carriages that includes remnants of the original Battle Road but also leaves the road as the minutemen did, traversing fields, wetlands, and forests. The preserved landscape of crumbling foundations and cobblestone walls conveys an eerie sense of what it was like to be a minuteman dodging redcoat bullets. Markers along the way point out historic spots, such as where Paul Revere was captured. Some restored buildings, including the Hartwell Tavern, are open for tours in season.

A multimedia presentation at the **Minute Man Visitor Center** provides background on the Revolutionary War and its participants. *Route 2A; 781-862-7753.*

The Revolutionary War started on Concord's North Bridge when minutemen responded to their first orders to fire against British troops, an act of high treason against the crown.

Munroe Tavern, south of the visitors center, served briefly as field headquarters for British relief troops and a field hospital for the wounded. A bartender was reportedly shot in the back when he ran for the door, and a bullet hole is still visible in the ceiling. Visited by George Washington in 1789, the preserved tavern is now a museum. *1332 Massachusetts Avenue; 781-674-9238.*

■ CONCORD *map opposite page*

At the time of its settlement in 1635, Concord (then known by its Native American name Musketaquid) was the frontier. The settlers purchased a 6-square-mile plantation, then sealed the deal with a peace pipe. The town's name commemorates that friendship.

Today, this charming place is too well bred to beat either its Revolutionary or literary drum too loudly. Ralph Waldo Emerson, Nathaniel Hawthorne, Henry David Thoreau, and Louisa May Alcott lived and wrote here in the birthplace of transcendentalism, but you get the impression that Concord took them in its easy stride. Even the river is sedate; so sedate that Hawthorne said he lived beside it for weeks before working out which way it flowed.

Still, Revolutionary history is amply preserved in the Concord sections of **Minute Man National Historical Park.** At the park's North Bridge, on Monument Avenue, minutemen received their first command orders to fire (the shots fired by the colonials at Lexington were an impromptu response), an act that constituted high treason against the crown and thus launched the war. Emerson's famed poem "Shot heard 'round the world" reflects on that moment; it is etched on the base of the *Minute Man Statue,* also located at the North Bridge. The small span of the bridge shows just how close these armed adversaries once stood to one another. *North Bridge Visitor Center, 174 Liberty Street; 978-369-6993.*

Wright's Tavern, the Hill Burying Ground, Monument Square, and a few lesser sites also preserve the Revolutionary part of Concord's history. The literary part is more widely dispersed but is easily accessible from Route 2A.

Rev. William Emerson built the historic **Old Manse** in 1770. Legend has it that he watched the North Bridge battle from here, but locals don't buy it. They say more than likely the good minister was out on the field preaching to his soldiers. William's grandson, Ralph Waldo, lived here in 1834 and 1835 and wrote his first book, *Nature,* in a second-floor study. Nathaniel and Sophia Hawthorne rented the house for three years, first occupying it on their wedding night in 1842, and

Hawthorne wrote *Mosses From an Old Manse* in the second-floor study. The Hawthornes scratched graffiti on a couple of window panes, and their first child, Una, was born upstairs. Emerson and Hawthorne memorabilia are exhibited at the house. Henry David Thoreau planted the vegetable garden as a wedding gift to the Hawthornes. *269 Monument Street; 978-369-3909.*

The **Orchard House** is a shrine to the Alcotts, who lived here from 1858 to 1877. Louisa May Alcott wrote her first novel, *Moods,* at the house, as well as her most famous novel, *Little Women,* thus keeping the family out of poverty. The Alcotts left in 1877, but family items and many of her books are displayed here. *399 Lexington Road; 978-369-4118.*

Little Women was based partly on Louisa May's girlhood memories of the family's other Concord house, the **Wayside,** where they lived from 1845 to 1848. Nathaniel Hawthorne bought it in 1852 after the publication of *The Blithedale Romance,* a novel that satirized a utopian community akin to one started by Bronson Alcott, Louisa May's father. Built in 1688, the house is known primarily for its literary heritage, but it has a military history as well, having once provided storage for seven tons of gunpowder. During

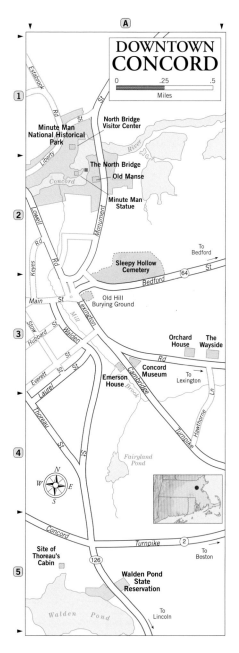

Ralph Waldo Emerson wrote in his study and entertained other writers and intellectuals here. The contents of the study are now on exhibit across from his house. (Concord Museum)

Revolutionary times, Wayside was home to the muster master of the Concord minutemen, who was charged with readying the troops for battle. Exhibits include a few pieces of furniture that date back to the Hawthornes and the Alcotts, as well as Nathaniel Hawthorne's writing tower, the place where he plied much of his craft. The house is operated as part of Minute Man National Historical Park. *Open May–Oct.; 455 Lexington Road, adjacent to Orchard House; 978-369-6975.*

The writer Ralph Waldo Emerson lived at **Emerson House** from 1835 until his death in 1882. Thoreau, Hawthorne, and the Alcotts visited often; Thoreau is said to have crafted the dollhouse in the nursery. The house is open seasonally. *28 Cambridge Turnpike; 978-369-2236.*

The original furnishings of Emerson's study are exhibited across busy Cambridge Turnpike at the **Concord Museum,** as is the simple furniture from Thoreau's Walden cabin. The museum houses the largest collection of Thoreau artifacts in the country, but its Revolutionary War–era memorabilia and period rooms are equally impressive. *200 Lexington Road; 978-369-9763.*

Rejecting a society in which "the mass of men lead lives of quiet desperation," Henry David Thoreau built himself a cabin by **Walden Pond** on Emerson's wood lot and lived there from 1845 to 1847. *Walden, or Life in the Woods,* published in 1854, was an account of that experience and its lessons. Were he living at Walden today, Thoreau would hear the soundtrack of that desperation as rush-hour traffic roars by on Route 2. A cairn of stones marks the cabin's original location, but the site is now largely dedicated to recreation, not contemplation, and the writer's solitude is literally unimaginable. *Route 126 off Route 2.*

■ TRAVEL BASICS

Getting Around: Boston's winding streets and historic neighborhoods are compact and easily explored on foot—it's an easy walk from the waterfront to downtown and Beacon Hill, for instance, and even into Back Bay. Driving through Boston is challenging, and rush hour is a veritable endurance test—you'll spare yourself great anxiety if you stick to public transit. The city's easy-to-master subway system can take you virtually anywhere in Boston proper, though you might need an occasional taxi. You can get to the sights in many of the outlying towns by car or by taking the commuter rail.

Climate: Summer temperatures range from 70 degrees Fahrenheit to the muggy 90s. Spring and autumn are unpredictable but glorious, while winter temperatures typically hover around freezing with an Atlantic bite. Ice makes quaint pavements treacherous, dictating sensible (not sleek) footwear.

Dress: The thousands of students at the Boston area's universities contribute to an anything-goes style of dress. Ultra-hip duds are definitely not a necessity, although you'll find no shortage of trendsetters strutting chic Newbury Street or taking in the scene at local nightclubs.

You will feel perfectly comfortable in slacks and jeans in cooler months, and shorts during the sultry summer. Carry a sweater in summer—the air-conditioning in some places can be downright chilly.

NORTH SHORE
& THE LOWELL AREA

The knob of land known as the North Shore juts out from the northeast corner of Massachusetts and is bounded on two sides by the Atlantic Ocean and on one side by New Hampshire. Sometimes referred to as "the other Cape," it is a beautiful, seductive place punctuated by the granite knuckle of Cape Ann.

Although less famous than Cape Cod, the North Shore is far from impoverished. This area north of Boston witnessed the death throes of Puritan zealotry, the flowering of global maritime trade, and the birth of the industrial city. You have to squint at times to bring that past into focus, but a trick of the light or a change in the wind can do it. On the wild stretch of coast here, the ocean's mood has always meant the difference between a fortune gained or lost, a prosperous life or an early death.

Today, even the fishing villages here are caught up in the modern bustle—the daily ebb and flow of commuter traffic from nearby Boston, overhead flights from neighboring Logan Airport, and the annual inundation of fair-weather visitors. There are, however, quiet times. Bright, bustling summer is flanked by two seasons of glorious suspense: spring, when the human wave has yet to reclaim the beaches, and autumn, when that wave has receded and cold, raw winter is poised to empty the streets of traffic and refurnish them with snowbanks.

■ HISTORY

In 1623, a group of fishermen and farmers from Dorchester, England, came ashore at Cape Ann hoping to fish, trade, and air their religious views. The Dorchester they left behind is better known to us as Thomas Hardy's Casterbridge, a town described by the heroine of *The Mayor of Casterbridge* as "huddled all together and shut in." Cape Ann was certainly the opposite, its windswept shores rewarding the settlers with space—but little else. "No sure fishing place in the Land is fit for planting," wrote John White of the Dorchester Company in organizing the settlers' crossing, "nor is the fishing good where farming is."

The Dorchester enterprise failed within three years. In 1626, however, its last manager, 34-year-old Roger Conant, led 20 followers along the Indian trail to Naumkeag, where they faced the encroaching winter in a cluster of hastily built

The Launching of the Ship "Fame" *(1802), by George Ropes. (Peabody Essex Museum)*

thatched huts. Naumkeag was renamed Salem in 1629, by which time Conant's group had been placed under the austere rule of the Massachusetts Bay Colony's Puritan regime.

The Massachusetts wilderness of the time was hardly enticing, as one settler's wife testified. "The air of the country is sharp," she wrote, "the rocks many, the trees innumerable, the grass little, the winter cold, the summer hot, the gnats in summer biting, the wolves at midnight howling." Governor Bradford also warned that "they are too delicate . . . that cannot enduer the biting of a muskeeto; we would wish shuch to keepe at home till at least they be musketo proofe."

More importantly, though, the fish were biting. Ideal for salting and drying, the codfish caught in these northern waters were soon nourishing not only Colonial farmers but also much of Europe, and salt cod became a key element in the expanding West Indies trade. By the mid-17th century, the area north of Boston, although still the frontier, supported a string of flourishing trading towns and fishing villages, all dependent on ships built with native white oak and pine. By 1643, ships were ferrying cod and lumber from Salem's port to the West Indies and sailing back to Europe or New England with molasses and rum, trading along the way for manufactured goods. In Salem, Gloucester, Ipswich, and Newbury, shipbuilding was a major industry by 1660.

Increasing interference from the Crown was first ignored and then resisted by colonists on the North Shore, who protested the appointment of Sir Edmund Andros in 1686 as governor of New England with rallies in Ipswich and neighboring towns. Imperial control was further tightened in 1691, and the following year

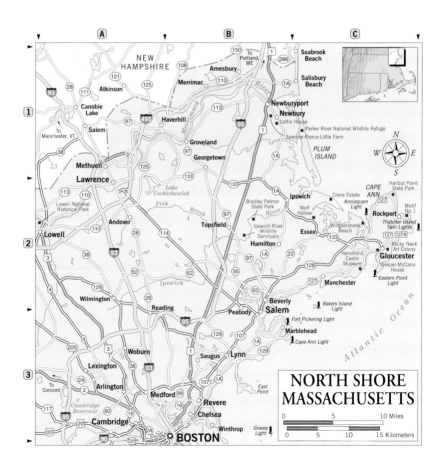

NORTH SHORE
MASSACHUSETTS

Indian Encampment at Salem Harbor *(ca. 1920s), by John Orne Johnson Frost, is the artist's vision of Salem 300 years earlier. (Shelburne Museum)*

the witch hysteria in Salem Village briefly threatened to destabilize the entire region. Prosperity would weather not only superstition, but also the impending revolution, which was in fact financed largely by Massachusetts ship owners.

The launching of the first Gloucester schooner in 1713 galvanized the fishing industry, and by 1744 the small town of Marblehead had 90 vessels at work. Later in the century, Massachusetts merchants began charting new international trade routes. In 1784, the *Empress of China* completed her maiden voyage to the Orient, and two years later *Grand Turk,* owned by Salem's Elias Hasket Derby, reached the Chinese port of Canton. The opening of the Indies and China trade was the dawn of the North Shore's golden age, which would last until the early 19th century, with Salem at its center.

Thomas Jefferson's 1807 embargo on shipping to and from England and France during the Napoleonic Wars effectively closed foreign trade to a Massachusetts fleet that was earning about $15.5 million in freight money annually. The War of 1812 dealt North Shore merchants a further blow, and by mid-century the region's trading dominance was lost to Boston's deeper harbor.

Commercial fishing remained healthy, particularly in Gloucester, but Massachusetts was increasingly a manufacturing state. First water and later steam powered huge new textile mills at Lowell and Lawrence from the 1820s onward, and in 1848 Salem entered the factory age with the opening of the Naumkeag Steam Cotton Mills.

■ SALEM *map page 103*

"To the farthest port of the rich East" is Salem's motto, but its souvenir T-shirts are more likely to read, "I did it every witch way in Salem." In a delicious twist, the Salem witch trials of 1692 have spawned a tourist industry that would confound the Puritan zealots who inspired the phenomenon.

Salem's 18th-century merchants, on the other hand, would instantly recognize the impulse to trade on past infamy. Trade, after all, was their business. It was also the key to Salem's considerable political influence and the source of the city's extraordinary cultural and architectural wealth.

Despite its modest beginnings as Roger Conant's tiny settlement in 1626, Salem has never been a backwater. Each era—maritime, industrial, and commercial—has left its distinct mark on the city, as have the immigrants who continue to arrive. The resulting townscape, while small and eminently walkable, is also somewhat fractured.

Salem's 1.7-mile **Heritage Trail,** indicated by a red line on the sidewalk, connects the major historic sites. Entire streets are meticulously preserved, but the spaces in between run the gamut from intriguing shabbiness to phony charm. Most of the phony charm can be found on the **Essex Street Pedestrian Mall.** Farther along toward Salem Common, however, the Peabody Essex Museum houses genuine riches in its exquisite and informative exhibits.

Founded in 1799 by the East India Marine Society, the **Peabody Essex Museum** is the oldest continuously operated museum in the country, having started out as a repository for artifacts acquired by Salem's mariners. Its porcelain collection alone is remarkable, but there are also paintings, sculpture, furniture, and textiles from Asia and the Americas. Exhibits related to New England history and to Salem's seafaring tradition provide an invaluable background to any exploration of the city. The museum's long-awaited expansion and renovation should be complete by the end of 2003. The Peabody runs tours of several historic houses, among them the 1684 John Ward House, the 1727 Crowninshield-Bentley House, and the 1804 Gardner-Pingree. Behind the last of these is a small architectural

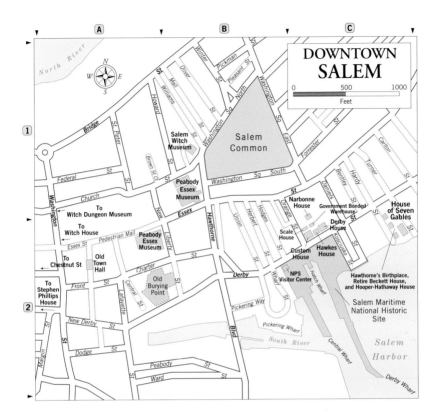

jewel—the Derby-Beebe Summer Tea House, built in 1799 for Elias Hasket Derby. The architectural critic Peter Vanderwarker described the 12-foot-square teahouse as "a delicate confection in a community of stuffed shirts." *Main entrance, Essex Street at Liberty Street; 978-745-9500.*

The **National Park Service Salem Visitor Center** provides general information for visitors strolling downtown. There are exhibits on the early settlement of the city, the maritime era, and the leather and textile industries. A film covers the history of Essex County. *2 New Liberty Street; 978-740-1650.*

Salem's handsome **Common** is ringed by elegant houses bearing the stamp of architect Samuel McIntire. Nearby is the Salem Witch Museum, in front of which stands a statue of Roger Conant, described by the historian Samuel Eliot Morison as a "moderate and kindly puritan, conciliatory and peaceful." Conant would

The John Ward House, built in 1684, is open for tours. (Peabody Essex Museum)

doubtless have been horrified by the exhibits in the museum, which include dioramas chronicling the events that led to the imprisonment of 150 townspeople and the execution of 20. *19½ Washington Square North; 978-744-1692.*

Although nearby Danvers, then called Salem Village, was the town contorted by witch hysteria, Salem, the scene of the trials, capitalizes on the 17th-century aberration. Throughout the summer, trials are reenacted in the **Witch Dungeon Museum** (16 Lynde Street; 978-741-3570), and during the summer and fall, **Old Town Hall** (Essex Street Mall) becomes the setting for *Cry Innocent: The People vs. Bridget Bishop* (978-927-2306, ext. 4747), a reenactment of the trial of purported witch Bridget Bishop. Farther down Essex Street is an authentic site—the **Witch House** (310½ Essex Street; 978-744-0180), the residence of Magistrate Jonathan Corwin, where the accused were subjected to intimate preliminary examinations in rooms that today seem more cozy than sinister.

Ships no longer dock at the historic Salem waterfront, but on a brisk May morning when a northeast wind corrugates the sea, it is easy to imagine the air being perfumed by the exotic spices of a schooner's hold. Of the 50 wharves that once ridged Salem Harbor, only Derby, Central, and Hatch, which date from 1762 to 1819, remain. The wharves are the centerpiece of the 9.5-acre **Salem Maritime National Historic Site** (978-740-1650), which includes several houses and warehouses as well as the Custom House. Rangers lead tours of some of the buildings and the *Friendship,* a work-in-progress replica of a 1797 East Indies trading vessel.

Facing the wharves is the maritime site's 1819 **Custom House** (178 Derby Street), where Salem novelist Nathaniel Hawthorne worked as surveyor of the port of Salem from 1845 until 1849. Fortunately for Hawthorne, Salem's port was declining at that time, so the writer was able to fill his notebooks as well as his ledgers during idle work hours. Behind the Custom House in the **Scale House** and **Government Bonded Warehouse** are exhibits that reveal the variety and value of Salem's 18th-century imports.

The **Derby House** (168 Derby Street) was built in 1762 by Richard Derby for his son Elias Hasket Derby and his new wife, Elizabeth Crowninshield. Probably America's first millionaire, Elias Derby took over the family business and expanded its European and West Indies trade. He profited immensely from privateering during

A golden eagle perches on the pediment of the Custom House in Salem.

the Revolutionary War and was instrumental in opening the East to Salem. His ship *Grand Turk* was the first Salem vessel to reach China, trading its load of ebony, ginseng, gold thread, cloth, and betel nuts for tea, silk, spices, porcelain, and cassia.

Samuel McIntire designed the 1780 **Hawkes House,** next door, for Derby, who used it as a privateer warehouse during the Revolution. Samuel Hawkes, owner of the Hawkes Wharf, bought and completed the house in 1801; these days the park rangers use it as an office. Behind the Hawkes House is the 17th-century **Narbonne House,** which was the home and workshop of various Salem craftsmen as well as the "Cent Shop" described by Hawthorne in his 1851 novel, *The House of the Seven Gables.*

A short walk from the maritime site is the **House of the Seven Gables,** also known as the Turner-Ingersoll Mansion. Built in 1668 but extensively restored in 1910, the house was the inspiration for Hawthorne's novel. The interior secret staircase is often credited by energetic tour guides with everything from hiding witches to being a part of the underground railway. Ominous as it looks (the painfully narrow passage requires all who visit to breathe in hard to pass through), curators say it is simply an original staircase that got cloaked when the newer parts of the house were built. Part of the Seven Gables complex is **Nathaniel Hawthorne's birthplace,** a less stately abode moved to this location from its original site a few blocks away on Union Street. The Hawthorne house shares a charming harborside garden with the **Retire Beckett House** (1655) and the **Hooper-Hathaway House** (1682)—an arrangement that would surely have displeased a writer who liked to choose his neighbors. *54 Turner Street; 978-744-0991.*

Arguably Salem's grandest thoroughfare and one of the nation's finest architectural sites, **Chestnut Street**—a wide, tree-lined street of mostly Federal-style houses—was laid out between 1796 and 1804. Its elegant 19th-century residences, many of them influenced by McIntire's architecture, were owned by merchants and sea captains and even today have an air of uninterrupted prosperity. Chestnut Street is particularly lovely in late spring, when its exquisite private gardens overrun their brick walls and impudent sparrows play hopscotch on the herringbone brick sidewalks. The **Stephen Phillips Memorial Trust House** (34 Chestnut Street; 978-744-0440) is open for tours, but you should, above all, dawdle on the street itself to appreciate the remarkable security created by Salem's high-stakes maritime gambling.

A statue of Roger Conant, Salem's first leader, stands in front of the Salem Witch Museum.

■ **MARBLEHEAD** *map page 100, C-3*

Arriving in Marblehead in 1715, the Rev. John Barnard wrote: "Nor could I find twenty families that could stand upon their own legs, and they were generally as rude, swearing, drunken, and fighting a crew as they were poor."

Now the respectable yachting center of the eastern seaboard, Marblehead nonetheless retains a delightfully chaotic demeanor, particularly in its historic district, where narrow streets weave toward the harbor and pre-Revolutionary houses are positioned to compose complicated labyrinths. Attempting to drive and park in such mazes is frustrating and time-consuming, particularly in July and August. Far better to relieve yourself of your car in the Front Street public lot, or on one of the streets skirting the older part of town, and proceed on foot or two wheels.

Fishermen from Devon and Dorset (and later from Cornwall and the Channel Islands) first settled Marble Harbor, as they called it, in 1629. Clinging to a terrace of granite ledges regularly pounded by northeast gales, the town rapidly became a leading fishing, shipbuilding, and trading port. With its fine mansions and thriving businesses, Marblehead became the sixth-largest city in the colonies and a center of Revolutionary and privateering activity. Superstition and wild imaginings also flourished.

As you tour, keep in mind the "screeching woman of Marblehead," a poor lass who was purportedly killed long ago by pirates at Louis Cove and was said to haunt the harbor in the 17th century, and the town's "Mammy Redd," hanged in Salem as a witch for turning butter to wool. Moll Pitcher, a famous psychic, was born here in 1743; the wizard Edward Dimond defied gales atop Old Burial Hill; and Marblehead was the model for the fictional Kingsport in the horror writer H. P. Lovecraft's *Kingsport: City in the Mists*.

The charming harbor into which the old town tumbles is mesmerizingly peaceful these days, especially on a luminous June or July morning, when you might picnic at **Fort Sewall** on Front Street or at **Chandler Hovey Park** on Marblehead Neck. Pretend you're a local by referring simply to "the Neck" and by merely raising an eyebrow when confronted by such mansions as **Carcasonne,** off Ocean Avenue, or by the viewpoint at Castle Rock. Faking it is tougher during hectic Race Week in July—a nautical spectacle more than a century old that attracts hundreds of boats—and during the Labor Day Regatta, when individuals who don't know their lanyards from their spinnakers are advised to keep a respectful distance from those who do.

Marblehead, ca. 1920, by John Orne Johnson Frost. (Marblehead Historical Society)

Still, you don't need arcane knowledge or waterproof clothing to appreciate Marblehead's unique buildings (more than 200 date from before the Revolutionary War) and their gardens, both ranging from grand to pocket-size. The **Jeremiah Lee Mansion,** across from the Marblehead Historical Society on Washington Street, shows what 18th-century profits could buy. Completed in 1768, this is one of the finest Georgian houses in the country, with original wallpaper, furniture, and paneling as well as a lovely sunken garden of lavender and boxwood. Lee, a shipping magnate and Revolutionary, was attending a seditious meeting in Arlington when the British passed through that Massachusetts town on their way to Concord in April 1775. He escaped through the fields but died a month later from exposure. *161 Washington Street; 781-631-1768.*

The nearby **King Hooper Mansion** was begun in 1728 by candlemaker Greenleaf Hooper. In 1745, Hooper's son, Robert, expanded the property, which now serves as the home of the **Marblehead Arts Association** (8 Hooper Street; 781-631-2608). A few doors down, on elegant Washington Square, is **Abbot Hall** (188 Washington Street; 781-631-0000), which holds America's favorite Revolutionary War painting, *The Spirit of '76.* Gen. John Glover assembled his men here before marching to Boston.

In Market Square, the beautiful **Old Town House,** built in 1727, is one of the most symmetrical in Marblehead. It was constructed with identical entrances so that it could face two directions at once. The recent removal of the stairs on the east side, however, makes it clear that the west side is the official entrance. *Washington Street at the top of State Street.*

Good Harbor Beach, in the Cape Ann area.

■ CAPE ANN TOWNS *map page 100, C-2*

You can circumnavigate the small, rugged knuckle of Cape Ann in an hour's drive along the shore road, but the towns of **Essex, Gloucester,** and **Rockport** may—and should—divert you. Essex and Gloucester in particular are still seafaring towns with ramshackle appeal. Stellar views provide at least part of the charm, but the fried clams and lobster rolls are equally enticing.

■ GLOUCESTER *map page 100, C-2*

In its mid-19th-century heyday, Gloucester had a 350-vessel fleet that once landed almost 10 million pounds of fish in a single day. Today Gloucester is still a seaman's town, with an expansive harbor that shelters a fleet of fishing boats, although the catch is not quite so large. On a bone-chilling November day, when black-backed gulls hunker down on the quay and sleet pockmarks the water, the heroic mariner's statue on the waterfront seems to be heading the town into the wind, beyond Ten Pound Island, toward fair weather.

A Storm Lands in Gloucester

By midafternoon the wind is hitting hurricane force and people are having a hard time walking, standing up, being heard. Moans emanate from the electric lines that only offshore fishermen have ever heard before. Waves inundate Good Harbor Beach and the parking lot in front of the Stop-n-Shop. They rip up entire sections of Atlantic Road. They deposit a fifteen-foot-high tangle of lobster traps and sea muck at the end of Grapevine Road. They fill the swimming pool of a Back Shore mansion with ocean-bottom rubble. They suck beach cobble up their huge faces and sling them inland, smashing windows, peppering lawns. They overrun the sea wall at Brace Cove, spill into Niles Pond, and continue into the woods beyond. For a brief while it is possible to surf across people's lawns. So much salt water gets pumped into Niles Pond that it overflows and cuts Eastern Point in half. Eastern Point is where the rich live, and by nightfall the ocean is two feet deep in some of the nicest living rooms in the state.

—Sebastian Junger, *The Perfect Storm,* 1997

Long before Sebastian Junger chronicled his storm, artists rendered the tough seas around Gloucester. (National Oceanic & Atmospheric Administration)

THEY THAT GO
DOWN TO THE SEA
IN SHIPS
1623 ━ 1923

Settled in 1623, Gloucester is the oldest fishing port in Massachusetts, and one whose occupational hardships have become legendary. Rudyard Kipling's novel *Captains Courageous* was set aboard the Gloucester fleet, and Sebastian Junger's *The Perfect Storm* recounted the chilling tale of the 1991 gale that annihilated a Gloucester vessel.

Reminders of sacrifice and endurance are everywhere in this port, which was losing 100 fishermen annually at the end of the 19th century. "Full many a gallant ship/ When we were lost/ Weathered the gale" reads the inscription on the bas relief in the stairwell between the first and second floors of the beautiful 1870 **City Hall.** A sobering mural on the second floor bears the names of more than 5,000 men lost to the seas since the late 19th century. *9 Dale Avenue.*

The nearby **Sargent-Murray House,** built in 1782, displays the wealth generated by such hardship, in particular by the port's fish and molasses trade with Dutch Guiana. The structure factors into the area's literary past as well, having been built and inhabited by the author Judith Sargent-Murray. An early feminist, Sargent-Murray wrote in the 1790s, "The idea of the incapability of women, is, we conceive, in this enlightened age, totally inadmissible; and we have concluded, that establishing the expediency of admitting them to share the blessings of equality, will remove every obstacle to their advancement." *49 Middle Street; 978-281-2432.*

The **Cape Ann Historical Museum** gives visitors a taste of the town's glorious past. A modest boat in the museum testifies to Gloucester's most exceptional seafaring story. The sloop *Great Republic* belonged to Howard Blackburn, a dory fisherman who lost all his fingers to frostbite while long-lining off Newfoundland in the late 19th century. Despite his disability, Blackburn completed two solo transatlantic voyages: the first from Gloucester, Massachusetts, to Gloucester, England, in 1899; and the second from his home town to Lisbon, Portugal, in 1901. The voyage to Lisbon, which Blackburn achieved in his second sloop, the *Great Western,* set a new world record of 39 days.

Another local fisherman, Alfred Johnson, was the first man to sail the Atlantic solo in 1876, and his boat, *Centennial,* is also displayed at the museum. Joshua Slocum started his 1895 solo circumnavigation of the globe from Gloucester. In 1980 Gloucester resident Philip S. Weld, then 65, departed from here in his trimaran the *Moxie,* crossing the Atlantic in 18 days and winning the Observer Single-Handed Trans-Atlantic Race.

The heroic mariner's statue on the Gloucester waterfront.

Gloucester's artistic pedigree is flaunted in the museum's collection of marine paintings. So popular was this coast with 19th- and early-20th-century artists that one of them, John Sloan, once wrote to the literary critic and cultural historian Van Wyck Brooks that "there was an artist's shadow beside every cow in Gloucester, and the cows themselves were dying from eating paint rags." The clear, rain-washed light that inspired Milton Avery, Childe Hassam, Marsden Hartley, Maurice Prendergast, Edward Hopper, Cape Ann native Fitz Hugh Lane, and others is just as striking today, and the skeleton of Gloucester's streets remains virtually unchanged. *27 Pleasant Street; 978-283-0455.*

At the Cape Ann museum you can view Lane's famous *The Western Shore with Norman's Woe,* which depicts the landmark in Henry Wadsworth Longfellow's "Wreck of the Hesperus"—a poem that ends with the ominous lines "Christ save us all from a death like this,/On the reef of Norman's Woe!" A good way to see the actual Norman's Woe (a rock, really) is from the **Hammond Castle Museum.** The palatial and intriguing residence, with artifacts such as Roman gravestones on the walls, was built in the 1920s by John Hammond Jr., a quirky millionaire fascinated by things medieval. *80 Hesperus Avenue; 978-283-7673.*

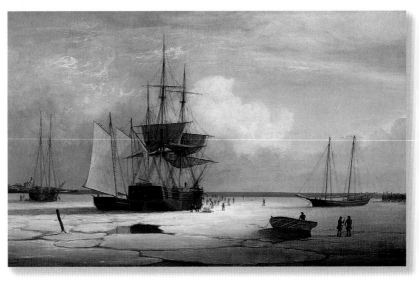

Ships in Ice off Ten-Pound Island, Gloucester *(ca. 1850), by Fitz Hugh Lane. (Museum of Fine Arts, Boston)*

Just outside town, overlooking Smith's Cove, **Rocky Neck Art Colony** is the nation's oldest working art colony. Studios along this scenic strip house more than 30 artists in residence. From Gloucester's East Main Street, head south on Rocky Neck Avenue, and the scenery unrolls like one long canvas of magnificent seascapes. Beyond the Neck, with its galleries and waterside restaurants, Eastern Point Boulevard skirts Niles Beach and proceeds past impressive mansions that command even more impressive views.

Beauport: The Sleeper-McCann House, an eccentric monument to one man's obsession, was built and furnished here between 1907 and 1934 by Henry Davis Sleeper, an interior designer whose fine antiques collection is artfully arranged in period rooms. The house was purchased after Sleeper's death by Charles and Helena McCann, whose heirs donated it to the Society for the Preservation of New England Antiquities. *75 Eastern Point Boulevard; 978-283-0800.*

Beyond Rocky Neck on East Main Street is the rocky outline of Back Shore and the elegant sweep of Good Harbor Beach. The largest summer crowds, however, favor Cape Ann's biggest beach, **Wingaersheek** (Route 128, Exit 13). At the north end of the Annisquam River, it is a sandy expanse with dunes, salt marshes, and plentiful parking. A mile away, the **Cape Ann Camp Site** (Atlantic Street; 978-283-8683) provides 300 shaded tent and trailer sites overlooking the same river, and the smaller **Little River Campgrounds** (Stanwood Point; 978-283-2616) has a tidal beach.

Larger thrills are provided by the numerous whale-watching cruises sailing out of Gloucester, Salem, and Newburyport. Experienced boaters are even encouraged to approach the whales in kayaks launched at sea. Less energetic mariners may ship out aboard the schooner *Thomas E. Lannon* for cod jigging (a method of fishing), lobster bakes, and sunset cruises. *Rogers Street: 978-281-6634.*

Each June during the three-day **St. Peter's Fiesta,** parades, boat races, fireworks, competitions, and a blessing of the fleet turn the town into a street party. This is a good time to sample Gloucester's food, much of which has sublime Portuguese and Italian flavors. You should not wait for the Fiesta, however, to enjoy the remarkable breakfast and lunch in the **Two Sisters Coffee Shop** (27 Washington Street; 978-281-3378) or the Sicilian pastries and breads in **Caffe Sicilia** (40 Main Street; 978-283-7345). During the September Seafood Festival, you can sample Gloucester's famous catch.

■ ROCKPORT *map page 100, C-2*

After robust Gloucester, Rockport, at the tip of Cape Ann, seems almost demure—if only because this has been a dry town since the seamstress and herbal healer Hannah Jumper preached abstinence almost a century ago. Or perhaps the reason is the abundance of old-time gift stores and quaint, quiet restaurants. Reproduced in painting after painting, Rockport seems to be permanently admiring itself. And who could blame it? On a cloudless June morning, even the herring gulls screeching and wheeling above the harbor are choreographed players in a picture-perfect scene. Tidy lobster boats rock contentedly beside snooty yachts, and the quay is littered with fishing nets, old rope, and lobster pots like so many still lifes.

It is hardly surprising, then, that Rockport's most famous site is **Motif No. 1,** a fish shack at the breakwater on Bearskin Neck, a short walk from downtown's Dock Square. The original shack, which collapsed into the harbor during a 1978 storm, and the current replica have been favorite subjects for generations of painters. The shack is annually venerated in May, on the Saturday before Memorial Day, when local artists paint it and sell their work—often still wet—to onlookers. Lifting your head from the canvases, you will notice that Bearskin Neck offers its own stunning views of the Atlantic.

In this town teetering on the edge of cuteness, there are some down-home holdouts. The humble **Portside Chowder House** (7 Tuna Wharf; 978-546-7045), a quick right turn as you're leaving Motif No. 1, serves some of the best chowder and shellfish in Rockport, and **Pigeon Cove,** north of Dock Square, is preserved as a lobstering and fishing harbor.

Those wishing to live, however briefly, in old Rockport style will appreciate the **Yankee Clipper Inn.** Perched on a dramatic promontory, it comprises a 1920s art deco mansion, a shingled captain's quarters, and a quarterdeck-style promenade. Katherine Anne Porter was sufficiently inspired to stay here while finishing her only novel, *Ship of Fools,* published in 1962. *127 Granite Street; 978-546-3407.*

For natural curiosities, there is **Halibut Point State Park,** an oceanside spot where even on the most hectic summer weekend, you can find a secluded spot between massive rocks from which to gaze at the coastline. Rockport's coastline was once lined by granite, the hardy substance contributing to the town's moniker. In the mid-19th century the town's quarries, still visible at Halibut Point, were the primary source of its prosperity. Today bathers plunge into some of the quarries (access is limited), and waders stand heron-like on the rocks, supervising the ankle-licking

Lobster boats and yachts share Rockport Harbor.

waves, exploring the many crab pools, or waiting for inquisitive seals to pop up only feet from the shore. Visit the same spot in winter and you'll encounter nature at her moodiest, sullenly hurling about gray waves under leaden skies or shrieking her winds at gale-force pitch. At such moments, the sight of Thacher Island's Twin Lights—the only surviving double lighthouses in the world—seem as practical as they are picturesque and provide a kind of visual punctuation for the area just outside Rockport harbor. The best way to get onto the island is by kayak; you can rent one from North Shore Kayak Outdoor Center (9 Tuna Wharf; 978-546-5050). *Halibut Point State Park, off Gott Avenue; 978-546-2997.*

■ **ESSEX** *map page 100, C-2*

Shipbuilding has shaped the town of Essex since at least 1668, when the Story and Burnham families established shipyards here. Over the centuries, many vessels have been launched in these waters, from dories and traditional Cape Ann "Chebaccos" (named for Chebacco, the original name of Essex, where the boats were developed) to modern schooners and trawlers. The first Essex boat was reportedly built by a Burnham in the 17th century, and today young Harold Burnham builds traditional wooden vessels on the same spot. Along with other

local craftsmen, Burnham in 1997 built the *Thomas E. Lannon*—the first traditional North Shore fishing schooner to be launched in almost 50 years. It now takes visitors on summer fishing heritage cruises from Seven Seas Wharf in Gloucester Harbor. *Lannon tours: 978-281-6634.*

Clams are taken seriously in what food writers Jane and Michael Stern have christened "America's fried-clam belt," and the more venerated these bivalve mollusks are, the more casually they are served. **Woodman's of Essex** (121 Main Street; 978-768-6057), a not-so-glorified clam shack only minutes from the water, has been a New England institution since Chubby Woodman first dropped some clams into a pot of lard at his roadside stand 80 years ago. Serving no-frills chowder, steamers, and fried clams that can silence any food snob, Woodman's reportedly dips its raw clams in evaporated milk before coating them with fresh cornmeal. That suspiciously prosaic explanation cannot, however, account for something that tastes like toasted sunshine. The **Essex Clam Fest,** in September, is an ideal opportunity to put Woodman's and other local clam shacks to the test

■ IPSWICH *map page 100, B/C-2*

Ipswich, north of Cape Ann, was an isolated frontier settlement when John Winthrop Jr., the son of Gov. John Winthrop of the Massachusetts Bay Colony, founded the town in 1633 with a dozen other pioneers. The younger Winthrop's wife and baby daughter died here the following year, and when Governor Winthrop visited his son, he reportedly had to walk the 30-mile Indian trail from Boston.

Winthrop Jr. was a broad-minded man of science, and under his influence this outpost quickly became a 17th-century intellectual and cultural center. Home to Anne Bradstreet, one of America's first female poets, and to satirist Nathaniel Ward in the 1630s and 1640s, Ipswich is also the setting for many of John Updike's novels. This affluent center of equestrian activity, one of New England's most beautiful towns, has more 17th-century houses preserved and occupied than anywhere else in the country.

The Ipswich Historical Society maintains two homes near the town Common. The neoclassical **John Heard House** (54 South Main Street), built between 1795 and 1804, is a fine local museum with 19th-century furnishings. The **John Whipple House** (1 South Village Green), facing the Common, is the most

Lobsters, live and cooked, at Woodman's of Essex.

Canoeing gentle waters. Ipswich River Wildlife Sanctuary. (Massachusetts Audobon)

dramatic of the town's restorations. The oldest part of the house was built in 1655; additions were built in 1670 and around 1700. The house was saved in the 1890s by Rev. Thomas Franklin Waters, who called it "a link that binds us to the remote Past and to a solemn and earnest manner of living, quite in contrast with much in our modern life." Waters's benediction aside, the Whipple House, with its lovely 17th-century garden and graceful proportions, is more beguiling than solemn—a reminder that Puritanism was not all severity. *Historical Society; 978-356-2811.*

Reinforcing that impression are the many poignant gravestone inscriptions in the **Old Burying Ground** on High Street, Ipswich's main thoroughfare. "Warm from his lips the heavn'ly doctrine fell," the 1775 testimony to Rev. Nathaniel Rogers begins, with imagery befitting a love poem. Anne Bradstreet's secular poetry scandalized the neighbors of her 33 High Street home. She acknowledged "I am obnoxious to each carping tongue/ Who say my hand a needle better fits."

Houses built in the 17th and early 18th centuries line High and East Streets, but even the town's side streets evoke its uninterrupted prosperity and architectural creativity. A great American elm at the corner of East Street is also a reminder of how such towns looked when these giants shaded every thoroughfare.

The Ipswich River is stocked with trout, and much of its watershed is protected in conservation areas between Ipswich and neighboring Topsfield. One of the North Shore's best-kept secrets and the most impressive of the areas, the 2,800-acre **Ipswich River Wildlife Sanctuary** was the private estate of the early-20th-century amateur horticulturist Thomas Proctor, who favored plantings that would encourage birds and wildlife throughout the year. The riverside parkland is most exuberant in early spring, when the Ipswich is in full flow—its creeks roaring, its banks daubed with wildflowers, and the air shimmering with butterflies. Ten miles of nature trails border 8 miles of river here; you can also canoe the gentle waterway, putting in at Foote Bros. (230 Topsfield Road; 978-356-9771), a canoe-rental outfit, by the Willowdale Dam. Children particularly approve of Proctor's most outlandish construction, the **Rockery,** a gigantic rock garden constructed out of glacial boulders. Its caves and tunnels are ideal for hide and seek. Also here is another fabled local residence—a beaver lodge, the natural home of some dam-building critters. *87 Perkins Row, off High Street; 978-887-9264.*

At **Wolf Hollow,** Joni Soffron has studied American timber wolves in natural enclosures for six years and invites you to visit with Wolf Hollow's resident pack. *144 Essex Street (Route 1A), outside Ipswich; 978-356-0216.*

CHOWDER HEADS

There is a terrible pink mixture (with tomatoes in it, and herbs) called Manhattan Clam Chowder, that is only a vegetable soup, and not to be confused with New England Clam Chowder, nor spoken of in the same breath. Tomatoes and clams have no more affinity than ice cream and horse radish. It is sacrilege to wed bivalves with bay leaves, and only a degraded cook would do such a thing.

Representative Cleveland Sleeper of Maine recently introduced a bill in the State legislature, to make it illegal as well as a culinary offense to introduce tomatoes to clam chowder. And immediately a chowder battle ensued—with high-class chefs asserting that a tomato and clam should never meet, and the low maestros of Manhattan advocating their unholy union.

Anyone who wants tomato soup can have it; but Manhattan Clam Chowder is a kind of thin minestrone, or dish water, and fit only for foreigners.

—Eleanor Early, *New England Sampler,* 1940

The Great House is the architectural centerpiece of the 2,000-acre Crane Estate.

■ **CRANE ESTATE** *map page 100, C-2*

Outlying Ipswich is a dreamy place of marshes and estuaries, much of it part of the sprawling Crane Estate. The **Great House,** perched atop Castle Hill, a historic mound of land overlooking the ocean and prized by the early colonists for its stellar farming, remains the estate's focal point and is a National Historic Landmark. Built between 1910 and 1928 for the Chicago plumbing magnate Richard T. Crane Jr., the elegant mansion can be toured in season and remains a popular year-round locale for public and private festivities. But tony soirees are only part of the estate's allure. Its more than 2,000 acres are traversed by about 4 miles of walking trails, and the Crane Wildlife Refuge has more than 180 species of birds and other wildlife. On nearby Hog Island (reachable by boat), visitors can take in the **Choate House,** a 1725 structure built for one of the area's oldest families. The island was the setting for the 1996 film version of *The Crucible,* Arthur Miller's tale about the Salem witch trials. The Crane Wildlife Refuge tour, via boat and hay wagon, takes in the "Proctor House," which was built by the film crew for two of the main characters, and travels to other islands. The ocean views on the tour are spectacular.

In spring and summer, **Crane Beach,** below Castle Hill and once part of the estate, is an idyllic, pastel arrangement of low-lying dunes, azure sea, and bleached sky, and you can see why Native Americans of the Agawam tribe were attracted to the tidal creeks and plentiful shellfish. In winter, however, when the shore is concussed by relentless surf, Crane lives up to its designation as a barrier beach, shielding Essex Bay and its estuaries from the Atlantic's ferocity. Sea ducks ride the waves on even the stormiest days, however, and a winter walk along the mile-long interpretive beach trail leading to a peaceful woodland may raise a snowy owl, red fox, or resident deer. The estate and beach are owned by the Trustees of Reservations; admission fees cover the costs of managing the property and safeguarding its wildlife. *Crane Estate, Argilla Road; 978-356-4351. Crane Beach information line; 978-356-4354.*

■ **NEWBURY**   *map page 100, B/C-1*

The old highway that is Route 1A meanders along the coastline between Newbury and Newburyport, dictating a leisurely pace—a Newbury pace, you might say. This sleepy town, settled in 1635, has an Upper Green and a Lower Green, with a duck pond in the middle for excitement.

Just off Route 1A is the **Spencer-Pierce-Little Farm,** one of the country's most atmospheric 17th-century sites, with land that has been continuously farmed for 350 years. John Spencer, one of Newbury's first settlers, was granted the original 400-acre parcel (now whittled to roughly 230 acres) in 1635. The stone-and-brick manor house came later, built by Col. Daniel Pierce toward the end of the 17th century. The Little family, a local farming clan, occupied the farm from 1851 until 1986, when it became part of the Society for the Preservation of New England Antiquities. The society has continued the tradition of working the land, leasing out parcels to local farmers who raise market vegetables and commercial flowers. Visitors to the manor are taken step by step back through its history: beginning in the mid-20th-century dining room; heading through the turn-of-the-20th-century kitchen and the late-19th-century living room to progressively older rooms; and ending in a chamber built in 1690, when the house was originally constructed. The attic walls have some original graffiti, including a painstaking sketch of a sailing ship. During the Draft Horse Plow Match, a New England–wide competition held on the farm's flat, dreamy fields each April, the clank of harnesses and the presence of docile equine giants reinforces the sense that this is a place suspended in time. *Open July–Oct., 5 Little's Lane (follow signs from Route 1A); 978-462-2634.*

The **Coffin House,** north of the town center, was the 1654 residence of tailor Tristam Coffin and his family—and ultimately six generations of Coffins. Its two early kitchens, a buttery, and Coffin family samplers and other artifacts illustrate how New England life evolved over three centuries. *14 High Road; 978-462-2634.*

■ **NEWBURYPORT** *map page 100, B-1*

Originally an outpost of its sleepy neighbor, Newburyport capitalized on its position at the mouth of the Merrimack River to become an important shipbuilding and trading center in the 18th and early 19th centuries. Specializing in the West Indian and European markets, the town also developed many rum and whiskey distilleries as well as goldsmithing, textile, and printing industries. The many editions of Nathaniel Bowditch's *New American Practical Navigator* (the seaman's bible) and Captain Furlong's *American Coast Pilot* were printed here.

The society created by such enterprises was considered one of the most sophisticated in post-Colonial America, far ahead of Salem in manner and style. Lavish balls and liveried servants were the order of the day in 1809, when the town had just 8,000 inhabitants but a merchant's cellar typically held 1,200 gallons of wine.

The decline of the Federalist party in the early 19th century punctured Newburyport's political power; Jefferson's 1807 embargo on foreign commerce wounded its shipping; and an 1811 fire destroyed 15 acres in the city center. Shipbuilding was revived, however, in the clipper era, when Donald McKay opened a shipyard here in 1841. His shipbuilding reputation was made on the

Newburyport Marshes: Passing Storm *(ca. 1865), by Martin Johnson Heade.*
(Bowdoin College Museum of Art)

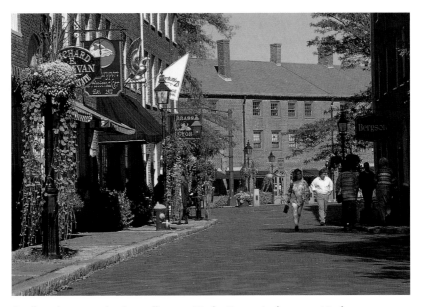

Inn Street is now a pedestrian walkway on Market Square, in downtown Newburyport.

basis of several great vessels, including the triple-decker *New World*; the clippers *Lightning* and *James Baines*; and the *Glory of the Seas*, which in 1869 made a landmark voyage from New York to San Francisco in 94 days.

Newburyport's **Market Square Historic District** has preserved many commercial waterfront buildings, including the **Custom House** (25 Water Street; 978-462-8681), built in 1835 and now a maritime museum. One theory suggests that ship carpenters designed and built Newburyport's mansions, and the originality of the ornamentation seems to support this view. Quirkiness of a more modest kind survives in the waterfront's early-18th-century dwellings, but practically every street in town demands attention, not simply for the unparalleled examples of Georgian, Federal, Greek Revival, and Victorian residential architecture, but also for the sense those streets give of Newburyport's vigorous heyday.

Conscience and commerce both had their say in Newburyport. Abolitionist William Lloyd Garrison exposed a merchant who was taking slaves as freight from Baltimore to New Orleans in 1829. Today, Garrison's statue dominates **Brown Square,** which is also the site of the **Garrison Inn** (11 Brown Square; 978-499-8500), a handsome brick mansion built in 1809 for Moses Brown, a rum merchant.

Newburyport's main outlying attraction is **Plum Island,** a small barrier island with sandy beaches, extensive marshes, and the **Parker River National Wildlife Refuge.** A residential area since Colonial times, Plum Island continues to attract newcomers, with the northern tip home to an increasing number of year-round inhabitants. Though there are a couple of very small restaurants, the highlights are undeniably the beaches and the birds—this is one of North America's prime bird-watching spots. Some of the beaches close from April to mid-June to accommodate the endangered piping plovers, but the remainder of the refuge is accessible. *Parker River National Wildlife Refuge (take Plum Island bridge); 978-465-5753.*

■ **AMESBURY** *map page 100, B-1*

Upriver from Newburyport, practically on the New Hampshire border, is the modest town of Amesbury, settled in 1654. The contrast with Newburyport is immediately evident and, on Amesbury's part, quite deliberate. Amesbury's Main Street tells the story. Instead of stripping itself down to a Federal core that was never particularly glorious and attempting to attract upscale antiques and specialty stores, the town preserved local businesses such as **W.E. Fuller Co.** (45 Main Street; 978-388-0287), which has been in the same family for four generations and continues to peddle men's and women's formal attire. Assistance was given by the National Main Street Center, a branch of the National Trust for Historic Preservation, which selected Amesbury precisely because it was so average.

Although never comparable to Newburyport, Amesbury was an important ship-building center until the steam revolution of the 1850s. Impressive 18th-century shipwrights' houses line the beautiful sweep of Point Shore Road on the Merrimack's banks. Dories, skiffs, and other small vessels are still built in the **Lowell Boat Shop** (459 Main Street; 978-388-0162), America's oldest dory shop, started in 1793 by Simeon Lowell.

Amesbury's once teeming riverfront is a beautiful, soothing place today, and it is easy to see why Robert Frost spent his summers at 5 Evans Place. Experiencing the area's old-fashioned natural charm is best done by bike on the Merrimack River Loop, a quiet, shady riverside road that winds from Amesbury to the neighboring town of Merrimac; grassy banks at regular intervals are ideal for picnicking or stone-skimming.

Among the town's small, delightful surprises is the **Bartlett Museum** (270 Main Street; 978-388-4528), named after Josiah Bartlett, the first of the New

Hampshire delegation to sign the Declaration of Independence. The museum displays an idiosyncratic collection of Native American artifacts, natural science exhibits, and carriages. Also on Main Street is **The Millyard,** a complex of restored mill buildings housing offices and stores. Main Street contains an eccentric mix of storefronts, and steep, winding dead-end streets such as Union Street reveal the town's curious angles and roof pitches.

Perhaps Amesbury has always seen itself as more substantial and less frivolous than its southern neighbors. The **Rocky Hill Meetinghouse** certainly supports that view. Built in 1785, literally on a rocky hill, the large, austere building is an outstanding example of New England meetinghouse architecture. Little used, it has remained unchanged. The only fanciful detail is the crude marbleizing on its interior columns. *Elm Street and Rocky Hill Road; 978-462-2634.*

Regardless of its plainness, Amesbury attracted more than one poet. John Greenleaf Whittier lived here from 1836 until 1876, when he moved to Danvers. Although he died in New Hampshire, his funeral was in Amesbury, where he was buried at **Union Cemetery** (Haverhill Road). The Garden Room at his home, now the **John Greenleaf Whittier Museum** (86 Friend Street; 978-388-1337), remains as it was when the poet and abolitionist wrote his inspiring and lucrative works here.

Like most New England outposts, Amesbury also has its share of witch and ghost lore. Susanna Martin, better known as Goody Martin, was a famous Amesbury witch hanged in Salem in 1693. Legend insists that the loom that belonged to Goody Whitcher, another local witch, kept weaving long after she met a less gruesome end.

■ LOWELL *map page 100, A-2*

Most of the mills at Lowell are shuttered, but some looms are run for demonstration purposes—fueled by the Merrimack River and by the determination of this mill city to preserve its industrial heritage. "Many workers . . . wanted the good and the bad of the past preserved, rather than flattened and denied," the late legislator Paul Tsongas explained in 1978, promoting the restoration of the city's historical sites.

In the 1820s, a group of Boston investors—later known as the Boston Associates—found the ideal location for a modern mill city at Pawtucket Falls on the Merrimack River. The group was inspired by Francis Cabot Lowell, the man who founded the first American mill built with a power loom. Lowell had set his mill in nearby Waltham, using a Charles River waterfall for power. Although

Lowell died in 1817, the Boston Associates saw promise in his innovations and set to work building their own mills in what would become the city of Lowell. Workers here became part of a mill community, living in dormitories and taking advantage of educational, athletic, and religious activities. The goal was to better the conditions of the workers, but because the mills were dependent entirely on Southern cotton they paradoxically aided the expansion of slavery. Sen. Charles Sumner of Massachusetts described the arrangement as the "unholy union . . . between the lords of the lash and the lords of the loom."

Unperturbed by such criticism, new companies sprang up in Lowell between 1826 and 1840, and by 1846 the mills were producing almost one million yards of cloth a week. Equally remarkable were the power canals: 6 miles of waterways that, by the 1850s, powered the mills of 40 buildings. Lowell's population kept pace, growing from about 2,500 in 1826 to 33,000 in 1850, when 10 mills employed more than 10,000 people. New England farm girls, valued by the employers for their apparent virtue and tractability, were the earliest labor source for Lowell's "bale to bolt" cotton mills. Many of these mill girls were drawn to the promised attractions of town, but more were driven by economic burdens at home.

The mill girls were soon writing and editing two factory publications: the *Lowell Offering*, which idealized factory life, and the *Voice of Industry*, which criticized it. The workday began at 4:50 A.M. and ended at 7 P.M. Curfew was 10 P.M. The average pay in the 1830s was $3.50 for a six-day week. "Up before the day at the clang of the bell and . . . into the mill . . . just as though we were so many living machines," one worker wrote. Disillusionment grew as production was accelerated to keep pace in a newly competitive market.

Labor protest erupted as early as 1834 in response to wage reductions and continued through subsequent decades. By the mid-1840s, industrial accidents were increasing worker discontent. Barilla A. Taylor, a young mill worker, wrote to her parents in 1844 that a coworker "got her hand tore off" in the card room. "I heard she has got to have it taken off above her elbow," she wrote.

Lowell's female workers earned less in 1860 than they had in 1836, despite increases in productivity. First Irish immigrants in the 1840s, then French-Canadians, Poles, Portuguese, Russians, Greeks, Syrians, and others replaced the New England farm girls on the factory floor. By the end of the 19th century, Lowell was a city of distinct immigrant enclaves, each as squalid as the English

The Boott Cotton Mills buildings were erected between the 1830s and the 1920s.

slums that had originally shocked Francis Cabot Lowell. A general strike in 1912 won a 10 percent wage increase, but mill owners were already moving their operations to the cheaper South. Most of the mills closed in the 1920s and 1930s, and some were subsequently demolished. Others were restored in the 1970s and 1980s as part of **Lowell National Historical Park. Market Mills,** the park's gateway on Market Street, houses a **visitors center** (67 Kirk Street; 978-970-5000) where exhibits and an introductory video present industrial Lowell's major themes. The canal system was the key to Lowell's success, and a tour of the remaining waterways in the city takes in an 1820s industrial canyon, a series of gatehouses, a turbine exhibit, and several canal locks.

The **Boott Cotton Mills Museum,** part of the historical park, is in a complex of buildings erected between the 1830s and the 1920s and contains a working weaving room and exhibits about textile production and working life. A superb slide show and several video presentations put Lowell in its historical context, and displays in the adjacent 1850s boardinghouse reveal the everyday life of the closely supervised mill girls. "I object to the constant hurry of everything," one of them wrote, "We have only thirty minutes to go from work, partake of food and return to the noise and clatter of machinery." *400 Foot of John Street, at French Street.*

The nearby **Kerouac Park** (Bridge and French Streets) commemorates Lowell native Jack Kerouac, the author of *On the Road* and other books. He was born of French-Canadian parents in the Centralville area in 1922. Lowell natives are largely bemused by the interest in the city's most famous writer. Still, the park remembers him with an elaborate Kerouac commemorative sculpture— thousands of his words etched into granite columns.

The Bobbin Girls, *(1871), by Winslow Homer. (National Park Service)*

Gravesite of Lowell native Jack Kerouac draws visitors from around the world.

Lowell's other museums include the **American Textile History Museum** (491 Dutton Street; 978-441-0400) and the **New England Quilt Museum** (18 Shattuck Street; 978-452-4207). The **Whistler House Museum of Art** (243 Worthen Street; 978-452-7642) is the birthplace of artist James McNeill Whistler, whose father was chief engineer of the Locks & Canals Company in the 1830s.

The city vibrates in July during the popular **Lowell Folk Festival,** where salsa meets polka and everything in between. You may even hear Lenny Gomulka singing the official state polka of Massachusetts—"Say Hello to Someone in New England."

■ TRAVEL BASICS

Getting Around: A high-speed ferry connects Boston and Salem from July to October. Commuter trains serve Lowell, Ipswich, and Rockport. If you're driving, avoid hectic Route 128. Instead follow Route 127 around Cape Ann and Route 1A northward. I-495, a major truck artery, is the most direct route to Lowell.

Climate: As elsewhere in the region, summer temperatures range from 70 degrees Fahrenheit to the muggy 90s and can change in a heartbeat. Cape Ann, regularly pummeled by Atlantic storms, is a breezy retreat when city temperatures rise.

SOUTH SHORE
CAPE COD & THE ISLANDS

Like the best escape routes, the journey south from Boston to one of the world's most spectacular coasts is a form of surrender. As you venture from the solid deck of the South Shore out onto the bowsprit of Cape Cod, then cast yourself adrift on the sandy rafts of Nantucket or Martha's Vineyard, you submit to a landscape of shifting sands and milky light, where roses grow in the dunes and the setting sun lingers on the horizon like a reluctantly departing guest.

To most visitors, it is simply the beach—an excuse to shed clothes, walk barefoot, and eat with your hands. But this bewitching place has always hidden more than it has revealed. Its dunes conceal piping plovers, its waters harbor singing whales, and its fishermen's shanties accommodate summering software tycoons.

"A man may stand there and put all America behind him," wrote Henry David Thoreau of Cape Cod in 1849. If you visit the region's most popular spots at peak times, you may find all America not only behind you but ahead of you as well, in an inland sea of traffic. But if you travel out of season, you will reach a more ecstatic conclusion.

■ HISTORY

We can thank the Wisconsin Stage Glacier for Cape Cod, and for the islands in particular. Moving south 25,000 years ago, the glacier paused, depositing boulders, sand, and debris to form the fragile hook and its satellites. The deep, enchanting ponds dotting the interior are also a glacial legacy, having originated as enormous ice blocks that melted as the glacier retreated.

Though fleetingly referred to as Cape James, in honor of King James of England, Cape Cod earned its title from explorer Capt. Bartholomew Gosnold, who in 1602 sailed up the New England coast and noted "the great store of codfish" he observed in its waters. Landing on a nearby island, Gosnold and his fellow explorer John Brereton were so impressed by "the incredible store of vines and the beautie and delicacie of this sweet soil."

Many colorful 19th-century cottages built by Methodists on Martha's Vineyard still survive.

Gosnold noticed that he had not been the first white visitor. Encountering some Native Americans, he was surprised to see them "apparelled with a waistcoat and breeches of black serge, made after our sea-fashion," and to see that they understood "much more than we for want of language could comprehend."

■ PILGRIMS AT PROVINCETOWN

Though popular legend may have it that the Pilgrims first touched New World soil on Plymouth Rock, the actual story is more complicated. In fact, *Mayflower* Pilgrims came ashore first on Cape Cod, in Provincetown, in November 1620. They later disembarked at Plymouth after finding the former inhospitable. Like Gosnold on Martha's Vineyard, these Pilgrims were amazed to discover a sign that other Europeans had preceded them: a skeleton with blond hair in a Wampanoag grave. The coast had indeed been visited before both Gosnold and the *Mayflower* set sail, chiefly by Portuguese, Spanish, Basque, French, and Italian explorers content to chart its waters and shoreline.

The First Thanksgiving at Plymouth *(1914), by Jennie A. Brownscombe. (Pilgrim Hall Museum)*

The Pilgrims, though, were the ones who stayed. "There was the greatest store of fowl that ever we saw," they wrote, "and excellent black earth." This is surely a rosy recollection. Provincetown was mostly sand, and after a month of vicious weather, the Pilgrims decamped to the cleared and abandoned Indian cornfields across the bay at Plymouth, where, with the assistance of the native peoples, they managed to survive.

The existence of the Pilgrims nonetheless remained a borderline one. Though more hospitable than their previous anchorage in Provincetown, the Plymouth terrain was unforgiving, with acidic soil and an unpredictable harbor. By 1630, the Plymouth Colony numbered just 300, whereas the Boston-based Massachusetts Bay Colony, established in 1628 and bolstered by colonists arriving by the hundreds, had more than 2,000 inhabitants. Within a decade, however, the Plymouth settlers had founded communities along the South Shore at Duxbury, Marshfield, Hingham, and as far north as Quincy. Their first permanent toehold on Cape Cod was at present-day Bourne, quickly followed by Sandwich and, in 1639, by Barnstable and Yarmouth.

■ Shipbuilding, Fishing, and Whaling

From the late 17th century, the increasingly populous South Shore was set on a prosperous course that would make it a major shipbuilding, whaling, and, eventually, industrial center. Cape Cod and the islands would remain largely poor and isolated by comparison. There were, of course, good times: Nantucket's century-long reign as the globe's whaling metropolis and the rise of towns like Barnstable, which grew rich on the China and fur trade.

In hard times, Cape Codders and islanders alike depended on nature's generosity: fish, shellfish, cranberries, sea salt, the salvage from a wrecked schooner, the detritus blown in on a gale. Like their farming cousins inland doing battle with the rocky soil, these resilient seafarers cultivated thrift and endurance, waiting out repeated adversity as they waited out recurring storms.

By 1835, Cape Cod's fishing fleet was the largest in the state, with 359 vessels, and whaling was creating unimaginable fortunes. At its peak in 1843, Nantucket had 88 whalers and a population of almost 10,000. More refined oil and spermaceti candles were exported from here than from any other American port, and whaling merchants like Daniel Fisher, on Martha's Vineyard, made fortunes supplying lighthouses with highly prized whale oil.

Workers split and wash codfish in this 1912 photograph.

By 1850, however, inadequate harbors, antiquated fishing methods, and the lack of rail transportation had condemned Cape Cod to steady decline. The Cape's population of 35,000 was, at that time, 95 percent native born and wholly dependent on the sea; however, some prescient individuals, following the lead of Capt. Zebina Small of Harwich, had begun to sell their ships and set out cranberry bogs. Some entrepreneurs during the mid-19th century thought that in addition to capitalizing on cranberries as an edible crop, they could sell them for use as a dye—a purpose for which Native Americans had employed the fruit for centuries.

This was the insular world Thoreau entered when he first walked the coastline in 1849 and wrote what is surely the finest evocation of a mysterious, haunting seascape inhabited by eccentric, resourceful people. Wrote Thoreau of an old beachcomber, whom he described as a "regular Cape Cod man":

> He looked as if he sometimes saw a doughnut, but never
> descended to comfort; too grave to laugh, too tough to cry;
> as indifferent as a clam,—like a sea-clam with hat on and legs,
> that was out walking the strand. He may have been one of the
> Pilgrims,—Peregrine White, at least,—who has kept on the
> back side of the Cape, and let the centuries go by.

■ THE SOUTH SHORE

Some people think of the South Shore chiefly as the home of Fall River's factory outlet stores, but there's more here than suburban strip malls. Such institutions as Adams National Historical Park and Plimoth Plantation evoke a past markedly different from the area's suburban present. You can follow a more or less straight line from Quincy to Plymouth to Cape Cod, or you can detour south on Route 24 from just below Quincy to Fall River to visit the Lizzie Borden House—where one of the late-19th-century's most notorious murders took place—and Battleship Cove, a collection of warships. From here you can head to New Bedford to learn about the whaling trade, after which you can pick up I-195 or U.S. 6 and travel east to Cape Cod.

■ QUINCY *map page 135, B-1*

On a stretch of land between I-93 and the inlets leading to the Atlantic Ocean stands Quincy, once a part of the neighboring town of Braintree. The city was named for the esteemed military man Col. John Quincy, the grandfather of Abigail Smith—the wife of the nation's second president, John Adams, who was also born here. John and Abigail had a son, John Quincy Adams, who became the nation's sixth president. The Adams family is memorialized at the 14-acre **Adams National Historical Park,** where you can take guided tours of two 17th-century saltbox houses: the birthplace of John Adams and the Peacefield mansion, in which four generations of Adamses lived. Original furnishings include John Adams's law desk, on which it is believed the United States Constitution was drafted, as well as thousands of books from the Adams collection. *1250 Hancock Street; 617-770-1175.*

"My country has in its wisdom contrived for me the most insignificant office that ever the invention of man contrived or his imagination conceived," remarked John Adams about his role as vice president under America's first leader, George Washington. Adams, lauded as much for being a philosopher as a politician, did not toil in political obscurity for long; he succeeded Washington as president after two terms. The higher office evidently didn't change his opinion of politics: "No man who ever held the office of President would congratulate a friend on obtaining it. He will make one man ungrateful, and a hundred men his enemies, for every office he can bestow."

A mayflower design appears on the stern of Mayflower II, *a replica of the original ship.*

■ PLYMOUTH *map opposite page*

Plymouth makes the most of its status as New England's earliest successful European settlement. British specialty stores abound, and even the laundromat is called Ye Olde Pilgrim Washing Well. Despite these recent shows of pride, the town has failed to preserve some of its oldest dwellings.

The scene at **Plymouth Rock** can often seem comical, with vacationers snapping pictures of and throwing pennies at an unresponsive rock at the bottom of a pit. But in an age when the blockbuster mentality holds sway even at historical attractions, this old-fashioned veneration of the nation's symbolic doorstep is almost touching. The 690-million-year-old granite boulder no doubt was once a prominent shoreline feature that played an important navigational role (as in, "Turn right at the rock"), but centuries of sand accumulation have reduced its visibility considerably. The symbol of the Pilgrims' arrival was accidentally halved in 1774 and reassembled in 1880, at which point the date 1621 was chiseled into it. The Greek portico that currently houses Plymouth Rock dates from 1921.

This columned structure houses Plymouth Rock, the symbol of the Pilgrims' arrival in the North America in 1620.

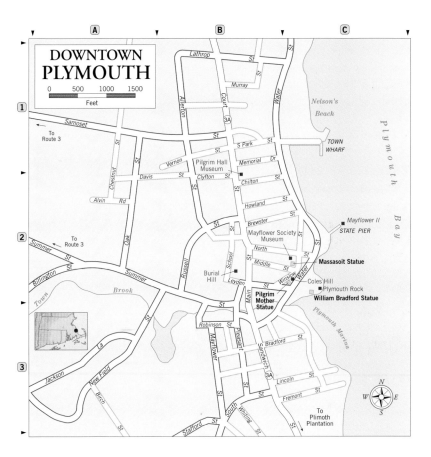

Coles Hill, across the street from Plymouth Rock, is the burial site of the settlers felled daily by disease and exposure during that first bitter winter of 1620. A nearby statue commemorates Massasoit, the Wampanoag chief who helped the remaining Pilgrims to survive.

If the rock is the teeming waterfront's still point, the ***Mayflower II*** is its eye-opener. Boarding the tiny, flamboyant ship, you will be astonished that 103 people, with their worldly goods and livestock, survived on board for 66 tempestuous days. Even the replica has proved itself: Built in England in 1955, it sailed the Atlantic to Plymouth two years later. *State Pier; 508-746-1622.*

In the fall the area's cranberry fields, flooded for harvesting, turn bright crimson. The site is as spectacular as the berries are tart and tasty. One way to appreciate the countryside is on harvest-time train rides offered by the **Edaville USA Family Fun Park.** The theme park, whose other diversions include a carousel and a Ferris wheel, closes during inclement weather, and the trains run only sporadically, so call ahead. *7 Edaville Avenue; 877-332-8455.*

Burial Hill saw the first Pilgrim constructions—a meetinghouse, fort, and watchtower. Its 17th-century cemetery contains the grave of Governor Bradford. *Leyden Street, behind First Parish Church.*

That the General Society of Mayflower Descendants takes its heritage quite seriously is evident at the **Mayflower Society Museum,** in the residence of Edward Winslow, the great-grandson of Plymouth Colony's third governor. The mid-18th-century home's nine period rooms present a graceful if decidedly selective evocation of the past. Fittingly, the *Mayflower II* is not far away. *4 Winslow Street; 508-746-2590.*

The **Pilgrim Hall Museum,** in the center of town, houses the largest collection of Pilgrim artifacts, including colonist Myles Standish's swords and Governor Bradford's Bible, as well as special exhibitions. A painting of the first Thanksgiving by Jennie A. Brownscombe is also in the collection. *75 Court Street; 508-746-1620.*

■ PLIMOTH PLANTATION *map page 135, D-3*

Nothing in Plymouth proper prepares you for the extraordinary immersion into the 17th century that you will experience at Plimoth Plantation, just south of town off Route 3A. Written descriptions of this living history museum sound hokey, but Plimoth Plantation is, in fact, mind-altering, even unsettling.

A dusty track descends from the visitors center and Carriage House Crafts Center, past corn planted in the hummocked, Native American manner, into the stockaded 1627 village. Everything here—the primitive wooden houses, agricultural and domestic implements, clothing, crops, animals, costumes, and speech—has been meticulously researched and reproduced. The livestock has even been "back-bred" for authenticity.

Questions you always wanted to ask about the *Mayflower* voyage, the early struggles, theological debates, and Native American reactions will be answered here by the people who appear to have lived through the events. When you wander past Myles Standish's house and a green-stockinged Pilgrim greets you with "Good day,

Mistress," the instinct to laugh him off evaporates quickly. These costumed interpreters, all living the historically accurate lives of their assigned characters from 9 A.M. to 5 P.M. daily, are too convincing to be dismissed. Appearing neither rehearsed nor programmed, they are consummate actors who effortlessly draw you into their world. Spend even an hour here—visiting women in their gardens, men building Governor Bradford's house, or the Wampanoags at their home site outside the stockade—and you will enter not only this life, but also this mentality. Afterward, getting back into a car seems positively surreal.

The daily life of Plimoth Plantation also includes reenactments of events such as the Patuxet Strawberry Thanksgiving in June, the 1621 First Thanksgiving in October, Colonial musters, and the arrival of Dutch messengers from New Netherlands (New York). There are regular lectures and workshops on everything from rare livestock breeds to 17th-century scandal, and the center's bookshop is a superb resource on the 17th century. An exhibition in the Nye Barn subtly examines the goings-on in Plymouth Colony. *Route 3, Exit 4 (follow signs); 508-746-1622.*

Costumed interpreters replicate the life of the Pilgrims at the Plimoth Plantation.

■ **FALL RIVER** *map page 135, A/B-5*

The area originally coveted by the Wampanoags for its river achieved later notoriety of a less idyllic sort when Lizzie Borden gave school children a rhyme to forever chant in schoolyards. The former mill town saw its favor further decline in the 20th century, when failing textile mills folded for good and left the once-thriving economy in tatters.

Tourism in the former mill town has picked up, with some visitors drawn by the legend of Lizzie Borden. The wealthy namesake of the **Lizzie Borden House** purportedly murdered her parents here in 1892. In addition to being a museum, the house is now a B&B whose owners invite you to spend a night "if you dare." Artifacts providing a window into Borden's psyche include her library, which contains the ominously titled gardening book *With Edged Tools.* Among the cozy accommodations is the room in which Lizzie's mother was found dead. *92 Second Street; 508-675-7333.*

The Lizzie Borden House may provide the ultimate Lizzie backdrop, but the **Fall River Historical Society** has the props—thousands of them. The killer artifacts include a blood-stained bedspread and a handle-less ax believed to be the murder weapon. *451 Rock Street; 508-679-1071.*

The fascinations are less morbid at **Battleship Cove.** The floating museum's collection of 20th-century war vessels, many of which can be toured, includes a battleship, a destroyer, and a submarine. The men who served on these gallant warships can often be seen paying homage to them. The 690-foot Battleship *Massachusetts,* dubbed "Big Mamie" by her crew, seems cavernous and endless. In her day, Mamie was a packed city of 2,000 people, with cannons enormous enough to inspire a chill just on sight. To dispel any romantic notions you might have of submarine life, tour the cramped and claustrophobia-inducing interior of the *Lionfish. 5 Water Street (take I-195, Exit 5); 508-678-1100.*

The Massachusetts. *(Battleship Cove)*

A Lady with an Ax to Grind

From the schoolyard rhyme, you might assume that Lizzie Borden was a convicted murderess—the brutal slayer of her father and stepmother, Andrew and Abby Borden. But the technical inaccuracies of the rhyme aside—there were only 19 and 11 "whacks" respectively—Borden was acquitted on all counts, leaving the citizens of Fall River to ponder forever who actually did commit the city's most infamous crime.

"Many people have strong opinions," says Michael Martins of the Fall River Historical Society, who with Dennis A. Binette edited the book *The Commonwealth of Massachusetts vs. Lizzie A. Borden.* "But the more research you do, the more confused you get."

The murders took place at the Borden home on the morning of August 4, 1892. Lizzie attracted immediate suspicion because she was home at the time and because she stood to gain financially from her parents' demise. Her shifting accounts of her whereabouts during the time of the murder also seemed to point to her guilt.

But the case was less open and shut than is widely believed. Lizzie's incoherent ramblings, taken during the initial inquest but never heard by a jury because she had no attorney present at the time of questioning, could have been the result of sedatives administered by the Borden physician. And if Lizzie did in fact slay her parents, why was it that just minutes after Andrew's death, she appeared not the least bit out of breath and without a single drop of blood on her? (The coroner pinpointed a precise time of death by analyzing the amount of breakfast that Andrew had digested—an advanced research method for the time.)

Salacious angles about Lizzie's motives—one theory had her committing the crime because she'd been caught in a lesbian affair—made the case a headline grabber. And a sensational cast of suspects, including the maid, a sister, and Andrew's purported illegitimate son, generated yet more curiosity about the case.

All the hubbub and reasonable doubt aside, attorneys on both sides of the case were not surprised by the acquittal. Victorian ladies of Lizzie's class, after all, were not convicted of such heinous crimes. But the mystery and allure persist, as steady sales of the Martins book attest. Of the mystery's enduring appeal, says Martins, "The fact that it's unsolved makes it fascinating."

—Lisa Oppenheimer

■ NEW BEDFORD *map page 135, B/C-5*

As a modern port disfigured by a modern highway, New Bedford cannot entirely immerse its visitors in its maritime past. Considering its handicaps, however, the town does a remarkable job. A vibrant whaling port for more than a century, New Bedford was in its prime in the mid-19th century, when it had a fleet of more than 300 whalers and a single-minded merchant class. "They hug an oil-cask like a brother," Emerson quipped.

Herman Melville's Ishmael spent time here, and Melville himself shipped out of New Bedford in January 1841 aboard the *Acushnet;* he jumped ship in the Marquesas Islands and returned three years later. Melville knew well the Seaman's Bethel on Johnnycake Hill and made it the setting for the sermon episode in *Moby-Dick.* Mused Ishmael, "Yes, the world's a ship on its passage out . . . and the pulpit is its prow."

New Bedford was an important station on the Underground Railroad, a series of safe houses that helped runaway slaves reach freedom in Canada. Abolitionist

BOUNTIFUL NEW BEDFORD

In New Bedford, fathers, they say, give whales for dowers to their daughters, and portion off their nieces with a few porpoises a-piece. You must go to New Bedford to see a brilliant wedding; for, they say, they have reservoirs of oil in every house, and every night recklessly burn their lengths in spermaceti candles.

In summer time, the town is sweet to see; full of fine maples—long avenues of green and gold. And in August, high in air, the beautiful and bountiful horse-chestnuts, candelabra-wise, proffer the passer-by their tapering upright cones of congregated blossoms. So omnipotent is art; which in many a district in New Bedford has superinduced bright terraces of flowers upon the barren refuse rocks thrown aside at creation's final day.

And the women of New Bedford, they bloom like their own red roses. But roses only bloom in summer; whereas the fine carnation of their cheeks is perennial as sunlight in the seventh heavens. Elsewhere match that bloom of theirs, ye cannot, save in Salem, where they tell me the young girls breathe such musk, their sailor sweethearts smell them miles off shore, as though they were drawing nigh the odorous Moluccas of the Puritanic sands.

—Herman Melville, *Moby-Dick,* 1851

The whaling museum in New Bedford displays a half-scale model of the whaling bark Lagoda. *(following pages) William Baker's colorful log of a South Atlantic voyage. (New Bedford Whaling Museum)*

Frederick Douglass himself hid here for a time after escaping from Maryland. As a child, the writer Conrad Aiken also found solace here with his aunt after the death of his parents in Georgia. He later referred to the city in his autobiography, *Ushant,* and in his novel *Blue Voyage.*

The **New Bedford Whaling Museum,** which opened in 1903, is the largest museum dedicated to American whaling, with extensive collections of scrimshaw, nautical equipment, marine paintings, and documentary photographs. An enormous textile panorama depicts a whaling voyage, and the museum's 89-foot-long half-scale replica of a fully rigged whaling ship, the *Lagoda,* is the world's largest ship model. Numerous ship's logs and mariner's journals vividly recall the town's golden age. The museum also has a reconstruction of the *Spray.* The 37-foot sloop, given to Captain Joshua Slocum by a friend, had been rotting in Fairhaven for several years. The captain rebuilt the vessel and, departing from Boston, circumnavigated the globe in three years—the first person to accomplish this feat solo. In his book *Sailing Alone around the World,* Slocum chronicled the voyage, which he completed in 1898. *18 Johnny Cake Hill; 508-997-0046.*

Although modern trawlers now call New Bedford home, the town still hosts **historic vessels,** particularly during the Fourth of July weekend, when such schooners as the *Ernestina,* an 1894 fishing vessel and arctic explorer, dock here.

Architectural evidence of New Bedford's previous wealth can be found on County Street, overlooking the waterfront. The magnificent **Rotch-Jones-Duff House and Garden Museum,** built here in the 1830s for the whaling merchant William Rotch Jr., contains period furniture and paintings and is surrounded by several beautiful gardens. *396 County Street; 508-997-1401.*

Wednesday Nov 21st 1838.

Commences with light winds from the N. W.
to the Southward saw right whales and chased sta
boat struck waist boat killed and about sunset
him alongside and took in sail, and shortly after
wind shifted to the S. W. middle and latter part
breezes at daylight commenced cutting, and after we g
through stood to the N. W.

So ends these 24 hours.   Lat. by obs. 36. 11.
     Long. By c⁰. 23. 30.

Thursday Nov 22d 1838.

Begins with fine breezes from the Westward a
about 5 P.M. saw a large sperm whale low
and chased but did not strike, whale bound to the
middle part light breezes latter part nearly calm saw a right w
All hands employed in bailing.
So ends these 24 hours.   Lat. by obs. 35.. 55
     Long. By c⁰ 23.. 40.

Friday Nov 23d 1838.

Commences with moderate winds from the No
standing to the Westward spake the Ship Hann
of Sag-Harbor with 90 bls. sperm oil and abo
same time we caught a porpoise, middle part
breezes latter part moderate employed in stowing down.
So ends these 24 hours.   Lat. by obs. 36. 16.
     Long. By c⁰ 24.. 19
     By Lunar.

Saturday Nov 24th 1838.

Begins with light winds heading to the N. E. saw
whale and chased and spoke the Ship Condor of New Bed
with 1650 bls of oil, middle and latter part light breezes
right whales starboard boat struck larboard boat killed and
So ends these 24 hours.   Lat. by D. R. 36. 6

Sunday Nov 25th 1838.

Commences with light winds from the Northward
saw plenty of whales lowered and chased starboard boat
struck and he stove the boat and were obliged to cut the
line and let him go, middle and latter part light
saw whales and chased waist boat struck and drawed.
So ends there 24 hours.   Lat. 36.. 08.
                                Long. 23.. 59.

Monday Nov 26th 1838.

Begins with very light breezes and chased a right
whale, middle part nearly calm latter part fine breezes
from the Northward saw whales and chased without
success, and caught two porpoises.
So ends there 24 hours.   Lat. By obs. 36.. 52.
                                Long. By ct. 24.. 25.

Tuesday Nov 27th 1838.

Commences with fresh breezes from the Northward
saw plenty of whales and chased middle part fresh
breezes latter part strong breezes saw right whales
and chased.
So ends there 24 hours. Lat By D.R. 36.. 38.

Wednesday Nov 28th 1838.

Begins with light breezes from the Westward and
fine weather saw right whales and chased but did
not strike, middle part much the same latter part
fresh breezes saw a right whale and chased.
So ends there 24 hours.   Lat. By obs. 36.. 43.
                                Long. By ct 24.. 07.

Thursday Nov 29th 1838.

Commences with light breezes from the Westward,
middle part light breezes latter part fresh gales from the Northward and
So ends there 24 hours.   No obs.

■ CAPE COD *map opposite page*

Bridges are punctuation marks between departure and arrival, often between work and play. Cross the Cape Cod Canal—the world's largest sea-level canal—on either the Sagamore or the Bourne Bridge, and the waterway beneath you suddenly becomes a ribbon decorated with canoes, puffing work boats, and elegant schooners.

■ BOURNE *map page 151, B-3/4*

Arriving in the village center of Buzzards Bay, you see what tourism here looked like 50 years ago. In the visitors center of the **Cape Cod Canal Region Chamber of Commerce** (70 Main Street; 508-759-6000), the only attempt at slick marketing is a highly informative video on cranberry growing. Here you may also first experience the Cape Cod accent, as the woman behind the desk repeatedly talks of *aahdfex.* It takes a moment to realize that she is referring to "artifacts." The menu at **Leo's Breakfast** (249 Main Street; 508-759-7557), up the road, has a distinct Portuguese accent.

Bourne, in fact, is an old hand at cross-cultural experiences. This was the site of the Aptucxet Trading Post, established in 1627 by settlers from Plymouth who bartered with Wampanoags who had arrived on the Cape some 3,500 years earlier. A reproduction of the trading post, the **Aptucxet Trading Post Museum** is bordered by 17th-century herb and wildflower gardens. *24 Aptucxet Road; 508-759-9487.*

■ FALMOUTH AND WOODS HOLE *map page 151, A/B-5*

Visitors to the southern Cape enclaves of Falmouth and Woods Hole are usually either headed to the Vineyard or involved with the world-renowned research center here. Falmouth offers warm-water benefits that its northern-cape counterparts do not—Nantucket Sound at this point is relatively shallow and protected from the harsh waters of the Atlantic Ocean. During summer, the water temperature can be downright balmy.

Finicky eaters will feel out of place in **Betsy's Diner** (457 Main Street; 508-540-0060), a Falmouth institution where the food is hearty, the portions large, and the service brisk. To walk off your indulgence, explore **Falmouth Green,** declared a common in 1749 and now surrounded by fine 18th- and 19th-century houses. A refuge for Quakers in the 17th century, Falmouth refused to surrender two cannons to the British in 1814 and was lightly bombarded for its impertinence.

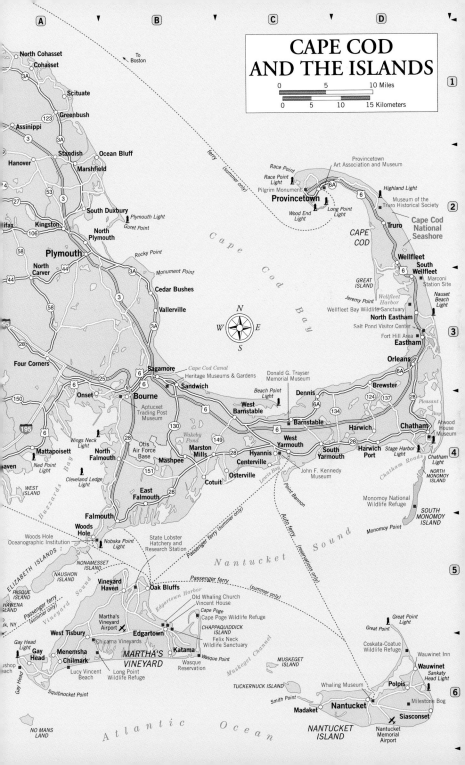

CAPE COD
AND THE ISLANDS

0   5   10 Miles

0   5   10   15 Kilometers

A   **B**   **C**   **D**

1   **2**   **3**   **4**   **5**   **6**

To Boston

North Cohasset
Cohasset
Scituate
Greenbush
Assinippi
Standish
Ocean Bluff
Marshfield
Hanover
South Duxbury
Plymouth Light
Guret Point
Kingston
North Plymouth
Plymouth
North Carver
Rocky Point
Monument Point
Cedar Bushes
Four Corners
Vallerville
Sagamore
Cape Cod Canal
Heritage Museums & Gardens
Onset
Bourne
Sandwich
Aptucket Trading Post Museum
West Barnstable
Mattapoisett
Ned Point Light
North Falmouth
Wings Neck Light
Otis Air Force Base
Mashpee
Marston Mills
Wakeby Pond
Cleveland Ledge Light
WEST ISLAND
East Falmouth
Cotuit
Osterville
Centerville
Hyannis
Falmouth
Woods Hole
Woods Hole Oceanographic Institution
Nobska Point Light
State Lobster Hatchery and Research Station

ferry (summer only)

Race Point
Race Point Light
Pilgrim Monument
Provincetown
Wood End Light
Long Point Light
Provincetown Art Association and Museum
Highland Light
Museum of the Truro Historical Society
Truro
CAPE COD
Cape Cod National Seashore
Wellfleet
South Wellfleet
Marconi Station Site
GREAT ISLAND
Jeremy Point
Wellfleet Harbor
Wellfleet Bay Wildlife Sanctuary
North Eastham
Salt Pond Visitor Center
Fort Hill Area
Eastham
Nauset Beach Light
Orleans
Brewster
Dennis
Donald G. Trayser Memorial Museum
Beach Point Light
Barnstable
West Yarmouth
South Yarmouth
Harwich
Harwich Port
Chatham
Atwood House Museum
Stage Harbor Light
Chatham Light
Chatham Roads
Pleasant Bay
John F. Kennedy Museum
Monomoy National Wildlife Refuge
Monomoy Point
NORTH MONOMOY ISLAND
SOUTH MONOMOY ISLAND

Cape Cod Bay

N
W   E
S

Buzzards Bay

ELIZABETH ISLANDS
NONAMESSET ISLAND
NAUSHON ISLAND
PASQUE ISLAND
HAWENA ISLAND
Vineyard Sound
Vineyard Haven
Oak Bluffs
Edgartown Harbor
Old Whaling Church
Vincent House
Cape Poge
Cape Poge Wildlife Refuge
CHAPPAQUIDDICK ISLAND
Felix Neck Wildlife Sanctuary
West Tisbury
Martha's Vineyard Airport
Chicama Vineyards
Gay Head Light
Gay Head
Menemsha
Chilmark
Lucy Vincent Beach
Long Point Wildlife Refuge
MARTHA'S VINEYARD
Edgartown
Katama
Wasque Reservation
Wasque Point
Squibnocket Point
NO MANS LAND

Nantucket Sound

Passenger ferry (summer only)
Passenger ferry
(summer only)
Auto ferry (reservations only)

Lewis Bay
Point Bannon
MUSKEGET ISLAND
Muskeget Channel
TUCKERNUCK ISLAND
Smith Point

Great Point Light
Great Point
Coskata-Coatue Wildlife Refuge
Wauwinet Inn
Wauwinet
Sankaty Head Light
Polpis
Whaling Museum
Madaket
Nantucket
NANTUCKET ISLAND
Milestone Bog
Siasconset
Nantucket Memorial Airport

Atlantic Ocean

(top) The Dexter Grist Mill operated for nearly three centuries.
(bottom) A 1912 carousel twirls at the Heritage Plantation in Sandwich.

Woods Hole is the jumping-off point for Martha's Vineyard, and from June to October the town may appear to be just one long queue for the ferry. You can escape the crowds by dawdling on the **Shining Sea Bike Path,** which runs for 3 miles from Falmouth to Woods Hole, or by visiting the exhibit center at the renowned **Woods Hole Oceanographic Institution** (15 School Street; 508-457-2000), established in 1930. The latter features a model of a deep-sea explorer vessel that, like the sub at Battleship Cove, is not for the claustrophobic.

■ SANDWICH *map page 151, B-3*

The road from Sagamore to Sandwich meanders between tidy shingled cottages bordered by rose-laden picket fences and shaded by overhanging locust trees. Sandwich, settled in 1637, is a real charmer. The town's earliest buildings were clustered around Shawme Pond, which was harnessed for milling by the colonists. Today the pond contents itself with being beautiful, although the **Dexter Grist Mill** (Town Hall Square; 508-888-4910), which ran for almost three centuries, still grinds corn for the edification of tourists. A leisurely ramble down practically any of Sandwich's side streets reveals a wealth of the small and midsize Victorian houses that the artist Edward Hopper found so pleasing.

The **Hoxie House,** overlooking Shawme Pond, was built in the 1670s and is Sandwich's—and perhaps the Cape's—oldest house. It is also one of the oddest, with a steep back roof and a few tiny windows placed apparently at random. A tour of the house is worthwhile, but it is also delightful to sit on the bench outside the back door, leaning against the sun-warmed walls, listening to the occasional creak and groan of the timbers. *18 Water Street; 508-888-1173.*

The **Dunbar Tea Shop,** across the street from the Hoxie House, is the best place to snap out of such reveries and slip into others. Tea fanciers surrender their place in the lunchtime line to examine the huge selection of teapots for spout angle, filtering capability, and heat retention. The shop has a fine selection of teas from Ceylon, South Africa, and elsewhere. *1 Water Street; 508-833-2485.*

Glassmaking became the town's chief industry in 1825, when the Boston and Sandwich Glass Company went into business. The **Sandwich Glass Museum,** down the hill from Water Street, displays nearly 5,000 samples of glassware, from vases and drinking glasses to serving bowls and glass animals. The Boston and Sandwich factory closed in 1888 after a labor dispute, causing the town's decline. *129 Main Street; 508-888-0251.*

Reliving childhood fantasies is as easy as visiting the **Thornton W. Burgess Museum** (4 Water Street; 508-888-6870), named for the naturalist and author best known for the Peter Cottontail stories. This home, once owned by the writer's Aunt Arabella, is now preserved with artifacts recalling his life.

You can further indulge your inner child at the antique carousel at the **Heritage Museums & Gardens.** About a mile from the village of Sandwich, the former Heritage Plantation has gotten a new name and has grown to 100 acres of gardens, automobiles, and art. The antique cars from the collection of J.K. Lilly, a descendant of pharmaceutical pioneer Eli Lilly and the founder of the museum, were manufactured from 1899 to 1937. The diverse exhibits at the American History Museum survey everything from antique firearms to antique toys. The on-site Art Museum is home to such folk art as wooden cigar-store figures. *67 Grove Street, at Pine Street; 508-888-3300.*

Leaving Sandwich, follow Route 6A, part of which traces the route of the Old Kings Highway and snakes through the woods once it reaches the Outer Cape. As you head toward Barnstable, the road crosses misty salt marshes ringed with pale pink roses and vibrating with birdsong.

■ **BARNSTABLE AND THE HYANNIS AREA** *map page 151, B/C-4*
The salt hay from these marshes was one key to the success of **Barnstable.** The other was the town's commodious harbor. In *Cape Cod,* Thoreau quotes a local observer as saying that "the duck does not take to the water with a surer instinct than the Barnstable boy. . . . He can hand, reef and steer by the time he flies a kite."

The whole town of Barnstable, which includes the villages of Barnstable, West Barnstable, Hyannis, Marston Mills, Centerville, Osterville, and Cotuit, was purchased from the Wampanoags for two breeches, four coats, three axes, three kettles, a broad hoe, a day's plowing, one house, and 20 English pounds. It proved to be a bargain. From its agricultural beginnings in 1639, Barnstable grew on trade and fishing to become the Cape's wealthiest port in 1850. Today, like every other Cape town, it is a tourist destination, but unlike most of its neighbors, it has not become one long strip of antiques and collectibles stores. In an unpretentious coffee shop like **Village Landing** (3226 Main Street; 508-362-2994), locals banter with the waitresses, and the miniature walnut tarts are inexpensive and delicate enough to encourage greed. Even James Otis, Barnstable's most esteemed 18th-century patriot, staring across from his pedestal on the courthouse lawn, seems tempted.

Miss Holly, *by golly, docked in Hyannis.*

The **Donald G. Trayser Memorial Museum** occupies the former Custom House, a Renaissance Revival building completed in 1856 on Cobb's Hill. Here you can really lose yourself, especially on a thundering humid June day when the building is a cool retreat. Exhibits in the museum itself are superbly arranged and delightfully non-interactive. There are no electronic buttons to push in the post office that occupies one corner of the ground floor, no China trade videos running in the dining room and parlor of sea captains Daniel C. Bacon and Thomas Harris. *Route 6A; 508-362-2092.*

On the edge of the museum's parking area, what appears to be a garden shed is actually one of the most unusual and haunting buildings in the country. The **Old Jail** is thought to have been built between 1690 and 1700, and the small, dark space you enter today immediately convinces you of its antiquity. Although a 1973 fire erased much prisoner graffiti, one remarkable example remains. On a cell wall, under the ghostly carving of a ship, are the words "N. Bartlett 13 October 1698 A.D. He Went Out." No other clues to sailor Bartlett's life exist, but caught in flight, his voice fills the darkness. Reemerging into the daylight, you would not be surprised to catch a glimpse of him, making for the harbor.

It is hard to avoid being drawn into the vortex that is **Hyannis.** A tourist hub and major ferry port, the village gained notoriety during the 20th century as the playground of the Kennedys. Clan sightings are frequent, with the family often paying visits to the famed compound Joseph P. Kennedy purchased in the 1920s.

The Kennedy connection makes Hyannis the appropriate site for the **John F. Kennedy Museum,** a small institution that pays homage to its favorite son with photos and videos, some of which can only be viewed here. You can keep track of who's who by looking at the Kennedy family tree. It starts with Joe and Rose and ends with the latest offspring. *397 Main Street; 508-790-3077.*

Unlike feverish Hyannis, which has largely obliterated its original allure, **Osterville** and **Cotuit,** to the southwest, retain the quaintness that first attracted tycoons and intellectuals. Known as "little Harvard," Cotuit became the summer retreat not only of academics but also of psychologists such as Erik Erikson. And when you stew in Hyannis traffic on a summer weekend, you may find Erikson's diagnosis of "identity crisis" particularly apt. **Mashpee,** northwest of Cotuit on Route 130, has significant Native American sites. And **Harwich Port,** on the coast between Hyannis and Chatham, has a beautiful historic district.

The shoreline near North Chatham.

■ **CHATHAM** *map page 151, D-4*

Surrounded by water on three sides, Chatham is sedate in the middle and wild around the edges. Main Street is pretty, the **Atwood House Museum** (347 Stage Harbor Road; 508-945-2493) enlightening, and the **Railroad Museum** (Depot Road; open June 15 through September 15 only), set up in a restored depot, is as charming as it is educational. The daily catch in the **Chatham Squire** (487 Main Street; 508-945-0945) usually includes swordfish, sole, and plenty of clams, mussels, and oysters. Chatham's dramas, however, center on its lighthouse and its barrier beach, which was split into North and South beaches by a fierce storm in 1987. At one time Chatham had two lighthouses, known as the Chatham Twin Lights; although erosion at one point claimed both, they were rebuilt in 1877. One of the "twins" was moved to Nauset in 1923, however, so today there is only one **Chatham Light,** on Shore Road.

■ **MONOMOY NATIONAL WILDLIFE REFUGE** *map page 151, D-4/5*

Having survived the sprawl of Hyannis, you'll want to keep the world at bay by rushing directly to the Monomoy National Wildlife Refuge, one of the Northeast's most spectacular birding areas. Located on two islands off Chatham, the refuge has marshes, ponds, beaches, and dwarf forests that attract clouds of migrating shorebirds from July to September. Among these birds are golden plovers and godwits. Peregrine falcons pass through during the autumn, seals congregate during the winter, and the vast nesting colonies also include the common tern, the oystercatcher, and the short-eared owl. *Visitors center, Morris Island Road; 508-945-0594.*

In season, the **Wellfleet Bay Wildlife Sanctuary** (Off U.S. 6, South Wellfleet; 508-349-2615) and the **Cape Cod Museum of Natural History** (896 Route 6A, Brewster; 508-896-3867) provide day trips to Monomoy's twin islands. The former also has trails, a salt marsh, and indoor exhibits. Displays at the museum focus on indigenous bird and marine life, and trails here lead through marshlands and woods.

■ **THE NATIONAL SEASHORE AND OUTER CAPE** *map page 151, D-2/3*

Heading north from Chatham, Route 28 skirts Pleasant Bay. Ahead of you, when you reach **Eastham,** lies the Outer Cape, the narrowest and historically poorest stretch separating Cape Cod Bay from the Atlantic Ocean. "The country looked so barren," Thoreau observed, "that I several times refrained from asking the inhabitants for a string or a piece of wrapping-paper, for fear I should rob them."

Another writer, Henry Beston, was so captivated when he came to Eastham in 1927 that he built a Walden-like shack on the beach and lived there for a year, chronicling his experiences in the supremely evocative book *The Outermost House.* The thin spindle of land veering north from Orleans is also the site of the peninsula's greatest natural treasure—the 50-mile-long **Cape Cod National Seashore.** Established in 1961, largely through the efforts of President John F. Kennedy, the 43,000-acre federal preserve seems to absorb its more than 4 million annual visitors without diluting its wildness.

At the **Fort Hill Area,** off U.S. 6 in Eastham, you will catch the seashore in one of its deceptively calm moments. Once you have recovered from the view across to Nauset Harbor and Coast Guard Beach, you follow a shell-strewn trail through watery fields into sandy groves of dwarfish red maples. Intoxicated by honeysuckle vapors, you are also bombarded with mockingbird arpeggios, cardinal whistles, and catbird squeaks, the combination of which sounds like heaven trying to get through on the shortwave. Bluebirds, indigo buntings, and other birds now rare on the Cape also favor this spot.

Near the Fort Hill parking area is the **Captain Edward Penniman House.** Built in 1867, it has a fine octagonal cupola and recalls another Eastham story. Born here in 1831, Edward Penniman ran away to sea at age 11. By the time he was 21 he was harpooning in the New Bedford fleet; at 29 he was commanding his own whaler, eventually amassing a considerable fortune. *Fort Hill; 508-255-3421.*

■ **WELLFLEET** *map page 151, D-2/3*

The Pilgrims soon discovered what the Native Americans had known for centuries—that oysters thrive in Wellfleet. The town was known for its shellfish as early as 1606, when they so impressed the French explorer Samuel de Champlain that he named the harbor Oyster Port. Wellfleet was New England's oyster capital from 1830 to 1870, and in 1850 it was second only to Gloucester as a cod and mackerel port. It was here that America learned about the banana, when Wellfleet Capt. Lorenzo Dow Baker returned from the West Indies with some of the strange fruit in the late 19th century. Rapturously received, the banana inspired the formation of the United Fruit Company in 1899. Finding a good banana in Wellfleet today is easy, but finding good shellfish requires a little more work—and luck. Oyster and clam shacks seem to open and shut down with mysterious regularity, and only a local can point you in the right direction.

OCTOBER ROAR

Away from the beach, the various sounds of the surf melt into one great thundering symphonic roar. Autumnal nights in Eastham village are full of this ocean sound. The 'summer people' have gone, the village rests and prepares for winter, lamps shine from kitchen windows, and from across the moors, the great levels of the marsh, and the bulwark of the dunes resounds the long wintry roaring of the sea. Listen to it a while, and it will seem but one remote and formidable sound; listen still longer and you will discern in it a symphony of breaker thunderings, and endless, distant, elemental cannonade. There is beauty in it, and ancient terror. I heard it last as I walked through the village on a starry October night; there was no wind, the leafless trees were still, all the village was abed, and the whole sombre world was awesome with the sound.

—Henry Beston, *The Outermost House*, 1928

Dune shacks on Cape Cod were inhabited by many famous artists and writers.

Locals do exist, despite the fact that Wellfleet and its neighbors, Truro and Provincetown, have long been fashionable summer destinations for artists and writers. The sleepy center of Wellfleet seems to have been unaltered by the presence of critics such as Edmund Wilson, novelists such as Mary McCarthy, and flocks of sun-worshipping psychoanalysts. The clock in the 1850 Congregational Church still strikes "ship's time" every half hour, and Newcomb Hollow beach (where Thoreau was once accommodated by a garrulous Wellfleet oysterman) has been significantly altered only by the ocean. Even the canoe tours of Wellfleet's ponds, organized by the Audubon Society, seem pleasantly antiquated.

Sitting beside **Horse Leech Pond,** in the middle of the sandy woods on a spring evening, you see why restless minds alighted here. It is not simply that "meditation and water are wedded for ever," as Melville observed. It is the mist in the air, the honeysuckle that seems to grow out of the water, and the hypnotic bellowing of reverberating bullfrogs. Sharp things lurk just out of sight—snapping turtles, pickerel, sharks, and salesmen—but this part of the Cape, more than any other, lulls the visitor with its dreamy softness, even on its ocean side, where tremendous gales regularly devour the dunes. Spending a morning on any Wellfleet beach, equipped with a book and a companion, you may find yourself ignoring both; instead, you may spend the hours hypnotized by the Atlantic, which endlessly unfurls and refurls its long bolts of gray-blue silk.

■ TRURO *map page 151, D-2*

The painter Edward Hopper captured the softness and luminosity of the Outer Cape, even in his painting of a local gas station that still stands on U.S. 6 near Truro. The pumps are gone, but the building remains practically unaltered—a shanty of a store selling a few Hopper postcards but otherwise ignoring the association.

North Truro is home to Cape Cod's first lighthouse, **Highland Light,** built in 1797 and reconstructed in 1857. According to locals, it is the Cape's oldest, highest, and most important lighthouse. Over the years, severe erosion threatened the lighthouse, and in 1996 it was moved 453 feet inland. The light is still in operation and tours are scheduled during summer. *27 Highland Light Road, North Truro; 508-487-1121.*

At the nearby **Museum of the Truro Historical Society,** open only in the summer, displays focus on local history, fishing tools, boats, and ships that came to grief on nearby rocks. Nineteenth-century furniture on the second floor recalls the

Edward Hopper painted a gas station near Truro in 1940. (Museum of Modern Art)

days when the building was a hotel, and there's a bookstore with titles about Truro history, the lighthouse, and other, mostly nautical, subjects. *7 Highland Light Road, North Truro; 508-487-3397.*

Writers also washed up in Truro. During the 1920s, Eugene O'Neill spent his summers in a converted Coast Guard station at Peaked Hill Bar, which was subsequently claimed by a 1930 storm. The shack the playwright inhabited at Race Point, outside Provincetown, suffered a similar fate. Fifteen years later, Mary McCarthy recalled her summer here with Dwight MacDonald, James Agee, and others: "I remember our beach picnics at night around a fire and our discussions of Tolstoy and Dostoevsky."

Thoreau—being Thoreau—visited Truro before it became fashionable. The town's harbors began to silt up in the early 18th century, and arriving here in 1849, the writer found it and neighboring Provincetown practically empty. "Nearly all who come out must walk on the four planks I have mentioned," Thoreau wrote, referring to Provincetown's gangplank sidewalks, "so that you are pretty sure to meet all the inhabitants . . . who come out in the course of a day, provided you keep out yourself."

(top) Fishing boats docked at the end of MacMillan Wharf, with flags for the annual Blessing of the Fleet. (bottom) The sun backlights the Pilgrim Monument in Provincetown.

■ PROVINCETOWN *map page 151, C-2*

Today, many Provincetown residents are out in every sense of the word. The site of the first Pilgrim landing and once a busy fishing and trading port, the town is now more popularly known as a lesbian and gay playground, where flamboyance and sensitivity walk—often literally—hand in hand.

Between June and October, you may find yourself gridlocked on Commercial Street, coveting a parking spot already being claimed by two dueling cars and trying not to stare at the colorful folks passing on either side. Even in the off-season, Provincetown seems to be all clever restaurants, pastel guest houses, and art galleries, but there are still fishing boats in the harbor and the town remains heavily Portuguese. During the **Blessing of the Fleet weekend festival** in mid- to late June, Portuguese flags and food stalls are everywhere. If you miss the feast, you can still sample the fine soup and seafood specials at **Tip-for-Tops'n** (31 Bradford Street; 508-487-1811), which has been preparing Portuguese-American fare during the summer since the 1960s.

Provincetown—historically known as Helltown—has always been wayward. For almost a century after the Pilgrims departed, fishermen here drank and gambled with visiting Wampanoags, prompting respectable Truro to refuse jurisdiction over its scandalous neighbor until 1727. "Mooncussing," the pirate art of using unnatural light to simulate the moon and lead ships to wreck so that they could be pillaged, was a common practice. In the shadow of the dunes, smuggling and rum running also thrived.

Founded in 1914 as a showcase for a group of prominent local artists, what is now the **Provincetown Art Association and Museum** turned to collecting in the 1970s. On display are the works of Hans Hoffman, Robert Motherwell, and other artists, some of them locals or summer residents. *460 Commercial Street; 508-487-1750.*

The best view in town is from the **Pilgrim Monument & Provincetown Museum.** The monument, a 250-foot granite tower, was erected between 1907 and 1910 and modeled after the Torre del Mangia in Siena, Italy. From here you can see dramatic Race Point Beach, calm Herring Cove, and remote Long Point, as well as the ridge of the Outer Cape. The museum displays whaling equipment and ship models and has a *Mayflower* diorama.

On exhibit at the superb **Expedition Whydah Sea Lab and Learning Center** are items recovered from the pirate ship *Whydah,* which sank off Wellfleet in 1717. *MacMillan Wharf, just past the whale-watching fleet; 508-487-8899.*

■ MARTHA'S VINEYARD *map page 151, A/B-5/6*

Despite being the closest island to the mainland, within easy reach of day-trippers, Martha's Vineyard is more than just a floating buffet of tourist attractions. The island's eccentric history—crowded with religious zealots, Native Americans, writers, and dilettantes—has created a distinct sense of island identity while the intensely varied landscape and architecture preserve a sense of real, not just photogenic, life.

All of which is best appreciated in the early spring or late autumn, when the crowds have thinned, the beach restrictions have eased, and the island seems welcoming rather than besieged. The golden rule of the maverick visitor—travel out of season—is particularly applicable here. One statistic says it all: the baseline population of Martha's Vineyard is 11,000, but the population swells to 90,000 in July and August. It is not just a matter of breathing space. Hours spent in a ferry line, even in a picturesque port, are not usually the happiest.

■ VINEYARD HAVEN *map page 151, B-5*

Boat lovers in Vineyard Haven's harbor have long reveled in the fine art of sea craft, and the area seems almost to grow wooden ships, some of the loveliest vessels on the eastern seaboard. You glide past the schooner *Shenandoah* and her neighbor *Alabama,* both of which take schoolchildren and other visitors sailing to the nearby Elizabeth Islands and beyond.

Your first instinct may be to sample the pastries and coffee near the ferry terminal at the **Black Dog Bakery** (1 Water Street; 508-696-8190)—from which President Bill Clinton is said to have procured a tote bag for Monica Lewinsky, his White House paramour—before leaving Vineyard Haven to explore the island. Still, the town deserves more than a backward glance. An important port throughout the 18th and 19th centuries, Vineyard Haven was a vital refuge for British ships during the Revolution.

The intersection of Colonial Lane and Main Street marks the spot where young Polly Daggett and two friends destroyed the town's liberty pole to thwart the British captain who wanted it for a spar. The British of that invasion were ruthless in their plundering of livestock and produce, and islanders were saved from starvation only by a northeast blizzard that drove a school of sea bass into Lagoon Pond, where they froze and could be harvested throughout the winter.

Such deprivation is unimaginable today on Vineyard Haven's Main Street, where even the thrift store is full of designer clothes—some of the island's best bargains, especially at the summer's end. Frenzied souvenir selling is largely concentrated on the waterfront; back roads like Williams Street are perfect for quiet strolls.

Try to avoid renting a noisy moped. The island is better explored in quiet on a bicycle, which you can rent from shops near the harbor. There are three excellent bike trails here and numerous tiny roads.

■ **OAK BLUFFS** *map page 151, B-5*

On the way to Oak Bluffs from Vineyard Haven, lobster fanciers should visit the **State Lobster Hatchery and Research Station,** reportedly the world's oldest such operation, where prospective meals may be viewed in their infancy. "Man needs to know but little more than a lobster in order to catch him," Henry David Thoreau concluded, and an insight into crustacean intelligence may force you to agree. *Shirley Avenue; 508-693-0060.*

Vineyard Haven and Oak Bluffs are contrasting neighbors. Vineyard Haven is a dry town (alcohol is not sold there); Oak Bluffs is a distinctly wet one (alcohol is sold at every turn). Vineyard Haven has elegant, wooden boats in its harbor; Oak Bluffs has the fiberglass variety, typically with crews that often include a rottweiler as mascot. Oak Bluffs offers an irrepressible, unapologetic welcome to the visitor. If you're looking for restraint, it seems to say, go to Edgartown.

Yet restraint, paradoxically, was the making of Oak Bluffs. In 1835, Jeremiah Pease, a Methodist minister, thought the site perfect for a summer campground, and soon thousands of fervent believers were living in tents, and then eventually in small cottages built beside the Methodist Tabernacle, which still stands in Trinity Park at Wesleyan Grove. The result today is a unique maze of about 1,000 houses, jammed into an improbably small space, each one bristling with intricate fretwork on roof, wall, porch, and doorway and competing with its neighbor for outrageous colors and candy-striping.

The **Cottage Museum** (1 Trinity Park; 508-693-7784) provides a view of life inside one of these architectural confections, and in July and August, services are still held in the **Trinity Park Tabernacle** (508-693-0525), built in 1879 to replace the tent the Methodist congregation previously used. On **Illumination Night,** in August, thousands of Chinese and Japanese lanterns are strung throughout the village, an end-of-summer tradition that dates from 1869.

(following pages) A beautiful day in Vineyard Haven.

This 1841 engraving shows Edgartown Harbor, as seen from Chappaquiddick Island. (National Oceanic & Atmospheric Administration)

■ EDGARTOWN *map page 151, B-5/6*

The road from Oak Bluffs to Edgartown skirts Sengekontocket Pond, which is surrounded by the 200-acre **Felix Neck Wildlife Sanctuary.** Cleverly planned trails snake through this dreamy saltwater estuary, leading you through marshes, fields, and diminutive woodland to Waterfowl Pond, a favorite meeting point for migratory and nesting water birds. This is an osprey nesting site; about 70 pairs live here. Visitors are encouraged—by the Massachusetts Audubon Society, not the birds—to observe the birds' predatory and domestic habits. *Edgartown–Vineyard Haven Road; 508-627-4850.*

Like Oak Bluffs, Edgartown was established on a religious impulse. But there the resemblance with its exuberant neighbor ends, for Edgartown is the island's aristocrat. Founded in 1642 by Thomas Mayhew—who established missions for the conversion of the island's 3,000 or so Wampanoags—the port grew rich on Arctic whaling, which financed the town's elegant architecture.

The loftiest example of this architecture is the austere **Old Whaling Church,** built in 1843, whose soaring white columns make it seem like a ship under sail. It is magnificently oblivious to the commercial detritus bobbing in its wake on Main Street. High-end gift shops, galleries, and restaurants line this thoroughfare and waterfront, but the streets behind this strip are quiet, residential, and glorious. On a still autumn evening, shadows dye the sloping lawns a deeper green, and the white clapboards appear merely to be etched on the buildings. *Main Street, next door to Duke's County Superior Courthouse; 508-627-4442. Touring info: 508-627-8619.*

Although today's islanders have become accustomed to such luxuries, Vineyard dwellings were not always so grand. The modest **Vincent House,** a farmer's shack built in 1672, is the oldest house on the island. Furnishings in the house reveal the creature comforts of New Englanders through the centuries. *Behind the Old Whaling Church; 508-627-8619.*

■ CHAPPAQUIDDICK ISLAND   *map page 151, B-5/6*
It takes about half a minute to reach Chappaquiddick Island from Edgartown by ferry (passengers and cars), and when you arrive you will have left the shops behind. Armed with a picnic, you can instead lose yourself for hours in either of its nature reserves. The 516-acre **Cape Poge Wildlife Refuge,** at the far end of the island—a roughly 3-mile drive on Chappaquiddick Road from the ferry dock—is a mesmerizing arrangement of sand, water, hummock, and marsh teeming with hawks, terns, plovers, ducks, and songbirds. Not far away at the southeastern corner of Chappaquiddick—take Chappaquiddick Road to School Road to Wasque Road—the **Wasque Reservation** catches nature in one of its melodramatic moments as Wasque Bluffs sweep up out of Katama Bay in a flourish of grassland and wildflowers. *508-627-3599 for information about both parks.*

■ WEST TISBURY AND GAY HEAD   *map page 151, A-6*
After all that drama, the road from Edgartown to West Tisbury seems disappointingly functional, but quieter beauty lurks nearby at the **Long Point Wildlife Refuge.** This 633-acre preserve encompasses Long Cove, an exquisite saltwater inlet; Tisbury Great Pond, which shimmers whatever the season; and many other ponds that are home to otters, muskrats, ospreys, harriers, swans, and water fowl. *Edgartown–West Tisbury Road; 508-693-3678.*

Less ambitious ducks bob contentedly on the pond in **West Tisbury,** a perfect rest stop for bicyclists who wish to donate their crumbs to the web-footed supplicants. You may think twice, however, if you have paid the inflated sandwich rates farther up the road at **Alley's General Store** (784 State Road; 508-693-0088), an island institution that at least does not charge for a seat on its front porch.

Martha's Vineyard is named for the wild grapes its earliest settlers found here.

Winding from West Tisbury to Gay Head, **South Road** is one of the loveliest on the island, particularly for bicycling. It swoops and twists between small stretches of woodland, wildflower meadows, and sheep pastures, affording tantalizing views of glinting ponds and creating a sense of rural calm. Following South Road through **Chilmark,** you might stop at the **Chilmark Store** (State Road; 508-645-3739) to stock up on emergency rations—or better still at **Chilmark Chocolates** (State Road; 508-645-3013), to stock up on emergency handmade treats—before pushing on to Gay Head at the island's westernmost tip. The undulations become a little steeper outside Chilmark, but it is the view and not the gradient that forces you to stop when South Road cuts between Menemsha Pond and Squibnocket Pond. On your right, a boat rocks on the glassy water, and on your left, a blue heron hunches in the reeds, seemingly hypnotizing his prey.

The multicolored cliffs at **Gay Head,** rising 150 feet out of the ocean, are most impressive when viewed from the water, particularly at sunset, when their layers become positively gaudy. But even the lookout point near the parking area provides rewards. For a closer inspection, find **Maushop Beach,** on Maushop Trail Road, where a short walk brings you underneath the strange protuberances. Surely the glacier's most outrageous handiwork, the cliffs contain 70-million-year-old deposits in which the fossils of early marine creatures and even horses are preserved. The souvenir stalls lining the route to the lookout also seem an oddly antique part of the island's tourist machine. But then Gay Head has always been apart. In 1711, the Society for Propagating the Gospel—oblivious, no doubt, to the irony of the transaction—bought the lands here for the sole use of the original inhabitants, the Wampanoags. Today, the tribe owns the National Historic Landmark on which some of its members live.

■ **MENEMSHA** *map page 151, A-6*

Lighthouse Road skirts Lobsterville Beach and returns to Menemsha, a fishing village where the nets and lobster pots on the dock are in use, not for sale. Despite having an unofficial anthem written for it by Carly Simon and being used as one of the locations for the movie *Jaws,* Menemsha is still a place where people would rather watch the water than the celebrities. And everybody's favorite special effect is still the flamboyant sunset, attended nightly by adoring fans. You may join them on the beach or enjoy the drive-in performance from your car. Instead of popcorn, you can snack on the fine crabcakes and fish cakes from either **Poole's** (508-645-2282) or **Larsen's** (508-645-2680), the fish market behind you on the dock.

North Road passes **Menemsha Hills,** where the view from Prospect Hill is more than worth the easy ascent along marked trails. You can see everything from here—the delicate chain of the Elizabeth Islands, Cuttyhunk to the north and No Mans Land to the south; Menemsha and Squibnocket Ponds; and Gay Head. Descend through the scrub and you arrive at one of the island's most secluded public beaches, where you may recline, seal-like, on a glacial boulder.

The lighthouse at Gay Head Cliffs.

■ NANTUCKET *map page 151, C/D-6*

In *Moby-Dick,* Herman Melville described Nantucket as "a mere hillock, an elbow of sand; all beach, without a background." Even today, approached by high-speed ferry, the small sandbar seems more an act of faith than a destination. Roaring along for an hour through dense sea fog, you begin to doubt the existence of this place, known to Native Americans as Canopache, or "the Place of Peace," and renamed Nanticut, or "the Far Away Island." The island seems about as real as Brigadoon until, suddenly, the engines' hum drops an octave, the fog lifts, and there it is, a fragile sliver 14.5 miles long and just 3.5 miles wide.

Your foggy doubts give way to a disorienting first impression: the ferry seems to have docked in a shopping mall. Tourists stroll from one gray-shingled specialty store to the next along a cobblestone thoroughfare that you expect to terminate in a food court. Sleek young women wearing Ralph Lauren carry demure "lightship baskets" that were first made by lightship keepers but are now manufactured and sold by artists, often for thousands of dollars. No wonder the writer Russell Baker said that if you listen closely on a summer's night you will hear "the sound of the island eating money." It would be understandable if, like Melville's Ishmael, you immediately headed seaward, fleeing corruption. But it would also be a pity. Despite the relentless merchandising, Nantucket Town is still one of the nation's loveliest—part Manhattan chic, part California casual, and, miraculously, part native Nantucket.

■ NANTUCKET TOWN *map page 151, D-6*

To discover the island's extraordinary past, head to the **Nantucket Historical Association Research Library** (7 Fair Street; 508-228-1655), formerly the Peter Foulger Library. A gold mine of information, the library has books, maps, manuscripts, prints, photographs, and documents about Nantucket's maritime history.

The **Whaling Museum** (13 Broad Street; 508-228-1736), in a former spermaceti candle factory, further celebrates island lore with documents and artifacts—including the skeleton of a 43-foot-long finback whale—of what was once Nantucket's most important industry. The museum store sells copies of a classic Nantucket poem in which Eliza Brock, born in 1810, testifies to the liberating side of being a whaler's wife. "Then I'll haste to wed a sailor, and send him off to sea," Eliza wrote in her journal, "For a life of independence, is the pleasant life for me."

A lamppost stands in the center of a Nantucket Town street intersection.

Also worth a look is the splendid **Nantucket Atheneum** (1 India Street; 508-228-1110), now the public library, whose artifacts and other items survey Nantucket history and 19th-century life.

Nantucket was chosen by its first settlers because it seemed beyond Puritan reach. Fleeing theological severity on the mainland, Quakers from Amesbury and Salisbury emigrated to Nantucket in June 1661, accompanied by Peter Foulger of Martha's Vineyard. At that time, the island's native population was around 3,000, a number it would take the English settlers another 100 years to reach. In 1690, when the settlers began to hunt right whales from small boats, Nantucket's Native Americans, already accomplished at whaling close to shore, made up a large portion of the crews. By the mid-18th century, however, when the lucrative sperm whale was being hunted for fortune rather than for food, much of the Wampanoag population, living near Miacomet Pond, had been killed by a mysterious ship-borne illness. The victims are buried in a sacred site near the corner of Miacomet and Surfside Roads.

By 1775, Nantucket's products accounted for a substantial portion of New England's exports to England, and the island's residents of African descent were among those who benefited from the newfound prosperity. The first Africans had arrived on the island as slaves, but slavery was outlawed here in 1773, a decade ahead of the rest of Massachusetts. In 1822, Absalom Boston was one of those who went to sea, eventually becoming a master of his own whaling vessel, the *Industry,* with an all-black crew.

The **African Meeting House at Five Corners,** built circa 1827, served as a school for African children (who weren't allowed to attend public schools), a church, and a meeting-house for free blacks, who lived south of Nantucket Town. The modest structure has been restored by Boston's Museum of Afro American History. *29 York Street; 508-228-9833.*

A stone marker from 1841 marks the edge of Nantucket Town.

By 1840, many Nantucket Quakers had become millionaires, but remnants of the humbler past are in evidence at the **Jethro Coffin House** (16 Sunset Hill; 508-228-1894), the island's oldest home, built in 1686 for newlyweds Jethro Coffin—grandson to one of the island's first white settlers—and his wife, Mary Gardner. With a open hearth and large pantry, the house (not to be confused with the Jared Coffin House inn) evokes the days when farming was Nantucket's primary focus.

By contrast, the magnificent furnishings and elegant gardens of the 1845 **Hadwen House** (96 Main Street; 508-228-1894) hark back to whaling's heyday. Across the street from the Hadwen House is **Three Bricks** (93, 95, 97 Main Street; 508-228-1894), a trio of identical houses—now private residences—built by Joseph Starbuck for his sons in the 1830s. One mansion on an isolated island in the Atlantic Ocean would be surprising, but to find streets of them seems positively fanciful. Walking down leafy Main Street, the island's architectural showpiece, you pass elaborate entrances bearing silver escutcheons that read "Starbuck," "Coffin," and "Macy." Such affluence also had a downside—namely its appeal to criminals, which led to a high occupancy rate in the sturdy 18th-century **New Gaol** (Vestal Street; 508-228-1894), the refurbished version of the 1696 old jail. Prisoners were incarcerated in the new lock-up as late as 1933.

William Hadwen's house was just a year old when fire destroyed one-third of the town and the entire waterfront. The desolation continued decades later, in the 1870s, when an increasing reliance on petroleum sank Nantucket's whaling industry. The population dwindled from a peak of 10,000 to just 2,000. Decades of hardship followed, but, paradoxically, the economic stagnation helped preserve some historic structures. In 1955, a group of Nantucket enthusiasts created the nation's first historic district, preventing change or demolition and eventually dictating the style of future development by purchasing land and imposing a gray-shingle orthodoxy that some find charming, others cloying.

In the 20th century, the island reinvented itself as a tourist mecca. Crowded during the summer, Nantucket Town is loveliest in early spring, late autumn, or even winter, when footsteps echo on the narrow, cobblestone streets and winding lanes that tumble drunkenly down to the water. Squint a little on a gray February afternoon, and spiky bare tree limbs turn into the spars and rigging of a whaler back from an ocean voyage. Keep your eyes wide open on a May morning on the beach at Madaket and you will still be fooled by isolated funnels of sea mist hovering in the distance, mimicking whale spume.

When you leave Nantucket Town, you enter a dreamscape best experienced on a bicycle or on foot. In spring, whichever direction you take, you can push your way through the heavy scent of Russian olive and wild roses as red-winged blackbirds cheer you on from the marshes and red-tailed hawks hanging overhead seem to monitor your progress.

It is easy to feel heroic. The island is, after all, tiny, relatively flat, and equipped with five bike paths, the most arduous of which, terminating at Siasconset, is mercifully unchallenging. Walkers can also cheat by taking one of the municipal shuttle buses, taxis, or tour buses, then setting out on foot to explore the peaceful, sandy expanse of Great Point Reservation, for example.

■ **COSKATA-COATUE WILDLIFE REFUGE** *map page 151, D-6*
Almost one-third of Nantucket's 32,000 acres is protected as conservation land. One of the largest and best loved areas is the 1,400-acre Coskata-Coatue Wildlife Refuge. Comprising the wishbone of land that protrudes from Nantucket Harbor out to **Great Point Lighthouse,** the refuge includes 18 miles of shoreline, a textbook barrier beach that protects the harbor at one end and an extraordinary bird population at the other. Crossing the haulover at Wauwinet—so-called because fishermen once hauled their boats over the narrow sand bridge here rather than battling their way around Great Point—you enter a wind-blasted spit of land, apparently held in place by tufts of spindly beach grass. Here the ocean is constantly busy. Like a compulsive housekeeper rearranging the furniture, it ceaselessly picks up sand from one shore and dumps it on the other only to start all over again. Winter storms make particularly drastic alterations, wiping out as much as 20 feet of shoreline with one blow and threatening, with the cooperation of the tide, to wipe out the entire peninsula.

On a warm May or June afternoon, however, everything at Great Point seems calm and permanent. Snowy egrets stand immaculate and immobile at the edges of shallow ponds, black-breasted plovers strut between the dunes, pleased with their avant-garde plumage, and a harrier delivers lunch to his mate in mid-air. At land's end, presided over by Great Point Lighthouse, some seals dip their black heads politely underwater. *Coskata-Coatue Wildlife Refuge: Off Polpis Road north of Wauwinet; 508-228-5646.*

Great Point Lighthouse at the northern tip of Nantucket.

The front porch of the Wauwinet Inn.

The refuge borders the grounds of the 19th-century **Wauwinet Inn,** originally an inexpensive hotel patronized by fishermen and pioneer tourists. On a narrow ridge separating Nantucket Sound from the ocean, the inn's situation remains glorious, even if its menu, decor, and rates have changed beyond recognition. If you reserve the right room, you can lie in bed and watch as your window fills up with navy-blue ocean and paler blue sky. Only a herring gull flying through the frame disturbs the composition. Faced with the tariff, you may recall Melville's observation that "The act of paying is perhaps the most uncomfortable infliction that the two orchard thieves entailed upon us." *120 Wauwinet Road; 508-228-0145.*

On the way to the inn you can follow Polpis Road to Folger's Marsh and the **Nantucket Life-Saving Museum.** The displays here include a restored U.S. Coast Guard craft, lifeboats, original lenses from nearby lighthouses, and items recovered from the *Andrea Doria,* which in 1956 collided with another ship and sank off Nantucket. "She was listing to starboard, the ugly gash in her side covered by the Atlantic," reported CBS News. "Word came from the skipper that the *Andrea Doria* was done for . . . .Three minutes later the *Andrea Doria* settled gracefully into the Atlantic, a terrible sight to see." *158 Polpis Road; 508-228-1885.*

■ SIASCONSET *map page 151, D-6*

Just south of Wauwinet is the small, enchanting village of Siasconset (pronounced *Scon-set* by locals). A cluster of fishermen's shanties interwoven with narrow, grassy lanes, pretty Siasconset is blessedly relieved by its eccentricity. Rambling from the comically misnamed Broadway to Front Street, you enter a twisting lane that passes between ancient gray-shingled cottages—each different, each askew, and facing each other, not the sea, as if for reassurance. "Sea views are only for urban folk who never experience its menace," Jane Austen once remarked. "The true sailor prefers to be land-locked than face the ocean."

Today's residents are largely "summer people," recreational mariners, but the houses look, as they always have, like ship's cabins riding the waves of roses and honeysuckle that flood their gardens. The view from nearby **Sankaty Head Light,** tracking the sea in one direction and barren heath in the other, makes Siasconset's coziness seem not only beguiling but also miraculous. Returning to Nantucket Town on Milestone Road, you pass the **Middle Moors,** a desolate sweep of former sheep pasture that is particularly lovely in autumn, when the heath's vegetation throbs with color. **Milestone Bog,** to the southeast, was the world's largest natural cranberry bog, covering 234 acres, until it was bisected by ditches in 1959.

■ TRAVEL BASICS

Getting Around: Traveling to and on Cape Cod, expect heavy, often stalled traffic in peak season and holiday weekends, particularly in ferry ports such as Woods Hole and Hyannis. Getting out of Boston, you'll be stuck on Route 3 or, from points inland, I-495. Route 6A from Sandwich to the Outer Cape is pretty, and the 25-mile Cape Cod Rail Trail bike route, invigorating.

Year-round and weather permitting, ferries serve Martha's Vineyard and Nantucket through the **Steamship Authority** (508-477-8600) and **Hy-Line Cruises Nantucket** (508-778-2600). Reservations are a must—far in advance in season, particularly if you plan to bring a vehicle.

Climate: Summer temperatures along the Cape, Martha's Vineyard, and Nantucket are in the 80s and 90s Fahrenheit. Spring and autumn days range from the 50s to 70s. Hard freezes and heavy snowfall are rare, but the islands and even parts of Cape Cod can be cut off by winter storms. The region is beautiful year-round, though early autumn, when the crowds have thinned but Indian summer is still a possibility, may well be the best time to visit.

C E N T R A L
M A S S A C H U S E T T S

In central Massachusetts, the land is impatient for spring. When the sun wheels southward in March, skunk cabbage bulls its way through the lingering patches of snow in the woods, and ferns jab through the moist soil at the edge of coursing freshets. May's final frost is always a capricious date—a race between the apples and the almanac—but when the sun heats the hilltop soils, the orchards explode in a mass of white and pink. Daisy fleabane fills the roadside ditches, and central Massachusetts is launched on another season of growing.

Lacking the drama of the Berkshire Hills or the steeper reaches of the Connecticut Valley, central Massachusetts draws you into its intimate valleys and hillsides instead of keeping you at an awestruck distance. The region contrasts bucolic farm country, where little has changed since 1790, with handsome industrial valley towns just rediscovering their long-neglected red brick downtowns. Central Massachusetts is a place of subtle pleasures—the sudden burst of golden sunlight filtered through the branches of a weeping birch on a country road, a large bass lunging for a fly in a cleaned-up industrial river, an Edward Hopper epiphany in one of America's original all-night greasy spoons.

Until the construction of highways in the 1990s, central Massachusetts was surprisingly decentralized. This chapter recognizes that historical pattern of settlement by covering the region in tiers: the northern orchard country and mill communities, the regional hub of Worcester, and the old river roads southeast of Worcester down the Blackstone Valley. Our journey concludes at the man-made Quabbin Reservoir, where wilderness has swept over the surrounding land in a sudden half-century.

■ HISTORY

A large central plateau stretches across the heart of the state from the Boston suburbs to the Connecticut River. Elevated from 400 feet to 500 feet above sea level, the ancient tableland of central Massachusetts is drained in all directions by small streams and rivers. It is bounded by rolling hills that descend in the east to the coastal plain and in the west to the Connecticut Valley.

An "accidental wilderness" resulted when the Swift River Valley was flooded to create the Quabbin Reservoir.

In the years before European contact, half a dozen distinct bands of the Nipmuck people farmed the open valleys and hunted the forests of what would become central Massachusetts. Although the Nipmucks signed peace treaties with the English, they became some of the staunchest allies of Metacom, an Indian chief whom the English called King Philip, in the conflicts of 1675 and 1676 known as King Philip's War. By 1678, most of the tribes had either died or joined the Abenaki in northern New England. A small band remained in the region southeast of Worcester.

The removal of the Nipmucks opened central Massachusetts to settlement, which began in earnest in the early 18th century. The region's northeastern hills still harbor the apple and peach orchards that were the fruit bowl of Colonial New England. But farmland on the plateau proved less fertile than either the coastal plain or the Connecticut Valley, and the country west of Worcester was never thickly settled.

Between the hills that bracket the region, dozens of streams and rivers spawned mills that grew into industrial villages, none greater than those at Worcester, Leominster, and Fitchburg. The arrival of railroads and the Blackstone Canal in the second quarter of the 19th century gave the mill towns a decided boost, and for the next century, manufacturing became the region's chief occupation. The rapid growth of jobs also created a more diverse population, as successive waves of immigrants flocked to the factory towns. While the largest immigrant groups to central Massachusetts were the Irish and the French Canadians, the region also attracted large numbers of Swedes and Finns in the late 19th century.

The economic hardships of the 1930s undermined labor-intensive industry in central Massachusetts, and the region suffered a population decline that has only recently reversed. The construction of new interstate highways that link the communities north of Worcester to the Massachusetts Turnpike to the south has begun to transform many small towns into residential suburbs.

■ JOHNNY APPLESEED TRAIL

Wanting to develop a colorful appellation, such as the western portion of Route 2's "Mohawk Trail," the communities in the plateau country of north-central Massachusetts latched onto native son John Chapman as a local icon. This area, from Harvard west through Gardner, is now known as the Johnny Appleseed Trail.

Born September 26, 1774, in Leominster, Chapman was a Swedenborgian preacher and a practical nurseryman who kept moving westward at the vanguard of American expansion. Midwestern settlers were required by law to plant 50 apple trees their first year, and Chapman was usually there ahead of them, ready to supply seedlings. Chapman headed west about 1797, but there's more than adequate justification for naming the region after the country's first nurseryman. The communities at the east end of the trail—Harvard, Sterling, Bolton, Boylston, Lancaster, Shirley—constituted America's first fruit bowl.

Just west of the Concord River drainage (a point marked for modern drivers by the divergence of Route 111 and Route 2), the land begins a gentle rise into broad agricultural country dotted by market villages. Although many former farmsteads have been converted to suburban McMansions, the landscape on both sides of Route 2 and southwest to the Wachusett Reservoir retains its Colonial-era identity as upland orchard country.

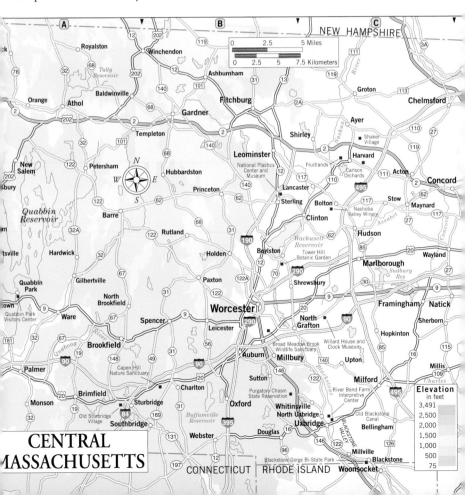

CENTRAL
MASSACHUSETTS

KNOCKING OFF WILD APPLES

The era of the Wild Apple will soon be past. It is a fruit which will probably become extinct in New England. You may still wander through old orchards of native fruit of great extent, which for the most part went to the cider-mill, now all gone to decay. I have heard of an orchard in a distant town, on the side of a hill, where the apples rolled down and lay four feet deep against a wall on the lower side, and this the owner cut down for fear they should be made into cider. Since the temperance reform and the general introduction of grafted fruit, no native apple-trees, such as I see everywhere in deserted pastures, and where the woods have grown up around them, are set out. I fear that he who walks over these fields a century hence will not know the pleasure of knocking off wild apples. Ah, poor man, there are many pleasures which he will not know! Notwithstanding the prevalence of the Baldwin and the Porter, I doubt if so extensive orchards are set out to-day in my town as there were a century ago, when those vast straggling cider-orchards were planted, when men both ate and drank apples, when the pomace-heap was the only nursery, and trees cost nothing but the trouble of setting them out. Men could afford then to stick a tree by every wall-side and let it take its chance. I see nobody planting trees to-day in such out-of-the-way places, along the lonely roads and lanes, and at the bottom of dells in the wood. Now that they have grafted trees, and pay a price for them, they collect them into a plat by their houses, and fence them in—and the end of it all will be that we shall be compelled to look for our apples in a barrel.

—Henry David Thoreau, "Wild Apples,"
in *The Atlantic Monthly,* November 1862

■ **HARVARD-WACHUSETT REGION** *map page 183, B/C-1/2*

The town of Harvard almost exemplifies this entire region. Incorporated in 1732, it appears the quintessential rural New England village. A clutch of Colonial and Victorian homes, churches, town hall, and library surround a green common. Roads pinwheel from the village center, following the ridgelines that link up highland farms. **Carlson Orchards,** one of the most productive of the region, is the largest producer of apple cider in the state and a significant grower of nectarines and peaches. *115 Oak Hill Road; 978-456-3916.*

But the apparent bucolic simplicity of Harvard hides a history of mystic yearning. During the third quarter of the 18th century, self-styled New Light preacher

Shadrach Ireland flourished here, teaching that death was illusory for true believers. A year after his decidedly permanent demise in 1780, the founder of the American Shakers, Mother Ann Lee, visited the area to proselytize to Mr. Ireland's followers and used Harvard as a base for her New England ridings. When the Shakers organized as a society after Mother Ann's death in 1784, Harvard was the fourth community called into the Gospel Order, in 1791.

The Harvard Shakers numbered 200 at their peak in the mid-19th century and operated successful garden-seed, broom-manufacturing, and dried-herb businesses. Before it closed in 1918, the community invented the circular saw, a machine for sorting broom corn, and the cast-iron chimney cap. A dozen buildings of the Shaker Village still stand as private dwellings along Shaker Road north of Route 2, and a trail leads to the Holy Hill, where members conducted secret rites during a brief era of ecstatic outdoor worship. Surrounded by a stone wall and shaded by tall pines, the burial ground on South Shaker Road contains at least 331 graves dating from 1792 to 1929 and is the only Shaker graveyard that retains the cast-iron "lollipop" markers that were substituted for headstones beginning in 1879.

A meeting of Shaker women at Hancock Shaker Village, Pittsfield, May 28, 1870, artist unknown. (Hancock Shaker Village)

The Trustees' Office of the Harvard Shakers—the structure where the community transacted business with the outside world—was moved in 1920 to the nearby country estate of Clara Endicott Sears, a wealthy Bostonian with a penchant for collecting. In 1922 the building opened as the first **Shaker Museum** in the country. Among the Shaker artifacts on display is a diminutive rocking chair that, according to tradition, was used by Mother Ann Lee when she made Harvard her missionary base.

The Shaker Museum is part of a museum complex on the Sears estate that includes the red farmhouse where philosophers Bronson Alcott and Charles Lane and a few starry-eyed followers launched an ill-conceived utopian community in 1843. Determined to create a "New Eden" and live as vegetarians off the bounty of the land, they called their community **Fruitlands,** and Sears used the name for her estate and museums. If you visit during the height of summer, Alcott's idea might not seem far-fetched. The west-facing slope of Prospect Hill rolls out into the distance down to the marshlands of the Nashua River, and the steady burr of cicadas is punctuated by the chortling song of redwing blackbirds and the chirping of goldfinches greedily stripping the grasses of their seed heads.

When Ralph Waldo Emerson visited the community on July 4, he wrote in his journal, "They look well in July, but we shall see in December." It was a prescient observation. All but the immediate Alcott family (including the precocious 10-year-old Louisa) left soon after the first frost. Prodded by his steel-willed wife, Abigail, Bronson Alcott threw in the towel on January 10, 1844.

The Alcotts took their belongings with them, but Sears managed to buy back a few objects, most of them associated with the family's prominent daughter, author Louisa May Alcott. Sears furnished the house with period country antiques that provide a sense of how the Alcotts and their fellow utopians lived for those seven months. Photos of Bronson Alcott and Charles Lane stand on the living room mantle. Although Henry David Thoreau never lived here, one tiny upstairs bedroom contains what purports to be his personal rock collection.

Two other buildings round out the Fruitlands museum complex. When Sears's gardener discovered Nipmuck arrowheads in the iris patch, Sears developed a fascination with Native American life and opened a small Indian Museum. One room displays materials of Eastern tribes, the other items from various western Indian groups. The most charming artifact, however, is the cigar box in which Sears stored the arrowheads found on her property—each in an envelope with notations in her own flowing script.

The Picture Gallery, opened in 1941, was Sears's final museum. Much of the collection is devoted to early- and mid-19th-century landscape paintings by Thomas Cole and many figures of the Hudson River School. The farm families who inhabited the landscape are represented by an extensive collection of portraits painted by itinerant artists between 1800 and 1850. *Open mid-May–Oct., 102 Prospect Hill Road, Harvard; 978-456-3924.*

For a sweet-scented May drive, follow Bolton Road south from the center of Harvard until it crosses the line into **Bolton,** where its name changes, in typical New England fashion, to Harvard Road. After crossing Route 117, the road ends on Wattaquadoc Hill Road. When a strong wind blows, a blizzard of white apple petals flutters across the landscape. From Colonial times until the advent of the temperance movement in the 1840s, apple cider was the region's primary beverage—safer than water and less heady than rum. Prohibition put the hard-cider makers out of business in the early 20th century, but in 1978 **Nashoba Valley Winery** began the movement to re-establish a fruit wine, cider, and perry (pear cider) industry in New England. The winery has expanded to include a restaurant and a large gift and wine shop. You can also picnic on the grounds and pick apples—as well as plums, peaches, raspberries, and blackberries—in season. *100 Wattaquadoc Hill Road; 978-779-9816.*

Wattaquadoc Hill Road continues through the uplands until it meets Route 70 in Clinton, at the head of the Wachusett Reservoir. This 6.5-square-mile man-made lake serves as a holding basin for water en route from the Quabbin Reservoir to Boston. South on Route 70, **Tower Hill Botanic Garden** provides both a grand view of the reservoir and a lesson in apple history. Settled in 1727, the Tower Hill farmstead has had only five owners. Originally a subsistence farm, it evolved into a successful dairy farm by the mid-19th century, became a gentleman's farm in the mid-20th century, and in 1986 was sold to the Worcester County Horticultural Society. The Belvedere at the top of the hill looks westward over the reservoir to nearby Mount Wachusett. Literally hundreds of varieties of landscape and flowering plants grow in Tower Hill's outdoor gardens. Of perhaps greatest historic interest, however, is the orchard of 119 apple varieties grown in the region before 1900—an unusual living genetic repository. *11 French Drive; 508-869-6111.*

At the south end of the reservoir, a right turn onto Route 140, followed by another right onto Route 12, leads north into the picturesque village of **Sterling,** which calls itself Apple Town. With its mix of Federal and Greek Revival architecture (and a few structures that can only be called "New England Barn"), Sterling

The town of Gardner is proud of its Big Chair, a symbol of the area's furniture-making roots.

seems untouched since the Civil War. In late summer and early autumn, the triangular green—located, of course, between Town Hall and the First Church—bristles with signs pointing uphill and out of town toward surrounding pick-your-own orchards. A lamb statue on the common asserts Sterling's claim that the nursery rhyme "Mary's Little Lamb" was written in 1817 about the town's own Mary Sawyer. One of Sawyer's descendants operates **Clearview Farm,** where vegetables from the fields are sold at a farm stand; pick-your-own opportunities start in July with raspberries, then move on to apples, peaches, and pears, and conclude in October with pumpkins. *4 Kendall Hill Road; 978-422-6442.*

■ **LEOMINSTER-FITCHBURG-GARDNER** *map page 183, B-1*
Leominster, at the crossroads of Routes 2 and 12, is the Pioneer Plastics City and the largest community on the Johnny Appleseed Trail. As early as 1770, Leominster was renowned for making ornamental women's hair combs from horn. The late-19th-century invention of "viscoloid," a type of celluloid, pushed the comb makers into plastics. The **Leominster Historical Society** (17 School Street; 978-537-5424) displays more than 400 pre-1900 combs. When bobbed hair became the rage in the 1920s, the plastics industry diversified. One surviving plastics manufacturer is Union Products, originator of the pink lawn flamingo. The tale of Leominster's plastics heyday is told at the **National Plastics Center & Museum** (210 Lancaster Street; 978-537-9529), an industry-funded effort a short distance off Route 12 as it leads north from Sterling into Leominster.

Just north of Leominster on Route 12, Fitchburg was one of the first industrial communities in the state, harnessing the Nashua River to run grist and sawmills as early as 1750. The city's manufacturing heyday was from 1870 to 1920, when immigrants from Quebec, Norway, Finland, and to a lesser extent Italy, Poland, and Germany flocked to Fitchburg for work. Paper and textiles were the dominant industries, and some specialty paper products are still produced in Fitchburg. Small companies, including e-businesses, now occupy historic mill buildings.

Fitchburg's well-to-do citizens formed the **Fitchburg Historical Society** in 1892. After undergoing extensive renovations and additions, the society's building is expected to re-open in 2004 with a central exhibition devoted to the Iver Johnson Company, one of Fitchburg's largest and most colorful manufacturers. Founded by a Norwegian immigrant, the company made a variety of products, from bicycles to motorcycles to handguns. In 1900, Iver Johnson outfitted the entire police force of Russia with pistols. *50 Grove Street; 978-345-1157.*

The **Fitchburg Art Museum** was founded in 1925 through the bequest of native Eleanor Norcross, daughter of the city's first mayor and an artist and art collector. She had lived in France for four decades and wanted her home town to have an institution along the lines of the regional museums she had so admired abroad. Norcross's own very competent paintings of china cabinets and museum interiors suggest a narrow, rather decorative artistic taste, but the museum owns an impressive collection of American art, especially from the early 20th century.

Among the highlights are paintings by George Bellows, Childe Hassam, Edward Hopper, Rockwell Kent, John Singer Sargent, Georgia O'Keeffe, and works by many artists who exhibited in the seminal 1913 Armory Show in New York City. Renovated and expanded in the 1990s, the Fitchburg mounts ambitious temporary exhibitions, including regular ones of arts and crafts from artisans who live within a 25-mile radius. The series is one of the oldest of its kind in New England. *185 Elm Street; 978-345-4207.*

West from Fitchburg and Leominster on Route 2, Gardner got into the chairmaking business in 1805 and has never entirely quit. Perhaps the height of the industry was 1868-78, when 12 companies produced 2 million chairs a year. In 1905, Gardner erected a giant chair downtown by the rail depot as a symbol of its signature industry. This first Big Chair set off something of a Big Chair competition with other furniture towns around the country. Gardner's current Big Chair, a 20-foot, 7-inch Heywood Wakefield replica erected on Elm Street in 1978, is not the nation's biggest, but it remains a source of local pride.

Even the Richardsonian Romanesque structure that houses the **Gardner Museum**—the Levi Heywood Memorial Building, named for a major chair manufacturer who also created chairmaking machinery—has an entry portico topped by architectural details that resemble a chair. The excellent local history collections are particularly strong on . . . chair making. *28 Pearl Street; 978-632-3277.*

Route 2 continues west beyond Gardner, becoming the Mohawk Trail at the French King Bridge in Turners Falls. (See the "CONNECTICUT RIVER VALLEY" chapter.) Route 68 leads southward from Gardner through hilly pastureland until it joins Route 122A to penetrate the industrial heart of Worcester.

Some unusual animal husbandry has replaced dairy cattle in the villages along the way. A farms in Rutland, for example, specializes in raising American bison, and **Westfield Farms** (28 Worcester Road, Hubbardston; 978-928-5110) makes exemplary goat cheeses with milk from surrounding farms.

Downtown Fitchburg.

■ WORCESTER *map page 183, B-2/3*

The state's second-largest city and the hub of central Massachusetts, Worcester ("Wooster," or "Woostah," in the local parlance) was founded in 1713 after an earlier settlement was abandoned due to frontier warfare. The farm community grew slowly until the 1828 opening of the Blackstone Canal waterway to Providence and the arrival of the railroad in 1835. The new transport routes transformed the town into an industrial boom city by the 1850s, resulting in a proliferation of handsome Greek Revival buildings, some of which still stand on Crown Hill. Several textile mills operated in Worcester, but the city was better known for making looms than cloth. While surrounding rural communities were losing population to post–Civil War westward expansion, Worcester profited by manufacturing plow blades, barbed wire, and farm implements. Its machine tool industry became one of the largest in the nation, and by the end of the 19th century, Worcester made equipment for factories, mills, and workshops all across America. By the onset of the Great Depression, the city boasted more than 1,000 factories.

Prototypical diners, the White House Cafés debuted in 1890. (Worcester Historical Museum)

Like so many centers that bloomed in the First Industrial Revolution, Worcester hemorrhaged industries and jobs by the mid-20th century. Still, some companies kept pace with changing times. The David Clarke Company, for example, debuted in 1934 as a small knitting concern. During World War II, the company developed a pressurized anti-gravity suit for military pilots and went on to develop the full-pressure suits used by NASA for manned space flights.

The **Worcester Historical Museum** has an excellent collection of photographs, paintings, and artifacts spanning nearly three centuries in Worcester—often personalized with vignettes about the daily lives of inhabitants great and humble. Many of Worcester's mechanical innovations have lost their impact over time, but one Worcester creation threatens to outlast us all—the Smiley Face, created by graphic designer Harvey Ball for an ad campaign that debuted in December 1963 for Worcester-based State Mutual & Life Assurance Company. The museum has a small exhibit of various uses of the Smiley Face. *30 Elm Street; 508-753-8278.*

The breadth of the Museum of Fine Arts, Boston sometimes leads Massachusetts residents to overlook the extraordinary **Worcester Art Museum,** which owns more than 35,000 objects covering 5,000 years, from dynastic Egypt

AMERICAN ICONS

You rarely hear a waitress yell, "Adam and Eve on a raft—wreck 'em," when a patron plops down on a stool and orders scrambled eggs on toast, but the diner is alive and well in Worcester, Massachusetts.

Founded in 1906, the Worcester Lunch Car and Carriage Manufacturing Company was one of three diner manufacturers across the country that transformed humble "lunch wagons" pulled by horses into American icons. The new diners offered three meals a day in a compact interior of slender galley kitchen, long counter lined with stools, and a wall of cozy booths.

Worcester Lunch installed its first car (#200) behind the Post Office on Myrtle Street in 1907 and sold its last diner in 1957. The company manufactured 651 distinctive diners, many of which are still central Massachusetts landmarks. Slow to adopt the stainless steel and streamlined look of other companies, Worcester diners are prized for the period graphics of their porcelain enamel exteriors and for the wood trim and booths inside.

Lovingly maintained Worcester diners—including the Miss Worcester, yellow with blue trim and built in 1948—are still slinging hash for cab drivers, shift workers, cops, and dreamers. The Boulevard, a National Historic Landmark, constructed in 1936, is guarded around the clock by surveillance cameras. It features an illuminated clock and extensive neon. Alas, the exterior of the 1934 Parkway Diner has been plastered with pebbled cement, but the vintage interior sports a second counter and row of stools in lieu of the usual booths. You can almost hear the ghosts of nighthawks past murmur into their porcelain mugs, entreating the waitress for a refill. *Miss Worcester Diner, 300 Southbridge Street; 508-757-7775. Boulevard Diner, 155 Shrewsbury Street; 508-791-4535. Parkway Diner, 148 Shrewsbury Street; 508-753-9968.*

to the most recent decade. Opened in 1898, the museum was an early collector of Mesoamerican art from the Yucatán and participated in the 1932–39 excavation of Antioch—the great Roman city, now in Turkey, that was destroyed in A.D. 585. The magnificent Worcester Hunt Mosaic from Antioch covers the floor just inside the Salisbury Street entrance.

Trying to do justice to the four floors of galleries in a single day is folly. Some of the most extraordinary works can be found in the tiny gallery of 14th-century

Italian religious painting, including two panels by the Fogg Pietà Master. In 1910, Worcester became the first American museum to actively collect Claude Monet and owns two stunning canvases, *Water Lilies* (1908) and *Waterloo Bridge* (1903). Not all the works have come "from away," as New Englanders say. The 1796 *Looking East from Denny Hill,* by native son Ralph Earl, is the earliest painted image of Worcester. *55 Salisbury Street; 508-799-4406.*

Worcester's central location also makes the city a hub for concerts and conventions. **Mechanics Hall** (321 Main Street; 508-752-5608) is generally recognized as one of the country's finest pre–Civil War concert halls. Concerts throughout the year include many free events. The **Worcester Centrum** (50 Foster Street; 508-755-6800) probably gets more use as a convention venue, but is best known for hosting rock concerts.

Two other unique museums lie a few miles from the city center. The **Higgins Armory Museum** seems itself encased in a suit of art deco armor. Founder John Woodman Higgins, proprietor of Worcester Pressed Steel, grew up on tales of days of old when knights were bold, and he longed to someday own one "real genuine suit" of medieval armor. By the time he finished collecting, he had more than a hundred. With 8,000 objects on five floors, the Armory claims to be the only museum in the Western Hemisphere dedicated to collecting, preserving, and exhibiting arms and armor. *100 Barber Avenue; 508-853-6015.*

Grafton Street leads east from downtown Worcester to **North Grafton** and the **Willard House and Clock Museum.** Joseph Willard was Grafton's first settler in 1718 and was among the proprietors who purchased the land from the Nipmucks in 1735. Benjamin Willard, his grandson, was born in 1766 and apprenticed with a Connecticut clockmaker. He returned to Grafton and trained his three brothers in the trade. In all, eight Willards over three generations built hand-made clocks that remain highly prized by collectors. Most of the Willards moved to Boston and Roxbury around the turn of the 19th century, but the ancestral family farm has been converted to this fine little museum, thanks to a modern collector of Willard clocks. The whole building seems to tick, and melodious chimes mark the top of each hour. Everywhere you look there are Willard clocks—from small mantle clocks to more elaborate wall-hung "banjo" clocks and tall case clocks. *11 Willard Street; 508-839-3500.*

Tales of knights brave and bold inspired the founder of Higgins Armory to collect armor.

■ BLACKSTONE RIVER VALLEY *map page 183, C-3*

Worcester's explosive industrial growth in the 19th century derived, in part, from the opening of the locks and canal along the length of the Blackstone River, which runs southeast to Providence, Rhode Island. Construction of the system was no mean feat—the Blackstone drops 438 feet over the 45-mile distance. The canal system included 48 stone locks and one wooden lock to step 70-foot-long barges up and down the waterway. The canal bed merged with portions of the river along about 10 percent of its length, but the rest was dug by hand using ox carts, picks, axes, iron bars, shovels, and black powder for blasting.

The National Park Service has designated the Blackstone River Valley as a National Heritage Corridor to recognize the region as the birthplace of the American Industrial Revolution. The historic industry, however, was almost entirely in Rhode Island. In Massachusetts, the Blackstone winds its way through a bucolic countryside with sudden interludes of dramatic landscape.

The 403-acre **Broad Meadow Brook Wildlife Sanctuary,** operated by the Massachusetts Audubon Society, is located on one of the many tributaries to the upper reaches of the Blackstone. As the largest urban wildlife sanctuary in New England, Broad Meadow has extremely diverse habitats that attract 78 recorded species of butterflies. Five miles of trails crisscross wetlands, brooks, pastureland, and hardwood forest teeming with creatures—white-tailed deer, red-winged blackbirds, several species of dragonflies, dusky salamanders, and wild turkeys. Leaves rustle in the forest as eastern towhees forage for juicy insects, and bullfrogs make their plaintive "jug-a-rum" calls from the banks of ponds. Hummingbirds hover at the deep-throated flowers planted around the visitors center, and on a warm spring day, you might encounter garter snakes warming themselves on sunny rocks. *414 Massasoit Road, Worcester; 508-753-6087.*

From the sanctuary, follow Route 20 west to Route 146 south, a major highway. Escape the roadway monotony by taking the second right after crossing the Massachusetts Turnpike and driving on Sutton Road. Follow the signs into the center of Sutton. It's easy to tell farm villages from mill villages. Agricultural centers like Sutton usually occupy the high ground and tend to coalesce around a common, while industrial villages stretch out along riverbanks. Pass through Sutton's central crossroads and follow Purgatory Road south into the cool green

A factory building in Uxbridge.

Sutton State Forest and **Purgatory Chasm State Reservation.** The boulder-strewn cleft in the granite bedrock has mesmerized visitors for centuries. In 1793, historian Peter Whitney wrote that many people visited to drop pebbles into the chasm, which is 70 feet deep in places, to marvel at icicles still visible in May and June, and to climb boulders and explore small caverns. He proclaimed his utter inability to convey the wonder of the setting: "After all, no description given of this place, by another, will enable persons to form just and adequate conceptions of it."

Modern science has dispelled some of the mystery, suggesting that the gash was ripped by the sudden release of dammed-up glacial meltwater about 14,000 years ago. So many people have picked their way across the boulders of the chasm that the rock has been worn smooth in many places. Wear hiking boots or rubber-soled athletic shoes and carry a good walking stick. Some of the rock formations have been given such fanciful names as the Corn Crib, the Coffin, the Pulpit, Lovers' Leap, and Fat Man's Misery. There are also terrific picnic facilities and good walking trails along the cliffs above the chasm. *Purgatory Road; 508-234-3733.*

Once you leave the chasm behind, you will find yourself on the flat and open farm country of a river floodplain. Keep going to the intersection with Route 122 at **North Uxbridge.** A left turn onto West Hartford Avenue leads to the **River Bend Farm interpretive center,** a center of information for the Blackstone River and Canal Heritage State Park as well as the National Heritage Corridor. A 4-mile walking tour, mostly along the ancient towpath, will give you a firm understanding of—and appreciation for—the Blackstone Canal. The canal company went out of business in 1849 and most of the granite locks were dismantled for building stone, but the Goat Hill lock (No. 25) remains intact about a mile north of the visitors center. *287 Oak Street; 508-278-7604.*

The best preserved lock is located in **Millville,** 6 miles south on Route 122. An old railroad bed, converted to a hiking trail, leads about a mile through the woods to the lock, then a little farther to the Triad Railroad Bridge, which was built to allow three separate train lines to cross the river simultaneously. As Route 122 approaches the Rhode Island border, follow signs in the village of **Blackstone** to the **Blackstone Gorge Bi-State Park.** Here the post-industrial Blackstone spills off Rolling Dam and runs wild through its last untamed stretch beneath rocky ledges that sprout hemlock and mountain laurel. The park is undeveloped—little more than a parking lot and a trail that plunges into the brush and makes a scenic loop on the river's east bank. Information on the park is available at the River Bend Farm interpretive center.

■ STURBRIDGE AREA *map page 183, A-3*

It's a paradox that modern highways should transport you so swiftly into the past, but Route 20 and the Massachusetts Turnpike bring you to **Old Sturbridge Village,** where you are promptly immersed in the early 19th century. The Wells clan of the American Optical Company in nearby Southbridge created the village, which began in 1935 as a one-building museum holding antiques the family began collecting in the 1920s. The collection continued to grow, and after World War II, Ruth Wells directed the completion of the museum complex that opened as Old Sturbridge Village in 1946.

The largest living-history museum in the Northeast, this re-creation of a circa-1830 New England community, set on 200 acres of farmland, is the most visited site in central Massachusetts. The meticulous research that went into its creation has resulted in an incredibly informative experience for visitors. Forty buildings were moved here from sites across New England, including the 1704 Fenno House from Canton, Massachusetts; the 1735 Stephen Fitch House from Willimantic, Connecticut; and an 1832 Greek Revival church. The costumed villagers herd livestock and work in the tin shop, pottery shop, mills, and other enterprises that contribute to this miniature rural economy. The village is set in a time when the American Industrial Revolution was already in gear and the West was just opening to settlement. New England villagers had no idea how swiftly their lives would change.

You get a strong feeling for a vanished way of life by visiting the village shops, church, common, mill district, and the traditional family farm. A day in the realistic world of Old Sturbridge Village puts to rest any tendency to sentimentalize this era of the American experience as a prelapsarian utopia. Since it stays open all year, visitors can follow the rhythm of the seasons from late winter calving to spring sheep shearing to the autumn harvest. Special programs focus on the celebration of various holidays, including Washington's birthday, Independence Day, Halloween, Thanksgiving, and Christmas. *Route 20 and I-84; 508-347-3362 or 800-733-1830.*

A more modest Wells legacy is the hilltop farm a few miles east of the town of Sturbridge. In 1977, Ruth Wells donated the farm to the town of **Charlton** to establish **Capen Hill Nature Sanctuary.** Pick up a map at the parking area and wander freely; every trail on the 72 acres circles back eventually. Depending on the season, you're likely to spy rabbits, deer, squirrels, skunks, foxes, opossums, wild turkeys, and owls. You may see a fisher (a member of the weasel family) or, more rarely, a bobcat or coyote. *Capen Road, off Route 20; 508-248-5516.*

The wool carding mill at Old Sturbridge Village.

People interested in that which is old also gather three times each year at nearby **Brimfield,** where more than 5,000 antiques dealers from across the country descend on a 1-mile stretch of Route 20 for the largest outdoor antiques show in New England. The three six-day shows generally begin the second Tuesdays of May, July, and September and continue through the following Sundays. Prices at the May event tend to fix benchmarks for the summer antiquing season.

■ QUABBIN AREA *map page 183, A-1/2*

You can't visit the villages of Dana, Enfield, Greenwich, and Prescott. Time stopped for them in 1938, when the last citizens departed and bulldozers arrived to scrape the Swift River Valley down to bare earth. The 150-foot earthen Winsor Dam went up at the southern end of the valley at Enfield, and water began backing up behind it on August 14, 1939. In 1946, water first flowed over the Winsor spillway and the Quabbin Reservoir was complete: a 39-square-mile, 412-billion-gallon lake to slake the thirst of 2.5 million residents in 46 cities and towns in Greater Boston.

History ran backward on the 187 square miles of lake and watershed forest known as the **Quabbin Reservation,** creating what some have called an "accidental wilderness" in the drowned valley. Access to the reservation is limited to protect the watershed and hence the purity of the metropolitan water supply. Motor vehicles are allowed only in Quabbin Park in Belchertown, near the visitors center at the southern stretch of the lake. The center contains exhibits on the heroic-scale engineering that created the Quabbin, along with nostalgic images of the lost towns. A cemetery of graves relocated from the inundated towns stands east of Quabbin Park along Route 9. *Quabbin Park Visitors Center: 485 Ware Road (Route 9), Belchertown; 413-323-7221.*

Most of the watershed is open for hiking, fishing, and even hunting. More than 40 public (if virtually unmarked) gates provide access from Routes 202, 122, 32A, and 9. Park in the turnouts, walk around the chains, and you are suddenly on a country road that once led to a Swift River Valley hamlet. Crumbling pavement or a dirt path overgrown with green moss entices you forward through the forest— down, down toward the lost towns.

Gate 8 is the crossroads of **Knightsville,** which lies south of Pelham where Packardville Road crosses Route 202. Before entering the Quabbin, stop across the street at **Knights Cemetery** to appreciate the potential for domestic strife in this rocky country. The tombstone inscription for Warren Gibbs, aged 36 when he died by arsenic poison in 1860, begins, "Think my friends when this you see/How my wife hate dealt by me/She in some oysters did prepare/Some poison for my lot and share. . . ."

Don't be misled by the oysters. The living was never easy on this begrudging land, and the stone walls bordering the roads and enclosing even the smallest pasture testify to the perseverance of farmers who endured until the promise of black soil lured them westward in the 1830s and forest began to reclaim the abandoned fields.

Packardville Road extends nearly a mile down to the Quabbin, with trails that were once the entrances to people's dooryards branching along the way. Step down one of these wooded trails and you will likely find a cellar hole, nearly overgrown with supple young birches or perhaps the rough trunk of a native hemlock. Struggling to bloom nearby will be the jaunty yellow heads of daffodils in the spring, the raucous orange trumpets of daylilies in midsummer. Look carefully and you will likely find—all in a row—six sturdy sugar maple trees. Six maples would sweeten the table for a year for a provident family.

THE EAGLE HAS LANDED

If you visit the Quabbin in the austere winter months, when the trees are bare and the landscape is cloaked in snow and ice, you may be rewarded by seeing the majestic bald eagles that flock to the region in late November and make the Quabbin their home until late March or early April. Eagles were first observed in the Quabbin as the reservoir neared completion in the mid-1940s, but the birds chose not to nest here, despite the nearly ideal habitat. Wildlife biologists hypothesized that bald eagles might only nest and breed in the habitats where they were hatched and fledged—and no living eagle had been born in the Quabbin.

In 1982 the Massachusetts Division of Fisheries and Wildlife initiated a bald eagle hacking program—introducing young birds into nests on platforms on the inner islands of the Quabbin. The program has raised more than 40 young birds, and biologists' hopes came true in 1989 when the first two pairs of eagles fledged at the Quabbin came to maturity, nested, and successfully fledged three young of their own. Birds continue to breed, building up the watershed's native eagle population. In 2002, three pairs nested at the Quabbin and raised two eaglets from each nest. Several birds now spend the entire year in the Quabbin, and the eagle population swells to around three dozen birds in the winter.

The best time to look for eagles is early in the morning. Good spots include Enfield Lookout, with its sweeping view of the reservoir; Goodnough Dike; and Gate 52. The birds are usually found near open patches of water because they prefer a steady diet of fish. Eagles like to ride the updrafts in search of food. Rising at the crack of dawn and standing in the cold morning wind, you might be rewarded by the sight of a mature bald eagle wheeling against the sky, suddenly banking, and making a skimming landing on the reservoir ice.

The gardeners and sugar makers are long gone from this territory, but the Quabbin Reservoir is far from uninhabited. Protected from intrusive human activity, the watershed forest teems with wildlife. Bobcats and shaggy Eastern coyotes prey on the overabundant white-tailed deer, and more than 50 species of songbirds trill in these woods. Much of the pleasantly undulating Route 202 runs along the edge of this forested preserve, and at the peak of the fall foliage season, the view from the lookout point just north of Pelham—and all along the highway—is nothing short of spectacular as maples and ash turn into color bombs detonated by the slanting sunlight.

Pine trees line the edge of the Quabbin Reservoir.

Those seeking more human inspiration may find it on the tombstone of Ephriam Pratt, who died in nearby Shutesbury in 1804, at the age of 117. "He swung a scythe 101 consecutive years," the stone declares, "and mounted a horse without assistance at the age of 110." As you traverse these roads you begin to see how old Ephriam did it. He just looked around him, at a landscape that was too beautiful to leave. Even vicious ice storms are bewitching here, transforming the trees into crystal wind chimes. Spring is a battle between sharp light and fuzzy foliage, summer a narcotic, and autumn a shameless display.

Nature occasionally hurls herself at you: when a moose steps onto the woodland path ahead, for instance, and fixes you with that implacable look; when a bow-legged bobcat suddenly appears in the mountain laurel or a bear trundles across the road at midday. But nature usually insinuates herself with a delicate midsummer firefly display or a distant coyote choral arrangement. And towns like Warwick, Royalston, Templeton, Petersham, Hardwick, and Barre (which has perhaps the prettiest town green in central Massachusetts) are equally sly, luring you into their shady commons, then bewitching you with their stillness and unforced beauty. The general stores and small country inns look real because they are, and you can drive for half an hour without meeting another car.

Among the Quabbin towns, **New Salem** is a special case, for its village center survived the amputation of most of the town's land. Resentment of the state legislature and of thirsty Bostonians still percolates here. With bittersweet exhibits of artifacts and photographs, the **Swift River Valley Historical Society,** in the Whitaker-Clary House and North Prescott Church, keeps the torch burning for the four towns that slipped under the flood. The hours of operation, however, are very limited. *Elm Street; 978-544-6882 or 413-548-9234.*

■ Travel Basics

Getting Around: Transportation in central Massachusetts hasn't changed much since days of the Nipmucks, with the east-west paths of Route 2, Route 9, and Route 20 following old Indian trade routes. Three interstate spurs—I-190, I-290, and I-395—off the Massachusetts Turnpike now connect Worcester, Leominster, and Fitchburg more efficiently to the interstate system. Interstate 495—a circumferential highway designed to give Boston a wide berth—forms the eastern boundary of the area.

Climate: Central Massachusetts endures some of the state's greatest weather extremes, because it is close enough to the ocean to pick up moisture yet far enough removed to miss out on the ameliorating effects of a large heat sink. Worcester Airport typically reports among the coldest temperatures in the state in the winter and is subject to frequent closures due to icing. The airport weather station often records the state's highest summer temperatures as well, frequently rising into the 90s Fahrenheit when Boston is basking in the low 80s.

Harvested apples in New Salem.

CONNECTICUT
RIVER VALLEY

Autumn in the valley is electrifying. Husky freight trucks load their cargo beds with Hadley pumpkins, tens of thousands of college students suddenly materialize like mushrooms after a rain, and the hardwood forests of the surrounding slopes ignite with their annual incandescent spectacle. The towheaded young man in overalls that you encounter in a bookstore could be a graduate student in philosophy or a farm boy from Whately—or both. The ancient Greek tradition of situating the groves of academe far from the corrupting influence of the city reaches its apex on the banks of the Connecticut, in the central part of the valley called the Five College Area. This is the land of gourmet coffee roasters, feisty political debates, social experimentation, and, above all, the life of the mind. Some denizens call Amherst "Cambridge with cows" and refer to Northampton as NoHo, but the valley's college towns are neither metro Boston nor metro New York. They are a set piece unto themselves, a melting pot of ideas and ideals, a prolonged identity crisis where even the old bask in perennial youth.

The road between colleges runs east and west. Perfectly perpendicular, the deeply agrarian traditions of the Connecticut Valley persist in a north-south axis along the river. Drive slowly down one of the bottomland river roads and you can almost imagine a Puritan farmer with his blunderbuss and a Pocumtuck brave with his tomahawk bursting through the wall of corn to fight each other to the death for the richest soils in New England. Tractors have replaced the oxen and draft horses, but the fields still yield astonishing crops. The valley may be dotted with colleges, but the land refuses to be ignored.

Life in the hill towns is quirkier, informed by pastoral traditions, yet leavened by the periodic sociological revolutions nourished in the valley below. Twenty years on, it becomes impossible to distinguish the back-to-the-land corporate refugee from the eighth-generation dairy farmer. They're both buying tofu at the co-op, milking goats and Jersey cows, and laboriously boiling down sap from 300-year-old sugar maples to make syrup in the spring.

(following spread) The long shadows of late afternoon set off golden fall foliage and verdant farms along the Connecticut River.

■ HISTORY

Some of the earliest evidence of settled agriculture in the Northeast is found in the Connecticut River Valley, where corn was a key crop a millennium before the Europeans arrived. The Pocumtuck peoples of the valley did not take easily to the encroachment of English farmers, who began moving upriver from Connecticut as early as 1636. Skirmishes and raids between settlers and native populations came to a head around 1675, during King Philip's War, when the Pocumtucks, led by Metacom, were decimated by attacks from the expansionist Mohawks on the west and the English on the south and east. The near-extermination of the Pocumtucks hardly spelled peace, for the palisaded towns of Hatfield, Hadley, and Deerfield

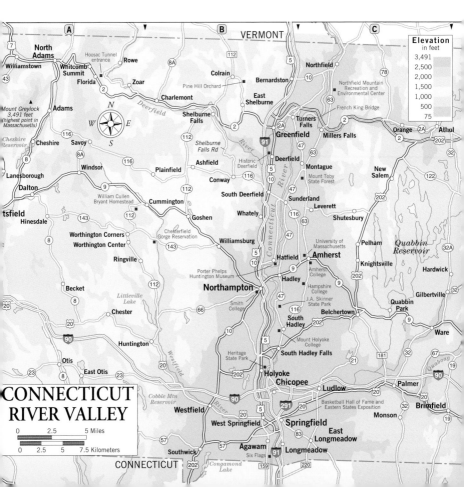

Rich soils made the Connecticut River Valley a key food- and tobacco-growing area in America's early years, and the river itself provided ready access to markets on the eastern seaboard. Following Springfield's emergence as an armaments manufacturing center around 1800, mills specializing in machined parts quickly sprang up wherever a falls could provide the power. Greenfield became known for its fine machinists, Holyoke for its papermakers. Much of this industry persisted until after World War II, leaving a legacy of brick mills along the riverbanks.

Ultimately, however, higher education shaped the Connecticut Valley's modern life. Amherst College had offered a first-rate education to men since 1821, Mount Holyoke and Smith Colleges to women since 1836 and 1875, respectively. The University of Massachusetts was established at Amherst in 1865, and for its first century remained a small but excellent college with strengths in agriculture and engineering. The Baby Boom generation transformed the school and surrounding communities in the 1960s, when UMass blossomed into a major research institution, with dozens of high-tech and knowledge industry spin-off companies.

■ **SPRINGFIELD** *map page 207, B/C-3*

With its aging brick factory buildings, pockets of immaculate Victorian neighborhoods, and Renaissance Revival–style public buildings, Springfield is a classic 19th-century industrial city. The soil along the banks of the Connecticut is no poorer here than farther north, but Metacom, whom the English called King Philip, set the city on a path away from the farm and into the mill. Legend has it that in 1675, at the height of hostilities between the English and the allied Algonquin tribes, Metacom stood on a bluff in what is now Forest Park and ordered the death and dismemberment of all the English settlers.

But half the population survived, and when they rebuilt, they huddled closer together and focused less on farming and more on sawmills and gristmills. Let the upriver farmers at Deerfield brave the arrows; Springfielders would stay indoors to process the grain and saw the timber. This mechanical bent was boosted when the Continental Congress established an arsenal at Springfield during the Revolution. George Washington was so impressed by the city's machinists that he pushed for the establishment of an armaments factory, and in 1794, Congress funded the Springfield Armory. During the bellicose years of the next century and a half, Springfield thrived making cannons and guns, including nearly half the firearms carried by Union soldiers during the Civil War.

REVOLUTIONARY SPIRIT

In 1786 the American Revolution had been over for three years, but many of the farmer-soldiers of western Massachusetts were beginning to wonder what they had fought for. The economic depression that followed independence forced those unable to pay their debts first into court and then to jail. Debt-ridden farmers petitioned the Massachusetts Legislature to issue a sound paper currency and halt foreclosures on their property. The Legislature, seen as the tool of Boston money men, turned a deaf ear, and the farmers took to arms in August 1786.

Under the nominal leadership of Daniel Shays from Pelham, they stormed through Worcester County, up and down the Connecticut River Valley, and throughout the Berkshires to prevent the local courts from making judgments for debt. In September, they forced the state supreme court, then sitting in Springfield, to adjourn. Desperate times called for desperate measures. In January 1787, Gov. James Bowdoin and his eastern Massachusetts business associates put up the money for 4,400 troops to put down the rebellion.

Before the troops could reach western Massachusetts, Shays and his men attacked the national arsenal at Springfield in hopes of better arming themselves. The arsenal garrison repelled them, however, and Shays's troops, always only loosely organized, dispersed. The army raised by Bowdoin caught up with the remnants in Petersham, and the rebellion was effectively quashed. But popular sentiment stood with the rebels. John Hancock roundly defeated Bowdoin in the gubernatorial election and pardoned the rebels. In one dramatic case where Shays's men stood accused of murder as well as treason, Hancock withheld his pardon until they had been paraded to the gallows—then gave them a last-second reprieve. Perhaps the most lasting effect of Shays's Rebellion was the impression it made on the Massachusetts Legislature, which hastened to ratify the U.S. Constitution rather than face future anarchy.

The armory closed in 1966, and most of the complex was turned over to Springfield Technical Community College. But the Main Arsenal, a Greek Revival structure built in 1847, was preserved as the **Springfield Armory National Historic Site.** Containing one of the world's largest collections of firearms, the museum here traces the evolution of guns produced at the armory and by private-sector gunmakers in the area as well. The armory was perhaps best known for the bolt-action .30-06 Springfield Rifle, still a popular deer-hunting rifle throughout New England. *1 Armory Square (Federal and State Streets); 413-734-8551.*

At the intersection of railroads, land routes, and the river barge system, Springfield was perfectly situated as a manufacturing center. By the end of the 19th century, it had one of the broadest industrial economies in New England. The first gasoline-powered automobile was built in Springfield, and so was the first production motorcycle. In 1901, bicycle manufacturer George Hendee and Swedish immigrant Oscar Hedstrom married Hedstrom's reliable little gas engine to Hendee's extra-strong bicycles and formed the partnership that eventually became the Indian Motorcycle Company. Within a few years of its founding, it was the top producer of motorcycles in the world. The **Springfield Indian Motorcycle Museum & Hall of Fame** (33 Hendee Street; 413-781-6500) celebrates the stylish motorcycle with the jaunty Indian-head ornament on the front fender, displaying almost every model made before the company folded in 1953.

Springfield's late-19th-century industrial wealth bred civic largesse, much of it concentrated in the **Quadrangle** at State and Chestnut Streets. Arranged around a central plaza are the Springfield Public Library, two art museums, a science museum with planetarium, and an extraordinary local history museum—a complex sometimes called "the people's college." *Quadrangle, Springfield Library & Museums Association, State and Chestnut Streets; 413-739-3871 for all museums.*

The **George Walter Vincent Smith Art Museum** was constructed by its Victorian namesake and his wife, Belle Townsley Smith, in 1896 to display their staggering collection of art. Because they were buying during an era of tumultuous cultural changes in the Far East, the Smiths managed to accrue the largest collection of Chinese cloisonné in the West; an array of Japanese arms and armor, screens, lacquers, textiles, and ceramics; and several exquisite Islamic rugs. Perhaps the high point of their collection is an elaborately carved Shinto shrine. The museum also displays the Smiths' collection of 19th-century American paintings.

The art deco **Museum of Fine Arts,** built in 1933, contains a solid survey of American and European painting, with some particularly strong works by Winslow Homer and John Singer Sargent. The two-story space at the heart of the museum is dominated by the compellingly strange *Historical Monument of the American Republic,* painted by local artist Erastus Salisbury Field (1805–1900). As busy and bizarre as a Hieronymus Bosch vision, the canvas was Field's meal ticket. He trucked it from town to town and charged admission to see it.

Springfield Symphony Hall is among downtown's neoclassical structures.

The **Connecticut Valley Historical Museum,** set in a Colonial Revival–style building, articulates local history from 1636 forward. The museum has extensive collections of hand-crafted furniture, pewter, and silver, as well as local portraits painted by itinerant artists, all of which conspire to conjure a rather personal, domestic history of the area. Because Springfield goes back to the roots of European settlement in North America, the museum's genealogical records are prized by scholars and ancestor-hunters alike.

The oldest American-built planetarium in the country, the Seymour Planetarium, is one of the highlights of the **Springfield Science Museum,** an institution that focuses on natural history. A huge model African elephant dominates the multi-level African Hall, devoted to the diverse wildlife and human cultures of that continent. The dinosaurs (including a replica tyrannosaurus) might be the biggest draw for the school groups that flock to the museum. T. Rex never stomped the Connecticut Valley, but hundreds of other species of dinosaurs inhabited the region during the late Triassic and early Jurassic periods. The peculiar nature of the valley soils, coupled with periodic floods, created one of the most extensive fossil records of dinosaur footprints anywhere in the world. The Science Museum takes advantage of this abundance by displaying prints throughout the galleries.

More-lovable monsters inhabit the central courtyard, where the **Dr. Seuss National Memorial Sculpture Garden** contains lifesize-plus sculptures of Theodor Geisel (more famous as Dr. Seuss) at his drawing board with the Cat in the Hat by his side. Various Seuss characters, including Yertle the Turtle, the Grinch and his dog Max, Gertrude McFuzz, and Thidwick the Moose, seem arrested in bronze. Geisel was born in Springfield, and his father took over

Do you like green eggs and ham? (Dr. Seuss National Memorial)

Colorful Milton Bradley games from days gone by. (Connecticut Valley Historical Museum)

the management of Forest Park after Prohibition closed the family brewery. Sharp-eyed observers will recognize some of his childhood landscapes (Myrtle Street and the zoo at Forest Park, for example) depicted in his books. During the winter holidays, the park glitters with its **Bright Lights** (413-787-1548) exhibit, including "Seuss Land," along a 2-mile drive.

In 1891, the Springfield YMCA challenged Dr. James Naismith to "develop an athletic distraction" for the young men. He nailed some peach baskets to the walls of the gym, grabbed an old soccer ball, and invented the game of basketball with nine players to a side. By 1892, the rules were published, and a year later Smith College women began playing the game. In 1894, a Chicopee factory was turning out the first basketballs, and braided cord nets on a cylindrical wire hoop became the standard basket. A year later, the first semiprofessional teams arose, and the game has been unstoppable ever since. The **Naismith Memorial Basketball Hall of Fame** in Springfield, dedicated in September 2002, tells the whole tale in loving detail. Historic games play almost continuously on giant monitors within the vast hemisphere that is the building, and the clamor nicely replicates the roar of a real contest.

Start on the third floor with the historical exhibits and the Hall of Fame plaques; work your way through the second-floor skills contests, where would-be stars measure themselves against the pros for height, wingspan, jumping skills, and reflexes; then come courtside to watch pickup games on the full-size court. Try your hand at a free-throw into a peach basket with no backboard and you'll see why the first game ended 1-0. *1000 West Columbus Avenue; 413-781-6500 or 877-446-6752.*

Across the Connecticut River, the **Eastern States Exposition** provides a reminder that Springfield lies in the heart of farm country. One of the nation's largest agricultural and cultural fairs, the Big E gives New Englanders a chance to bake pies, put up pickles, and raise piglets on a scale comparable to that of Midwestern farm-state fairs. In mid-September and early October, horse shows, crafts exhibits, parades, and indoor and outdoor pop and country music concerts take place. *Eastern States Fairgrounds, West Springfield; 413-737-2443.*

For another echo of times past, consider the merry-go-round at **Heritage State Park** (221 Appleton Street; 413-538-9838), north of Springfield in Holyoke. The 1929 carousel, one of the last from the famed Philadelphia Toboggan Company, has four dozen elaborately hand-carved horses, and two chariots, all serenaded by an Artizan band organ. The park also contains the **Children's Museum at Holyoke** (444 Dwight Street; 413-536-5437), where the permanent displays include a two-story climber and lots of interactive exhibits, including a building site, television station, and giant bubble maker.

■ SOUTH HADLEY *map page 207, B-3*

On a fall day, the drive from Springfield and Holyoke to South Hadley along Route 116 is golden, and the Tudor-style campus of **Mount Holyoke College** at the town center seems more a construction of leaf-filtered light than red brick. Established in 1837 as Mount Holyoke Female Seminary, the college retains a cloistered air and a single-gender student body. Founder Mary Lyon demanded that her students perform all the housekeeping and maintenance chores. "The domestic work would prove a sieve," she said, "that would exclude from the school the refuse, the indolent, the fastidious, and the weakly, of whom you could never make much, and leave the finest of the wheat, the energetic, the benevolent, and those whose early training had been favorable to usefulness, from whom you might expect great things." Educational fashions change, however: it has been a long time since Mount Holyoke women scrubbed floors. *50 College Street; 413-538-2000.*

AMAZING WOMEN

A few years ago I was invited back to my college, Mount Holyoke, to see a production of my play *Uncommon Women and Others.* The play is about five college seniors in the seventies who, faced with the real world, explore their feelings about marriage and careers versus their background in tea and gracious living.

When I arrived at the school several of the students told me how much they liked my play even though it was "a period piece." I could barely refrain from saying, "Who do you think I am, Sheridan?" When I asked them to explain what they meant by "period," they said, "Well, the women at your time were so confused about sex and graduate school. We're not confused. We know we're going to professional school, and we know all about sex."

In *Uncommon Women* there is a wistful refrain: "When we're forty we'll be pretty amazing." These students, most of them only twenty years old, seemed both competent and confident—already pretty amazing. In fact, most of them already had life plans mapped out. Blue for long-term personal goals, red for short-term career decisions.

—Wendy Wasserstein, *Bachelor Girls,* 1990

The **Mount Holyoke College Art Museum,** renovated, expanded, and reopened in 2002, displays a wide range of European, American, Asian, Egyptian, and Classical art as well as Medieval and Renaissance paintings and sculpture. *Lower Lake Road, on campus; 413-538-2245.*

Just after the equinox, the slanted autumnal light throws the peculiar geography north of South Hadley into elegant perspective. The drive north along Route 47 cuts through a geological interrupt where river and mountains appear twisted with indecision. **Mount Holyoke** itself, the northernmost spur of the Metacomet Range, is an unusual traprock formation, forced into its east-west orientation some 200 million years ago. Autumn inflames these slopes, and on September nights, the sunset seems to soak up its color from the trees below.

The mountain comprises **J. A. Skinner State Park** and its Summit House, a mountaintop hotel in the 1800s that is open for tours and programs on weekends and holidays from late spring to early fall. From the Summit House, the view of the Connecticut River's oxbow winding through the valley is as mesmerizing as it was for painter Thomas Cole. The passage between Mount Holyoke and nearby

The sylvan campus of Mount Holyoke.

Mount Tom is a bottleneck on the migration route for raptors in northeastern North America. In late September and early October, thousands of them can be seen riding the thermal updrafts on this celestial highway. *Route 47; 413-586-0350.*

A broad floodplain opens just north of the mountain pass. Amherst lies to the east, Northampton across the river to the west. The corridor between the two (Route 9) is a strip-mall-blighted rural traffic jam, but Route 47 continues through the floodplain, as if the depredations of the 20th century had never happened.

■ HADLEY AND THE RIVER ROAD *map page 207, B/C-2*

Hydroelectric and flood control dams have largely tamed the flow of the Connecticut River system, but every year with significant snowfall, the river swells over its banks along the river road, Route 47 between Hadley and Sunderland. These gentle floods and their renewing silt have been the farmer's friend since Native Americans began planting these bottomlands with maize roughly a thousand years ago. The sheer fecundity of this farmland astonishes the casual traveler. The seemingly inexhaustible soil produces prodigious crops.

Yet this agricultural world is virtually invisible to many residents of this part of the Pioneer Valley, as tourism promoters like to call the densely settled sections of the river basin from Springfield north to Greenfield. The main routes between towns, I-91 and Routes 5 and 10, simply bypass the farmlands, and commuters are too busy trying to avoid traffic accidents to cast a longing look down the side roads where tall corn sways in a gentle breeze.

The **Hadley Farm Museum** is like a Yankee farmer—amiable, generous, full of stories, and yet oddly reticent at the outset. The museum occupies a 1782 barn literally dragged to its current location in 1929 and expanded in the 1930s with lumber from barns torn down in villages now engulfed by the Quabbin Reservoir. Not a nail holds the solid structure together—it's assembled of rough-hewn timbers, notched and pinned with wooden pegs, planked with boards broader than almost any living tree in the valley.

Museum interpretation is haphazard at best, but the lack of signage seems a slight price to pay for the chance to handle hundreds of artifacts from a vanished rural world. A dozen implements for sowing small seeds, onions, and corn lie tilted willy-nilly against each other. A dusty table has several patent devices for candling or sizing eggs. Nearby is a centrifuge for testing butterfat in milk (local dairies paid the farmers based on butterfat content). Box, straw, and clay hives are heaped with

One-seater rocking horse at the Hadley Farm Museum.

a beekeeper's smoker, gloves, and veiled hat turned brittle with age. Wooden splint baskets line a wall, each of a different design: for corn, for goose feathers, for cheese, for winnowing. An earnest exhibit on broom-making stands at the head of one set of stairs—a reminder that Hadley began growing broom corn in 1797, and that by 1850 the town was riddled with small broom factories.

Along with cutters and sleighs and carriages on the ground floor are an early peddler's wagon, still stocked with goods, and a vintage Concord stagecoach—exactly the kind of vehicle featured in Western movies. If you make nice with the volunteer guide, you might receive an invitation to climb inside while he rocks the coach on its leather springs to simulate a ride. *Open mid-May–mid-Oct. At the junction of Routes 9 and 47; no phone.*

Precisely because its soil was so fertile, **Hadley** was one of the earliest communities in the valley. The original village, settled in 1659, stands a few hundred yards west of the current town center. Houses surrounding the long, rectangular common chronicle building styles through the 18th century. Just yards from the common, one of the large natural levees of the Connecticut rises behind North Street, a reminder of how tightly linked Hadley was to its life-giving river.

The early village had a palisade behind which settlers took refuge from Indian attacks. But the richest land lay beyond the pale, and those farm families were on their own. The 1752 house that became the **Porter Phelps Huntington Museum** preserves a sense of frontier life with remarkable verisimilitude. The structure is unchanged since 1799, and the belongings of seven generations of the same family fill the house with the quiet stories of the men and women usually overlooked in historical records. One shutter even bears the mark of an Indian hatchet from an attack in the 1760s, when the woman of the house huddled inside with her children and miraculously survived. Regarded as one of the best-preserved Colonial houses in New England, the museum serves a genteel afternoon tea with musical accompaniment on the porch during the summer and stages livelier concerts in its charming garden. *Open mid-May–mid-Oct., Sat.–Wed.; 1300 River Drive; 413-584-4699.*

Route 47 meanders northward, paralleling the twists and turns of the river, which is almost always out of sight behind the mud-bank levees or riverbank stands of swamp maples. This eastern bank of the river is planted largely in truck farm crops (asparagus, onions, pumpkins, leeks, strawberries) and field corn, which supports the dwindling dairy herds still found browsing the hummock, named, with some exaggeration, Mount Warner.

■ **COLLEGE SUBURBS** *map page 207, B/C-1/2*

The bottomlands suddenly rise as the road ascends into **Sunderland,** originally a village of Hadley called Swampfield. It was abandoned during King Philip's War and resettled under its present name around 1713. The floodplain extends east from the river here. Sunderland was under extensive tobacco cultivation until the 1960s, when population pressures from nearby Amherst began to turn its farmland into house lots. But the river road, Route 47, ignores the university encroachments, proceeding through the village past the largest sycamore tree east of the Mississippi. North of town, the road turns at last away from the river to circle the west flank of Mount Toby and rise into the relative highlands of **Montague Center,** a crossroads village with an unusual red brick Congregational Church.

Located on the edge of town on a falls of the Sawmill River, **Montague Mill** was built in 1834 as a gristmill to grind corn. Two of the old millstones still lie in the river below. About a century later, the Martin Machine Company purchased the mill and set six men to work for a year to rebuild the wooden crib dam. A pair of turbines created the power to make hydraulic marking machines sold all over the

Route 116, as it crosses the Connecticut River into Sunderland.

world to stamp wood and steel, including Louisville Slugger baseball bats. The company decamped for Turners Falls in 1987, but left behind large metal wheels throughout the mill. These had been used to open sluice gates and let water flow through the turbines. A major flood destroyed most of the dam in 1996, but the venerable mill complex has been restored to house the Book Mill discount bookstore, an antiques shop, a crafts gallery, a restaurant, and a seasonal café.

The Book Mill, on the river in Montague.

Woodsy Montague and the neighboring community of **Leverett,** just south on Route 63 heading toward Amherst, lost most of their industry during the Depression and most of their farms in the years immediately after World War II. Offering cheap land, beautiful vistas, and close proximity to Amherst, they were ripe for the picking when the University of Massachusetts suddenly blossomed in the 1960s. Old farms became communes, hayfields hid less traditional crops, and small institutes sprang up to teach meditation, yoga, and other spiritual practices of the New Age. This too mostly has passed, and driveways of both villages are more likely to harbor Volvo station wagons and SUVs than psychedelic microbuses.

Still, it is not impossible to wander the trails of the **Mount Toby State Forest** and hear the wind rustle the chimes on a log front porch across the valley. Drive slowly along the maple-blazed fall roads, and you will still encounter the occasional hand-lettered sign: "Llama manure for sale." Old habits die hard. *Route 63 and Reservation Road; no phone.*

■ AMHERST *map page 207, C-2*

The northern approach to Amherst on Route 63 is the least jarring of all the roads converging on this college town, although it does lead directly onto the campus of the **University of Massachusetts at Amherst** (413-545-0111), the flagship of the state's university system, with more than 24,000 students, 50 doctoral programs, and more than 100 undergraduate departments. Established as an agricultural college in the 1860s, it remained a modest state university until the mid-1960s, when the first bulge of baby boomers swelled its ranks to current levels. Rapid expansion meant a number of high-rise concrete structures in the International Style so roundly detested by traditionalists. To some taciturn Yankees brought up on the Little-Ivy good manners of Amherst College, UMass as an institution seemed boorish, strident, and uncultured, but the university has won many converts from the community for its extensive performing and visual arts programs (many of them free or nearly so) and its nationally competitive athletic programs.

Although its streets seem locked in a permanent traffic jam, the center of Amherst remains small and, in summer, when the student population plummets, relatively sleepy. The town is named for Lord Jeffrey Amherst, a British Colonial general who regularly sent smallpox-infected blankets to the Indians during the French and Indian Wars. Every few years there's a movement at Town Meeting to rename the community, but the ability of Amherst voters to talk interminably without reaching a conclusion inevitably dooms the proposal. For all its intellectual and politically correct fillips, Amherst remains a beautiful little town. The large, leafy common stretches between the business district and Amherst College, and small points of intense local cultural pride are located steps from the central intersection.

The town's public library, the **Jones Library,** is appropriately rich with literature. Robert Frost taught at Amherst College for 18 years, until 1938, and the library houses a large collection of items relating to the poet's life and work. The Emily Dickinson collection includes original manuscripts, letters, and illustrations. Massachusetts local history comes vividly to life in the correspondence, journals, and ephemera that comprise the Boltwood Collection, which includes the 18th-century letters of British general Lord Jeffrey Amherst and various Civil War diaries that evoke the voices as well as the events of history. *43 Amity Street; 413-256-4090.*

The 1774 **Strong House** displays 18th- and 19th-century rooms, one of which is dedicated to Mabel Loomis Todd, the late-19th-century neighbor of Emily Dickinson and the first editor of her poems. Loomis's steamy affair with Emily's brother, William Austin, is not commemorated here, but it was documented in the diaries kept by the couple and later in Polly Longworth's 1984 book *Austin and Mabel. 67 Amity Street; 413-256-0678.*

When Emily Dickinson limited her perambulations to her "father's fields," the reclusive poet was referring to his 14 acres of meadow, not the hillock on which the **Dickinson Homestead** stands. The 1816 house and the gardens at 280 Main Street are modest indeed, and most of Emily Dickinson's possessions are at Harvard, yet a tour of the rooms is strangely moving, perhaps because this space is so intimate. Dickinson lived here most of her life, and when you see the tiny white dress in her bedroom or the afternoon shadows bisecting her garden, her words materialize: "The soul selects her own society. . . . There's a certain slant of light." As the Amtrak *Vermonter* train rumbles across Main Street in the late afternoon,

DEATH KINDLY STOPPED FOR ME

The death of Miss Emily Dickinson, daughter of the late Edward Dickinson, at Amherst on Saturday, makes another sad inroad on the small circle so long occupying the old family mansion. It was for a long generation overlooked by death, and one passing in and out of there thought of old-fashioned times, when parents and children grew up and passed maturity together, in lives of singular uneventfulness unmarked by sad or joyous crises. Very few in the village, except among the older inhabitants, knew Miss Emily personally, although the facts of her seclusion and intellectual brilliancy were familiar Amherst traditions. There are many houses among all classes into which treasures of fruit and flowers and ambrosial dishes for the sick and well were constantly sent, that will forever miss those evidences of her unselfish consideration, and mourn afresh that she screened herself from close acquaintance. As she passed on in life, her sensitive nature shrank from much personal contact with the world, and more and more turned to her own large wealth of individual resources for companionship, sitting thenceforth, as some one said of her, "in the light of her own fire."

—Obituary written by Susan Dickinson, Emily's sister-in-law, published in the *Springfield Republican,* May 18, 1886 and in the *Amherst Record,* May 19, 1886

Emily Dickinson lived most of her life in this Amherst home.

you hear, "I like to see it lap the miles/ And lick the valleys up." Emily Dickinson is buried a short distance away in West Cemetery, on Triangle Street, where her simple tombstone reads "Called Back." *1 Pleasant Street; 413-542-8161.*

The next-door **Evergreens,** a wedding gift to William Austin, was the first Italianate house in Amherst. Austin's daughter, Martha Dickinson Bianchi, remembered Emily well—she was 20 when the poet died—and made a career of watching over the Dickinson literary estate. She kept up the Evergreens, retaining her parents' furnishings, and turned it over to her literary assistant when she died—with the provision that when the assistant no longer lived there, the house would be torn down. Local preservationists found a loophole in the will that has preserved the peculiar old house as historical. The exterior has been repaired and the interior continues to undergo restoration. It has been open for tours since 2001. *Open March–early Dec.; 214 Main Street; 413-256-3925.*

Founded in 1821 to educate men for the ministry, **Amherst College,** which borders the common, began accepting women in 1976. Its art and natural history museums, on the main quad, provide an edifying excuse for a stroll through the beautiful campus. *100 Boltwood Avenue; 413-542-2000.*

The National Yiddish Book Center is the world's largest repository for Yiddish-language books.

The 80,000 items of Amherst College's **Pratt Museum of Natural History** (413-542-2165) grew out of a 19th-century collect-and-catalog mind-set, but the museum's galleries have been handsomely updated to contemporary exhibition standards, and the museum is far more dazzling than many public natural history institutions. As you enter, you're immediately greeted by skeletons of extinct giants—a mammoth and a mastodon (with an Indian elephant skeleton for scale). Other Ice Age creatures stare down from the central dais: a saber-toothed cat, an Irish elk, and a cave bear. Local dinosaur footprint casts are located throughout the first floor, and the museum thrills children with its full mount of a standing duck-bill dinosaur and its triceratops and T. Rex skulls.

The college's **Mead Art Museum** (413-542-2335), meanwhile, established in 1839, holds approximately 14,000 works. Unusual among university art museums, it has extensive holdings in Latin American and Russian art as well as the more typical European and American collections.

Hampshire College, south of town in former orchard lands, is the town's third and newest college, having admitted its first students in 1970. (With Smith in Northampton and Mount Holyoke in South Hadley, the three Amherst campuses are part of the valley's "Five College Area.") Hampshire has long had a reputation as a school on the thin wedge of the counter-cultural edge. Although this may be less true than it used to be, the college still boasts a vibrant artistic and intellectual culture. *893 West Street; 413-549-4600.*

The college's green, rolling campus seems far removed from Eastern Europe, but the **National Yiddish Book Center** is housed here in a single building designed so that the exterior resembles a 19th-century shtetl. The only such institute in the nation, the center preserves a vanished culture in a stellar collection of volumes and exhibits. *Route 116, 3 miles south of Amherst; 413-256-4900.*

Children's book author Eric Carle (*The Very Hungry Caterpillar*) and his wife, Barbara, opened the **Eric Carle Museum of Picture Book Art** in 2002. Adjoining Hampshire College, it showcases the work of picture book artists, including Maurice Sendak, Lucy Cousins, and Carle himself. *125 Bay Road; 413-658-1100.*

One of the most relaxing travel routes from Amherst to Northampton is the **Norwottuck Rail Trail,** an 8.5-mile bicycle path that slips through cornfields from its starting point at Station Road in Amherst and vaults the Connecticut River to its conclusion at Elwell State Park on Damon Road in Northampton. Automobiles, alas, are doomed to overburdened Route 9.

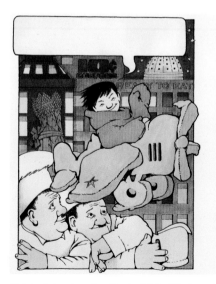

Original drawings from In the Night Kitchen. *(© 1970 Maurice Sendak)*

■ **NORTHAMPTON** *map page 207, B-2*

Jonathan Edwards no doubt spins in his grave if he is able to contemplate the fate of the community where he launched the Great Awakening of religious fervor in the 1740s. He was said to make small children swoon over the threat of hellfire when he launched into his perennial stem-winder, "Sinners in the Hands of an Angry God." Even Northampton, always a city of passionate extremism, finally had enough of Edwards, and the Puritan authorities spirited him off to preach to the Indians. But one wonders if the city ever got over the adrenaline charge of his sermons, for it remains a very hopped-up place. Overlays of youth cultures from the 1960s through 1990s create a strange time warp. Many inhabitants came to the region to attend college and became fixed like specimens in their particular generational amber. The city's local coffee roaster, Cafe Habitat, rails against the cultural imperialism and exploitation practiced by its better-known competitors, and cranks out such caffeinated favorites as Radical Roast and Wicked Women's Roast. Feminism in this home of Smith College long ago eclipsed mere analytical politics to make NoHo one of the nation's most lesbian-friendly communities.

From fire and brimstone to feminism, Northampton has been a city of passionate extremism.

Northampton residents proudly point out that some surrounding strip malls have failed because people would rather shop downtown. The 30 or so boutiques in the redeveloped building that is now **Thorne's Marketplace** (150 Main Street) have fluctuated in their success rate as well, but the peculiar mix of upscale housewares, natural foods, premium ice cream, New Age paraphernalia, and specialty books functions as NoHo's souk—the market that lays bare the soul of the place.

Cultural ferment bubbles incessantly, resulting in a proliferation of good bookstores, cafés, restaurants, and art galleries. The performance calendar is filled with concerts, poetry readings, dance, and theater. The **Iron Horse Music Hall** (20 Center Street; 413-584-0610), for example, has evolved into one of New England's top stops for touring blues, jazz, and folk musicians. The city-owned **Academy of Music** (274 Main Street; 413-584-8435) is a striking 1890 performance hall that has served as a vaudeville and dramatic theater since its inception; it showed its first motion picture in 1898. Live performances still light the stage occasionally, but it is best known for programming independent and art films.

Northampton and the surrounding hill towns have proved a magnet for fine crafts artists since the 1960s. Several galleries in town show their work, and twice a year, on Memorial Day and Columbus Day weekends, the city's Tri-County Fairgrounds hosts the **Paradise City Arts Festival,** a juried crafts show of about 240 exhibitors. *Route 9; 413-527-8994.*

Those assuming that the thoughts of Calvin Coolidge, America's notoriously taciturn president, would fill a postcard will be surprised by the extensive collection in the Calvin Coolidge Memorial Room at the town's beautiful **Forbes Library.** Coolidge was mayor of Northampton and governor of Massachusetts before he was president, and he returned here after retiring from politics. The man who emerges from these documents and photographs is more complex than the simplistic image of "Silent Cal." The president's mechanical bucking horse also conjures unlikely images. *20 West Street; 413-587-1011.*

In a city of contradictions and wonders, **Smith College** occupies the high ground. Founded in 1875 by Sophia Smith, of nearby Hatfield, to offer a nonsectarian Christian-influenced education to "the intelligent gentlewoman," Smith retains its all-women undergraduate program and its Seven Sisters manner. The campus, where Sylvia Plath walked (and had her first nervous breakdown) and where *Who's Afraid of Virginia Woolf* was filmed, is a tree-shaded delight on a midsummer day. *Elm Street; 413-584-2700.*

The **Smith College Museum of Art,** rebuilt on the same site in 2002, is filled with good teaching examples that span the ages and is unusually strong in art of the last century and a half. The collections began in 1879 with the purchase of a contemporary painting by Thomas Eakins, and the museum curators continued to exhibit excellent taste by acquiring works by Homer, Sargent, and other painters of the day. Although its first European painting was not purchased until 1919, the museum has compiled an impressive collection of French Impressionist and Post-Impressionist art. *Elm Street and Bedford Terrace; 413-585-2760.*

Many of the plants on Smith's stunning campus come from the college's own botanical gardens. The 19th-century conservatory at **Lyman Plant House** and **Smith College Botanic Gardens** foster more than 3,500 species of plants. The Victorian greenhouses, which appropriately overlook Paradise Road, are a miracle in the early spring, when snow and ice sterilize the outside world while the annual bulb show assaults you with riotous colors and the dimly remembered smell of hyacinths. *College Lane, off Elm Street; 413-585-2740.*

The main road past Smith College, Elm Street, continues west as Route 9 through the village of Florence, perhaps best known in the Five College Area for its vintage **Miss Florence Diner,** a Worcester Dining Car diner that serves breakfast day and night. *99 Main Street; 413-584-3137.*

■ HEADING NORTH *map page 207, A/B-2*

The hubbub of Northampton seems a lifetime away if you leave town for a circuit drive through the high country of dairy farms and timber lots northwest of the city. The main roads are long and curvy and well-maintained, alternating valley-spanning vistas with closed bowers of old oaks and maples. Turn off Route 9 and roads frequently turn to dirt. Wandering should be your aim, as you bear in mind Thoreau's advice. "What's the hurry?" he wrote, "If a person lost would conclude that after all he is not lost . . . but standing in his own old shoes . . . how much anxiety and danger would vanish."

Streams tumble off the mountains in **Williamsburg,** which had water power aplenty for a variety of mills and factories in the early 19th century. But in 1874 a dam that had been built three miles above the village burst, sending through town a wall of water that killed 136 people and washed away the entire manufacturing district. It was never rebuilt.

Out for a ride at Smith College.

THE QUADRANGLE

Instead, Williamsburg has developed into a bedroom town for writers, artists, and gentlemen farmers with real jobs in Northampton. Its landmark general store has evolved into a faux general store with all the gimcracks of "country life" and a very busy ice-cream counter.

Take the road less traveled west of Williamsburg to make a loop through dramatic mountain scenery. Route 143 branches off Route 9 to the left to sweep through the blink-and-you'll-miss-them villages of **Chesterfield.** Watch for signs to **Chesterfield Gorge,** a natural wonder on Trustees of Reservations property. The foot trails through a birch and beech forest along the bluffs above the gorge provide dramatic views of the sheer granite cliffs carved by glacial ice and millennia of rushing water. A more difficult trail leads down to the Westfield River at the entrance of the gorge, where swirling pools offer premier fly-fishing for trout. *River Road, 1 mile south of Route 43; information available from Trustees of Reservations, Notchview, 413-684-0148, or Ashintully Gardens, 413-298-3239.*

The back road from the gorge—beginning as Ireland Street, becoming Partridge Road and then Indian Oven Road—leads westward to Route 112, where the northbound highway rises dramatically into the stately hilltop village of **Worthington Center,** which actually has a traffic light. It's worth the trip to see Worthington's handsome buildings, including an elaborate red clapboard Congregational church across the broad main street from the austere white town hall. The gingerbread Carpenter Gothic house style was very much in vogue here in the late 19th century, and several outstanding examples of this idiosyncratic, colloquial style line Worthington's streets.

The land north of Worthington heading toward **Cummington** (on Route 112) seems stepped—one high plateau after another—as if each farmer had leveled his own land. In fact, this is a trick of geology, stacks of sedimentary rock juggled by periodic upheavals. The lanes of the old farms are lined with gnarled and weathered sugar maple trees that were strong enough to stand in the hurricane of 1938.

Before entering Cummington (where Route 9 returns to Northampton), the road pauses at Bryant Four Corners, and a triumphal bower of maples leads up a farm road to the region's most evocative literary site—the **William Cullen Bryant Homestead.** Born here in 1794, the poet spent his boyhood and old age on this hill where breezes rustle the maples he is said to have planted. The Rivulet Walk, below the house, winds through old-growth forest, and the view of the Westfield Valley and Hampshire Hills invites reveries. *207 Bryant Road; 413-634-2244.*

■ TOBACCO LANDS *map page 207, B-2*

The historic agriculture of the Connecticut River bottomlands, which includes small vegetable farms east of the river in the towns of Hadley and Sunderland, manifests itself on the river's west bank as broad tracts of corn, Hubbard squash, and broadleaf tobacco.

Start your tour of the area by driving up Routes 5 and 10 north from Northampton and then turning right onto Elm Street toward the water. This will bring you into **Hatfield,** a town whose claim to history is that it was "thrice attacked by Indians in the King Philip's War." Following one ferocious attack in 1677, Benjamin Waite and Stephen Jennings paddled from here to Quebec—about 300 miles through hostile territory—to rescue their captive wives and children with a ransom of 200 pounds.

You could easily find yourself dawdling at 5 miles per hour behind a tractor hauling a manure spreader, for farmers in Hatfield and neighboring **Whately** ignore the impatience of their more urbanized neighbors. The slow pace gives you time to contemplate the utilitarian beauty of the weathered tobacco barns, their slatted walls open after the August harvest, permitting air circulation to cure the dangling sheaves of broadleaf inside.

When you reach Whately, consider stopping at the **Fillin' Station One,** a large streamlined 24-hour diner where long-haul truckers chow down on eggs and bacon and home fries next to poets and fiction writers sobering up after marathon literary readings or the vicissitudes of UMass writing workshops. *Route 5 off I-91, Exit 24; 413-665-3696.*

Dead ahead in **South Deerfield** stands the sudden interruption of the horizon known as **Mount Sugarloaf,** a "sheepback," or knob of basalt bedrock carved by glacial action. A lookout tower at the 791-foot summit provides sweeping views of the Connecticut River and the patchwork of cropland along its banks.

A short distance north of town on Route 5 is **Bloody Brook,** the site of a major confrontation between Connecticut River Valley settlers and local Indians in 1675. Seventy-nine men accompanying a wagon train of provisions headed from Deerfield to Hadley were ambushed at the crossing of what was then called Muddy Brook. They had stopped and were, Increase Mather later wrote, "so foolish and secure as to put down their arms in the carts and step aside to gather grapes, which proved dear and deadly grapes to them." Only eight settlers managed to escape, and the trickle has been known as Bloody Brook ever since.

The Dwight House, built ca. 1730, is one of Historic Deerfield's 14 museum houses.

■ **OLD DEERFIELD**   *map page 207, B-1*

"Old Deerfield" is a term local residents often use to differentiate the original fron-tier village of the 17th and 18th centuries from the more populated areas of town that have sprung up over the ensuing two centuries. In effect, the name applies to the quaint ghost of a village along The Street, also known as Old Deerfield Street, or Old Main Street. Old Deerfield was first officially settled in 1673, although at least one English farmer had been squatting here since 1669. The English dis-placed the Pocumtucks from their very fertile Deerfield cornfields, and the little community bore the brunt of the struggle between English settlers and native pop-ulations that continued for nearly a century.

"Not long before the break of day, the enemy came in like a flood upon us," the Rev. John Williams wrote in *The Redeemed Captive,* his account of the 1704 Deerfield Massacre. In the gray light of a bone-chilling February morning in Old Deerfield, it is easy to imagine that terrifying moment. Under French command, 350 Indians attacked on February 29, 1704, killing 49 people and marching 112 prisoners 300 miles to Canada; 20 of them died on the way. John Williams's account of the attack quickly became a best-seller, but his lifelong effort to persuade his daughter Eunice to return from her captors failed, as John Demos recounts in his 1994 book, *The Unredeemed Captive.*

Today, the door of the 1698 John Sheldon House (which no longer exists), with its gaping tomahawk hole, provides graphic evidence of the ferocity of the attack. Indeed, the door serves as the touchstone exhibit in **Memorial Hall Museum** (open May–Oct., 8 Memorial Street; 413-774-3768), the original 1798 building of Deerfield Academy but now the museum of the Pocumtuck Valley Memorial Association. The **Indian House Memorial Children's Museum** (107 Old Main Street; 413-772-0845), a 1929 reproduction of the John Sheldon House, gives a sense of the besieged lives of the early settlers. Children can try on Colonial clothing, write with quill pens, and play with the toys of old. Indian House keeps regular hours in July and August, but school groups dictate its hours the rest of the year.

On Albany Road, off the south end of Old Deerfield Street, the **Old Burying Ground** provides further hints of the rugged characters who lived and died in Deerfield when it was a frontier town. Among the 493 gravestones—all placed according to Puritan tradition, facing east to meet the rising sun—you will find Lt. Mehuman Hinsdell, who died in 1736, aged 63, "the first male child born in this place and was twice captivated by the Indian salvages [sic]."

Deerfield, however, has long been a peaceful, even staid place, with its mile-long street of restored 18th- and 19th-century houses set in the river valley's farmland. Fourteen of the old houses are part of **Historic Deerfield,** founded in 1952 by Henry and Helen Flynt, of Greenwich, Connecticut. The Flynts' son, Henry Jr., was a student at Deerfield Academy in the class of 1940; the Academy's headmaster, Frank Boyden, in 1945 convinced Henry Flynt, a New York City lawyer and history buff, to purchase and restore the Deerfield Inn. That year the Flynts also bought a home in Old Deerfield, the Allen House, which they restored and filled with antiques. They donated money to Deerfield Academy to restore other houses along Main Street, and they bought some of their own, which they filled with antiques purchased from dealers throughout the country. Their enthusiasm for early American history and their philanthropic nature are what saved Old Deerfield from deterioration.

On paper, Historic Deerfield sounds like a Colonial theme park, with its museum store, inn and restaurant, and meticulously restored houses displaying 20,000 artifacts dating from 1650 to 1850. But the enticements here are restrained and tasteful. Except on holiday weekends, a tour of this National Historic Landmark is more of a stroll than an endurance test. Head first to Hall Tavern, a 1765 roadside hostelry moved here from Charlemont in 1950 to serve as the museum's visitors center. You can purchase tickets to the individual houses, but it is best to buy an All of Deerfield ticket, which includes admission to all historic houses plus Memorial Hall Museum (from May to October) and is valid for one week. *Old Main Street; 413-774-5581.*

On fall evenings the tree-lined thoroughfare of The Street is particularly soothing, and even a visitor uninterested in the town's architecture will linger on the porch of the **Deerfield Inn** to watch the shadows devouring the clapboards. Constructed in 1884, the spacious old country inn remains a pleasant hostelry with one of the area's most formal dining rooms. *81 Old Main Street; 413-774-5587 or 800-926-3865.*

Walkers can explore the Channing Blake Meadow Walk to the Deerfield River, or hike the nearby Pocumtuck Ridge, named after the valley's first inhabitants. The former begins about ⅓-mile beyond the inn, on the same side of the street. The Pocumtuck Ridge trail is about 2 miles away and requires a steep 1.2-mile ascent.

A prominent presence on The Street is **Deerfield Academy** (7 Old Main Street; 413-772-0241), a preparatory school founded in 1797. Originally only for boys, the school began enrolling local girls as day students in the 19th century but discontinued the practice during World War II. In 1989, the school, which now has 550 students, became fully co-ed. One of the best high schools in the country, it counts among its illustrious alumni the author John McPhee (1949), the late Sen. John Chafee (1940), and King Abdullah II of Jordan (1980).

Because it is such a well-preserved village, Old Deerfield has become the focus of research on life in early New England, and the Memorial Libraries welcome visitors from Monday through Friday throughout the year. Historic Deerfield and Memorial Hall Museum host special events, workshops, antiques forums, and hands-on activities for families; Historic Deerfield's curators occasionally sponsor "object identification days"; and in June and September, Memorial Hall puts on major fairs of traditional crafts, with objects for sale ranging from Shaker-style furniture to pottery, hooked rugs, and pewter.

Autumnal rusticity, Deerfield style.

■ GREENFIELD *map page 207, B-1*

The town of Greenfield was settled in 1686 as Deerfield's "Green River Settlement," but its parishioners, in a series of theological disputes, gradually broke away from their mother community and incorporated as an independent town in 1753. In some respects, the separation paralleled a change in valley life: Deerfield was principally a community of farmers, and Greenfield capitalized on its natural resources to become a community of merchants and mechanics.

Greenfield was originally sited to take advantage of the alluvial soil where the Green River flows into the Deerfield and the Deerfield into the Connecticut. But all that flowing water ultimately proved more important than the land. At the end of the 18th century, the Locks and Canal Company opened river trade on the upper Connecticut by building locks around the falls in Holyoke and Hadley, and in 1792 the company made the south side of Greenfield a major shipping terminus for agricultural products. The rippling falls of the Green River just upstream from the warehouse district provided power for mills, and by the 1820s, Greenfield factories began to specialize in metal cutting—producing tools, machine parts, and cutlery. Eventually, many of these firms merged to create precision tool companies, including the Greenfield Tap and Die Corporation and the Millers Falls Corporation.

Increasing competition and aggregation of the U.S. tool industry led to the departure of Greenfield's industry in the years following World War II. Only Lunt Silversmiths and the smokestack of Greenfield Tap and Die near the Green River hint at the town's erstwhile industriousness. In a sense, Greenfield has come full circle to its agricultural roots as the market town for the rural, agrarian northern Massachusetts towns of the Connecticut River Valley.

The town itself stands well above the Connecticut and retains hints of its former beauty in the view from its small common, in the heroic-style 1930s reliefs decorating the Sweeney Ford Garage on Main Street, and in the steep residential streets that wind up to Mountain Road and **Poet's Seat.** Frederick Tuckerman Goddard (1821–74) was a local poet ("much admired by Emerson," a memorial plaque suggests) who favored this aerie as inspiration for his verse. The high bluff is topped by Poet's Seat Tower, a stone monument built in 1912 as a memorial to Goddard and the site from which July 4th fireworks are launched.

Twisting Eunice Williams Drive leads to a covered bridge.

Each September since 1848, Greenfield has played its part as Franklin County's shire town by hosting the **Franklin County Fair** on the town fairgrounds. One of the more resolutely agricultural county fairs of Massachusetts, the event focuses on the hard work and handiwork of rural residents. Small children lead hulking bovines around the dusty show rings, people queue up for peach shortcake, and the John Deere dealers always seem to be touting a shiny new tractor model. *Thurs.–Sun. following Labor Day; 89 Wisdom Way; 413-774-4282.*

On the north side of town, off Green River Road, twisting **Eunice Williams Drive**—named not for John Williams's captured daughter, but for his wife of the same name—leads to the 95-foot Pumping Station Covered Bridge over the Green River. The original 1870 covered bridge burned in 1969, and this replica was constructed by townspeople in 1972. From here Green River Road, an unspoiled, verdant delight, winds north to Vermont; on the other side of the river, Leyden Road winds south back to Greenfield.

Water flows over the dam at the Watermill Lumber Company, south of Turners Falls.

■ TURNERS FALLS AREA *map page 207, B/C-1*

The small jog of Route 2A between Greenfield and Turners Falls follows the Connecticut River along banks that were favorite Native American fishing encampments. Just as Greenfield was powered by the falls on the Deerfield River, adjacent **Turners Falls** drew on the thundering drops of the Connecticut as it descended from Vermont and tumbled down to its rendezvous with the Deerfield. Although located within the township of Montague, Turners Falls early on developed a separate identity as an industrial community. Site of the first dam on the Connecticut River, the town was built on a series of terraces rising 100 feet above the water, and as late as 1913 these impressive waters were the final destination of enormous log drives.

Observant travelers might notice the Polish-American stamp on Turners Falls. Just as Polish and other central European agricultural workers flocked to the farmlands of the Connecticut in the late 19th century, many mechanics and machinists found work in Turners Falls and nearby Greenfield and Athol. Organizations such as the St. Kazimier Society on Main Street are the social backbone of the village, and the red brick church **Our Lady of Czestochowa** (84 K Street) attracts pilgrims to view its hand-carved altars, stained-glass windows, and shrine to the Blessed Kateri Tekakwitha, the "Lily of the Mohawks."

Turners Falls may be distinctly unfashionable, even decayed in places today, but its dramatic setting, 19th-century mill houses, and attractive main thoroughfare are not its only advantages. Most of the large mills stand vacant, but smaller-scale manufacturing is leading the town back toward prosperity. The **Shea Theatre** (71 Avenue A; 413-863-2281), built in 1929 as a movie theater, is one of the finest small performance venues in the area, and the old-time **Shady Glen** (7 Avenue A; 413-863-9636) is one of the best eateries. The diner still serves fried liver as well as a banana cream pie that would tempt even the seriously spandexed.

Waddle down toward the water to the small park on First Street to find the **Fish Ladder,** operated by Northeast Utilities (413-659-3714), the local power generating company. At the viewing facility—open from Wednesday through Sunday, from mid-May through June—you can descend below the water's surface to the concrete observation room, where a large window reveals the river's busy migration. Although the numbers vary from day to day and even hour to hour, the window is often dense with fish—salmon and shad and lamprey—struggling against the current to reach their spawning grounds upriver.

THE MAN WHO BUILT THE HOUSES

A few towns up the Connecticut River from Amherst there's a village, called Northfield, that belongs in an old lithograph. It has a wide main street, tall trees, and many large, elderly houses that were built to last. The village has a few structures that date back to Colonial times, but most of its old houses were built in the 1800s. Collectively these amount to a text on 19th-century architecture. Northfield has houses with hipped roofs and center chimneys, ones with pediments and columned porticoes, ones with the pointy-topped windows of the prototypical American haunted house. The late Georgian, the Federalist, the Greek Revival, and the Gothic, all are represented in the old houses of Northfield's streets. The curious fact about them is that most were designed and built, for about five hundred dollars apiece, by a carpenter named Calvin Stearns and by his sons and brother. You can usually tell a Stearns house. All have classical-looking proportions. In their gable ends, Stearns installed fanlights with shutters that swoop out at the bottoms like bells. Inside, the houses have simple banisters, hand-carved to roundness, and on the trim under most fireplace mantels, Stearns placed two small decorative buttons—his signature. His houses look straighter and squarer than most things one hundred fifty years old. An elderly man who lives in a Stearns Federalist likes to say that someone once put a cable around another Stearns house and tried to pull it over, and the cable broke.

—Tracy Kidder, *House*, 1985

■ NATURAL RESOURCES AND RECREATION

The high dam at Turners Falls no longer generates any electrical power, but its presence has created **Barton Cove,** a significant impoundment a couple of miles east of Turners Falls in the town of Gill. Northeast Utilities maintains the shores of the cove as a park, complete with campsites, picnic areas, and seasonal canoe and kayak rentals. Bald eagles craft huge nests here in winter and scavenge the river for fish, ducks, and other potential meals. Egg-laying time for the eagles is in March, and cameras permanently focused on the nests allow for constant viewing on the Internet (www.nu.com/eagles). *Route 2, Gill; 413-863-9300 from Memorial Day to Labor Day; out of season, call Northfield Mountain Recreation and Environmental Center (see page 244).*

The French King Bridge crosses the Connecticut River east of Barton Cove.

In addition to developing Barton Cove, Northeast Utilities established the **Northfield Mountain Recreation and Environmental Center,** which includes a visitors center and a recreation area on Northfield Mountain. Hiking, mountain biking, and bridle trails double as cross-country ski trails in the winter. The center also operates the *Quinnetukut II,* a 60-seat boat that travels 12 miles round-trip down the Connecticut, passing through the **French King Gorge** and under the magnificent French King Bridge, which crosses the river on Route 2 east of Turners Falls. The gorge's granite walls force the normally sedate Connecticut into wild and beautiful contortions. (The view from the bridge's 140-foot height is spectacular.) The power company undertook its recreational and environmental projects as part of an agreement that permitted it to create the Northfield Mountain Pumped Storage facility on Route 63. During periods of low power demand, water from the Connecticut is pumped into a high-altitude holding area—the upper reservoir—inside the mountain. The reservoir holds nearly six billion gallons of water. During peak-demand periods, it is released through turbines to generate electricity. *99 Millers Falls Road (Route 63); 413-659-3714.*

A tourist shop along the Mohawk Trail offers gifts and "live" entertainment.

■ MOHAWK TRAIL

Between the French King Bridge and the New York border, the 63-mile stretch of Route 2 more or less follows a centuries-old Native American footpath used by the Mohawk during the French and Indian Wars. Successively widened to accommodate horses, then wagons, and finally automobiles, the highway opened in 1914 as the **Mohawk Trail.** Although this section of Route 2 has been straightened and improved since, it still has the feeling of an old-fashioned byway from an era when motoring was an adventure rather than a chore.

Driving west on the Mohawk Trail, you encounter tourism at its most antique. Peeling totem poles and pockmarked wooden Mohawk braves stand beside faded tepees and trading-post gift shops. Signs invite you to "See Live Deer Free," and tiny pink motel cabins proclaim their vacancies. The effect is oddly comforting, like discovering a forgotten childhood toy at the bottom of the wardrobe.

Turning north on **Shelburne-Colrain Road** takes you through woodland, apple orchards, and farmyards to the hilly village of **Colrain** (the road's name changes to Greenfield Road when you pass the town line). Along the way, at 248 Greenfield Road, is the roadside farmstand of **Pine Hill Orchard** (413-624-3325) and a retail outlet for **West County Winery** (413-624-3481), which has won regional acclaim for its hard ciders. Here you can purchase fruit from the orchard, preserves from **Bear Meadow Farm** (413-624-0291), located next door in the old sugarhouse, and even cheese from one of the small goat-cheese makers of Colrain. There's a small pond and penned farm animals that children are encouraged to feed. West County Winery helps organize the annual Cider Days, held the first weekend of November. The event features orchard visits and a market of backcountry growers with their heirloom apples.

■ SHELBURNE FALLS *map page 207, B-1*

Back on Route 2, head west past **Gould's** (Mohawk Trail, Shelburne; 413-625-6170), a sugarhouse open for pancake breakfasts in the spring and fall. The turn to Shelburne Falls drops you into a green bowl of trees or a white bowl of ice, depending on the season. The village straddles the Deerfield River and sits half in the township of Shelburne on the east and half in the township of Buckland on the west. It's an unusual arrangement, but the people of Shelburne Falls cultivate eccentricity. In effect, the village is the market, cultural, social, and tourism center for all the surrounding hill towns.

On the Buckland side of the Iron Bridge—as the residents insist on calling the otherwise unremarkable metal bridge that spans the Deerfield River—**McCusker's Market** provides a precise barometer of the local psyche. Bins of organic produce and culinary herbs share space with patent herbal remedies. The deli counter prepares several vegetarian options and nondairy, vegan sweets. A superb selection of gourmet chocolates sits beside a large sign advertising Oats Crème, a dairy-free, cholesterol-free frozen dessert posing as ice cream. Don't try smoking at McCusker's—it's prohibited inside the store, on the steps, and even within 50 feet of the building. *3 State Street; 413-625-9411.*

Trolley cars used to rattle past the store on the 7-mile link that operated between Shelburne Falls and Colrain from 1896 to 1926. Trolley Car No. 10, built in 1896 as the first car of the line, is the only one that survives. The trolley is the prize of the **Shelburne Falls Trolley Museum,** a labor of love that includes a room full of memorabilia and a couple of electric-train setups. Five-minute rides are given on the vintage equipment. The modestly priced tickets are good all day—to the delight of children determined to get their money's worth. *Buckland Rail Yard, 14 Depot Street; 413-625-9443.*

The 400-foot-long, five-arch concrete bridge now known as the **Bridge of Flowers** was built in 1908 so the trolley could transfer railroad freight from the Buckland side of the Deerfield River to the Shelburne side. (The previous bridge had a 20-ton limit, so teamsters had to unload rail cars in Buckland and haul the freight over the Iron Bridge in wagons.) When the trolley line went belly up, the bridge became a pedestrian crossing and efforts began immediately to convert the eyesore into a garden walkway. The Shelburne Falls Woman's Club hires a gardener to maintain the display, which includes more than 500 varieties of flowers and ornamental plants that create a continuous bloom from early spring to late fall.

The Shelburne side of the village has the larger commercial center. The storefronts are filled with crafts galleries, jewelry artisans, cafés, a coffee roaster, and even a massage parlor with river view. The great flood of the New Age has washed over the town, but there are hints of an antediluvian village as well in **Baker Pharmacy,** which stubbornly retains its six-stool soda fountain, and venerable **Memorial Hall,** now home to Shelburne's town offices and an upper-level theater that once hosted vaudeville shows and lectures.

The theater is now a concert venue and site of Pothole Pictures, a revival movie series named for the community's geological oddity, the "**glacial potholes.**" The

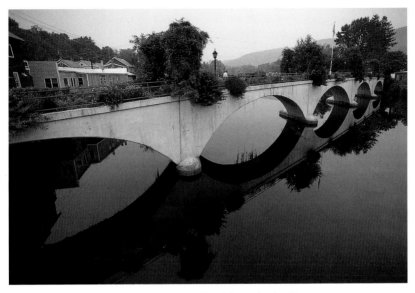

Along the Bridge of Flowers, footsteps have replaced the rattle of trolley cars.

granite bed of the Deerfield River was ground down by whirlpool action during high waters at the end of the last glaciation. Swirling pools spun huge boulders in circles until they bored into the rock. Many of the grinding stones are still visible in their holes, which range from 6 inches to 39 feet across.

The potholes are just downstream from a former mill dam reconstructed to generate hydroelectric power. Water pours steadily over the wooden lip of the dam, and due to an increase in accidents on the slippery rocks, the town of Shelburne has closed indefinitely the access stairs. There is, however, an observation deck, and in spring, when the swelling river forces the wooden wall of the dam to break down and a chilling spray fills the air, it is best to be out of the river's way.

A retail outlet for **Mole Hollow Candles** (3 Deerfield Avenue; 413-625-6337) occupies the mill building at the base of the falls. Started in this then-dilapidated building in 1969, when tourists were virtually unknown to Shelburne Falls, Mole Hollow Candles has grown into an international business. Just up the road, above the falls, is **North River Glass** (2 Deerfield Avenue; 413-625-6422), where glass blowers produce bowls, vases, and ornaments in a studio open to the street.

On a hill across the river is **Salmon Falls Artisans Showplace** (1 Ashfield Street; 413-625-9833), an impressive craft gallery filled with works of artisans from the Northeast. Pride of place goes to the "planets" of local glass artist Josh Simpson.

Both the Pocumtucks of the Connecticut River Valley and the Mohawks of the Hudson Valley considered the falls here to be important fishing grounds, calling them Salmon Falls. Although the tribes were bitter enemies, in 1708 they negotiated a treaty that lasted 50 years and set aside the falls and an area "one day's journey" away as a peaceful preserve for hunting and fishing. Salmon no longer get this far upriver, but the Deerfield has outstanding stretches of trout fishing, particularly in the upriver shallows in Charlemont.

■ ASHFIELD AND CONWAY *map page 207, B-1*

A spectacularly scenic drive from Shelburne Falls climbs Route 112 through Buckland to Ashfield, spirals downhill on Route 116 to Conway, and follows the Deerfield River back to Shelburne Falls along a road where Currier & Ives illustrators drew some of their most memorable images of winter sleigh rides.

Settled in 1743 but not incorporated until 1765, **Ashfield** occupies the rocky top of this portion of the Berkshire Hills. So stony is its soil that farms are spread far apart, and the town never bothered to set aside a common. There is a center of sorts with all the essentials: an 1812 Town Hall next to the firehouse, a Congregational church and an Episcopal church. It became briefly famous when essayist Tracy Kidder observed in his book *House* that ever since the first urban centers, there has always been a back-to-the-land movement. In Ashfield, he wrote, even breakfast was a reenactment of "the fantasy of local self-sufficiency," with maple syrup from your own trees, apple pancakes made with your own apples, and bacon from the neighbor's hogs.

Changing times have tempered the utopian vision, but no cultural shift can alter Ashfield's striking beauty. In the fall, the town is electric with color, from the flame hues of the Norway maples to the acid yellow flare of birch and beech and the deep purple tones of the black gum leaves. Yet in some ways Ashfield is most beautiful when naked. Stripped of the rich foliage, the craggy hillsides and long sloping pastures of its farms recall Theodore Roethke's line, "I knew a woman lovely in her bones." The very shape of the land, its contour under snow, is seductive.

Those fine bones of the landscape are nowhere more evident than on the twisting downhill route from Ashfield into **Conway,** which passes the 107-foot

Burkeville covered bridge (no longer in service) before entering Conway center. Originally a village of Deerfield, Conway was larger than Springfield around 1800 and reached its peak of industrial prosperity in the years before the Civil War, boasting a full range of woolen mills, sawmills, shoe factories, and toolmakers. By the end of the 19th century, it even had its own power company and street railway. The glories of Conway vanished in a flash in October 1896, when torrential rains cracked the granite reservoir dam and the South River washed away much of the town. Today, Conway is known for its dignified but quiet lifestyle, making it a prime refuge for professors and professionals who make their living at the academic mills in the valley below. Only the town's **Field Memorial Library** (Elm Street; 413-369-4646), a limestone temple of knowledge with a circular dome and copper roof, attests to former glories. It was the gift in 1885 from Chicago merchant Marshall Field, who was born in Conway. From the center of town, Shelburne Falls Road winds along the Deerfield River and returns to Shelburne Falls.

■ CHARLEMONT AREA *map page 207, A/B-1*

The Deerfield River changes character entirely as it babbles over a broad and shallow bed of pebbles along the Mohawk Trail between Shelburne Falls and **Charlemont.** The small agricultural village seems a remote musical venue, but this lovely town's annual **Mohawk Trail Concerts** (413-625-9511), performed on Saturdays in the acoustically perfect Charlemont Federated Church, attract the nation's most celebrated classical musicians and composers, and the journey here, along the Deerfield River, is part of the evening's pleasure. Route 2 follows the Deerfield for much of its length, and the waters at Charlemont and Zoar are particularly popular with canoeists and white-water rafters. Two rafting outfitters, **Zoar Outdoor** (413-339-4010) and **Crab Apple Whitewater** (413-625-2288), bracket the town to the east and west, offering group trips on selected portions of the river that can range from lazy floats down still waters to exhilarating, nervy bounces through Class III rapids.

Outside Charlemont, just before the Indian Bridge and the heroic *Hail to the Sunrise* statue of a Mohawk, the road on the right marked "Rowe and Zoar" is a flight into wilderness. Turn left after a couple of miles at the first intersection and follow the Deerfield's course between steep hills until you reach the gloomy entrance to the **Hoosac Tunnel,** open only to train traffic. Take the right fork instead, and you will continue climbing through hardwood forest.

You may find yourself rubbing your eyes when the sudden clearing becomes the village of **Rowe.** The handsome houses here represent a modest parade of early American domestic architecture, beginning with spare Colonial farmhouses and ending, circa 1830, with hints of Greek Revival in the column-shaped trim around the doorways. Wooden signs along the main road record where various businesses once stood: "Foliated Talc Mill: 1902–1922" or "Eddys Casket Shop: 1846–1948." Two old schools have been moved to the center of the village to serve as the **Kemp-McCarthy Museum of the Historical Society** (Zoar Road; 413-339-4700), open on Sunday afternoons in the summer.

Leaving behind the curious idyll of post-Colonial village life, retrace your route down Zoar Road to return to the Mohawk Trail. The highway winds along the precipitous banks of Cold River as it climbs steeply through the Mohawk Trail State Forest en route to **Florida,** a town named in the early days of tourism to suggest a balmy climate in the mountains. (Nathaniel Hawthorne mentions the town in passing in his travel piece "Ride Toward Charlemont.")

The view from the **Whitcomb Summit** (2,110 feet) embraces the highest points of Massachusetts, New Hampshire, Vermont, and New York. After cresting Hoosac Mountain at Florida, the Mohawk Trail begins a long series of switchbacks to descend into the Housatonic Valley. The last of these is the dramatic and appropriately named **Hairpin Turn,** where North Adams suddenly appears, a vision of industry in the bowl of the Hoosic River Valley.

■ TRAVEL BASICS

Getting Around: The Connecticut River Valley is oriented along the north-south course of the river, with I-91 providing the swift route and lazier U.S. 5 (known as Route 5), Route 10, and Route 47 following the river banks. Route 2 slashes across the north as the Mohawk Trail; Route 9 ventures from eastern hills through the colleges and into the western hills; and the Massachusetts Turnpike links the southern valley with eastern Massachusetts and the Berkshires.

Climate: The thermometer seldom rises above freezing in the winter, and snow falls on average once a week. Heat and humidity are the summer norm; even over the din of the cicadas, you can almost hear the tobacco and corn grow in the bottomlands. Autumn is a drawn-out, delicious season of deep-blue skies, golden sunlight, and frosty nights, with daytime highs in the 60s Fahrenheit and nights in the high 30s. There is no real spring—only mud season.

One of several covered bridges in the area.

THE BERKSHIRES

A lady in pearls studiously unpacks her picnic onto an Indian dhurrie. She sets out a silver bowl of ice with a scoop of black caviar on top, places the glazed roast duck on a carving platter, and brings out the pickle dish full of cornichons. Suddenly she is in a panic. She walks over to the couple sprawled on a bedspread, eating ham sandwiches. "Do you," she asks, blushing, "have any Grey Poupon?" It's a midsummer late afternoon at Tanglewood, and the patrons are dining on the rolling lawn before the concert begins.

The Berkshires. This valley where Massachusetts snuggles up to New York has long been a name with which to conjure the rustic magic of summer. For a busy nine weeks between late June and Labor Day, the rural towns of western Massachusetts blossom as a nexus of the arts. The Boston Symphony Orchestra explores the canon of orchestral music, Shakespeare & Company brings the Bard to life. Dance takes flight at Jacob's Pillow, and New Yorkers prowl the art galleries and antiques shops to find that special something for the guest room on Central Park West.

These sophisticated pursuits are balanced by a hospitable landscape of long valleys and mountains that are just high and steep enough to inspire admiration. Much of the Berkshire Valley has been allowed, even encouraged, to revert to something approaching a wild state. Yet these sanctuaries and parklands are crisscrossed with hiking trails. Follow the spirits of Melville, Hawthorne, and Thoreau and clamber up the topographic hiccup of Monument Mountain or the truly majestic summit of Mount Greylock. Wherever you find a cliff or a long waterfall, count on it having an associated legend of a tragic Indian maiden. Romantic poets of the 19th century made much of this landscape as the embodiment of the sublime; environmentalists of the 20th century framed the same praise in different, no less emotional terms.

What surprises first-time visitors to the Berkshires is the persistence of an earlier America. Stockbridge really does look exactly as Norman Rockwell painted it. Minutes from the conclaves of arts aficionados, the hill towns are still studded with tiny dairy farms and spreading orchards. "What thou lovest well remains," Ezra Pound wrote. "The rest is dross."

Autumn in the Berkshires.

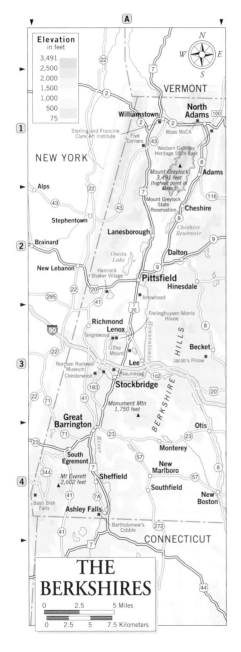

Elevation
in feet

3,491
2,500
2,000
1,500
1,000
500
75

VERMONT

Williamstown
North Adams

NEW YORK

Sterling and Francine
Clark Art Institute
Five Corners
Mass MoCA
Western Gateway
Heritage State Park

Mount Greylock
3,491 feet
(highest point in Mass.)
Adams

Alps

Mount Greylock
State
Reservation
Cheshire

Stephentown

Lanesborough
Cheshire
Reservoir

Brainard

Onota
Lake
Dalton

New Lebanon
Hancock
Shaker Village
Pittsfield
Hinesdale

Arrowhead

Frelinghuysen-Morris
House

Richmond
Lenox
Tanglewood

The
Mount
Becket

Jacob's Pillow

Norman Rockwell
Museum
Chesterwood
Lee

Naumkeag
Stockbridge

Monument Mtn
1,750 feet
Otis

Great
Barrington
Monterey

South
Egremont
New
Marlboro

Mt Everett
2,602 feet
Sheffield
Southfield
New
Boston

Bash Bish
Falls
Ashley Falls

Bartholomew's
Cobble
CONNECTICUT

THE BERKSHIRES

0   2.5   5 Miles

0   2.5   5   7.5 Kilometers

■ HISTORY

English settlement in the Berkshires proceeded from south to north up the valley between the Taconic and Hoosac ranges. But unlike the Connecticut Valley, the Berkshires towns did not take root until the second quarter of the 18th century, when the Mahicans at present-day Stockbridge and Sheffield had established friendly relations with the Massachusetts government. (The native populations of the Berkshires decamped for New York in 1785, and kept moving as the frontier shifted, finally settling in Wisconsin in the late 19th century.) The communities south of Mount Greylock date from 1750 or earlier. Permanent settlement in the northern Berkshires, however, was delayed until after the resolution of the French and Indian Wars in 1763.

As in the rest of interior Massachusetts, the people of the Berkshires farmed the valley bottomlands, grazed sheep and dairy cattle on the uplands, and built mills and manufacturing concerns wherever waterfalls provided power. Only Pittsfield and North Adams flourished as industrial centers, while the other communities remained agricultural.

This bucolic landscape attracted two kinds of dreamers, those who built castles in the air of heaven and those who built castles under the rubric of "summer cottages." The Shaker community at Hancock was one of the largest and most successful outposts of the sect, which reached its peak in numbers and influence in the years just before the Civil War. Just a generation later, wealthy rusticators began constructing country estates on British models. The untitled aristocracy carved up many a farmstead into a patchwork of exquisite Berkshire squiredoms. The institution of a federal income tax in 1913 put a stop to further estate-building, and now many of the old manses and their grounds house upscale hotels, spas, and performance venues.

■ NORTH ADAMS   *map page 254, A-1*

Route 2 freewheels in a long arc from the worn crags of the Hoosac Range westward into the fertile valley bottomland of the Hoosic River at North Adams, a former mill town now bubbling with cultural ferment. Boosters call the community "the Gateway to the Berkshires," a term it earned in 1875 with the opening of the Hoosac Tunnel. The 4.75-mile straight bore through the mountains from Florida to North Adams was one of the great engineering feats of its day. Crews tunneled from each end, and when they met, their alignment was accurate to less than an inch. The tunnel opened rail connections between Boston and Albany, New York, and thanks to a mid-1990s expansion to accommodate double-deck freight cars, it continues to serve as a major rail link between coastal New England and the Great Lakes via New York state. At the former rail station south of the city, **Western Gateway Heritage State Park** traces the development of the tunnel that put North Adams on the map the first time. *Route 8; 413-663-6312.*

It took the **Massachusetts Museum of Contemporary Art** (MASS MoCA) to put North Adams on the map again more than a century later. Exhibiting contemporary art too grand in scale for more conventional museum spaces, MASS MoCA occupies part of the gargantuan complex of 27 mill buildings constructed between 1872 and 1900 by the Arnold Print Works, in its day the largest finisher of cotton cloth in North America. When the textile company closed in 1942, the cavernous brick mill buildings adjacent to downtown were taken over by Sprague Electric Company, which used the space to manufacture electrical components until 1985. Sprague's departure shattered the North Adams economy and, to a great extent, the city's spirit.

But the opening of MASS MoCA in 1999 allowed North Adams to reinvent itself as a postmodern city, constructing a forward-looking future on the salvaged structures of its industrial past. Many of the museum's brick walls remain exposed, wire-brushed to reveal a century of paint layers. Industrial steel-plate supports frame the transitions from gallery to gallery, building to building. High windows and skylights allow light to flood into the galleries, some of which are two and three stories high. These enormous spaces are perfect for exhibiting outsized sculpture and installation pieces originally conceived for outdoor sites. Electronic media stations are positioned throughout, often suspended from steel wires in a practical implementation of industrial chic.

MASS MoCA neglects neither its context nor its past. Plaques throughout trace the history and evolution of the buildings. A small display in the lobby shows the Sprague company's VisiVox, a late-1920s precursor of the VCR and DVD player. The device had a phonograph turntable that operated at the conventional 78 rpm of the day—and the radically new 33 rpm format as well. Its wide-angle lens produced large pictures from both 16mm amateur and 24mm professional movie film. Although the advent of talking motion pictures kept the VisiVox from ever going to market, the ingenious device seems right at home in the cutting-edge technology of the museum.

Even the mill clock tower that governed the life of North Adams by ringing every quarter hour of the working day has been transformed into a contemporary work of art. Christina Kubisch created a digital database of tones by hammering, striking, and brushing the bells of the original carillon by hand. She installed solar sensors to read the intensity and location of sunlight and used software linked to the light conditions to create an environmental soundscape—clear and metallic during bright sun, soft and melancholy when it's cloudy. *1040 MASS MoCA Way; 413-662-2111.*

One wonders what the mill workers who once occupied the row houses across River Street think of the clock tower's change of tune, or the transformation of their once decrepit homes into the chic **Porches Inn,** which juxtaposes 1950s tchotchkes with high-speed Internet access and DVD players in every room. *231 River Street; 413-664-0400.*

North Adams derives its new vigor from precisely such a dialectic of past and future. Unable to use the entire Arnold Print Works complex, MASS MoCA rents out space to high-technology companies and Internet start-ups. The striking

A recent exhibition at MASS MoCA of contemporary Austrian works included (top) Franz West's sculpture Merciless *and (bottom) Peter Kogler's untitled wraparound video room.*

Second Empire mansion that houses the city **library** (74 Church Street; 413-662-3133) is dotted with computer work stations that sit next to 19th-century gaslight fixtures. Downtown, you're likely to find bright young chefs inventing new fusion dishes in colorful restaurants housed in stolid red brick structures from the 1860s. The grand art deco marquee of the **Mohawk Theatre** on Main Street blazes again, promising further interior renovations that will someday let it open as a community performance and meeting center. The final verdict won't be in for decades, but North Adams seems to be a perfect case study of an economic revival galvanized by the arts.

■ MOUNT GREYLOCK *map page 254, A-1/2*

Route 2 passes a picturesque Victorian graveyard on the west side of North Adams en route to Williamstown. But the 3,491-foot mass of Mount Greylock on the left defies even the most indifferent alpinist to pass by. Massachusetts's highest peak beckoned irresistibly to some of America's leading 19th-century literati, who climbed its slopes seeking alpine transcendence on the lines of Goethe and Byron.

A view over the Berkshires from Mount Greylock.

In 1838, Nathaniel Hawthorne was the first of the writers to reach the summit, and he took the easy route—by ox cart. Referring to the 100-mile views of the Taconic, Catskill, and Hoosac mountain ranges, Hawthorne wrote in his notebook, "Every new aspect of the mountains, or view from a different position, creates a surprise in the mind."

In 1844, it was Henry David Thoreau's turn. Typically, he walked up alone. "I made my way steadily upward in a straight line through a dense undergrowth of mountain laurel," he wrote, "until the trees began to have a scraggy and infernal look, as if contending with frost goblins, and at length I reached the summit, just as the sun was setting." Following a supper of rice, Thoreau settled in for the night beneath a Williams College weather observation platform. "But as it grew colder toward midnight, I at length encased myself completely in boards, managing even to put a board on top of me, with a large stone on it . . . and so slept comfortably." By contrast, on Herman Melville's sybaritic 1851 expedition up Greylock, he and his 11 fellow hikers fortified themselves with brandied fruit, champagne, port, cognac, and Jamaican rum and spent the night playing cards.

Today **Bascom Lodge,** built by the Civilian Conservation Corps in the 1930s and maintained by the Appalachian Mountain Club, provides a more conventional form of bed and board for weary hikers from mid-May through late October. *Mount Greylock summit; 413-743-1591.*

The 11,000-acre **Mount Greylock State Reservation** surrounds the mountain and encompasses five other major peaks. More than 100 bird species nest in the reservation, and coyotes, black bears, and bobcats are increasingly numerous, though rarely glimpsed. Fifty miles of hiking trails crisscross the hillsides, including a beautiful stretch of the Appalachian Trail. But more visitors emulate Hawthorne than Thoreau and opt to ascend by auto. As the road winds upward through forest and mountain meadows, the maples, hemlocks, and ash trees seem to cower on the hillsides, holding their ground against ferocious gales that batter this giant all winter. But Greylock also has its tranquil seasons. In May and June, painted trilliums, yellow violets, and many other wildflowers cover the slopes. The elusive blackpoll warbler nests here, and the forest is particularly rich in thrushes, who endlessly test its acoustics with their liquid riffs. Valley dwellers save special affection for the mountain in autumn. Since 1966, hundreds of people—from small children to great-grandmothers—have streamed up Cheshire Harbor Trail to the summit for the annual Columbus Day climb known as the Mount Greylock Ramble. *Rockwell Road, Lanesborough; 413-499-4262.*

■ WILLIAMSTOWN *map page 254, A-1*

Back at ground level, Route 2 leads to Williamstown, a renowned college town and cultural center where even the retirement community trailer park on the outskirts, the Spruces, has massive white lions flanking its entrance. The town largely consists of the 450-acre Williams College campus, with its exquisite 19th-century buildings. The **Williams College Museum of Art** spans the millennia, from two much-beloved 9th-century B.C. Assyrian reliefs to the rainbow-hued Sol LeWitt *Wall Drawing* commissioned in 2001. The museum's strength, however, lies with American art from the late 18th century to the present. Brothers Charles and Maurice Prendergast are represented by more than 400 works, the largest such collection in any museum. *15 Lawrence Hall Drive, off Main Street; 413-597-2429.*

From June through August, many film and television actors return to their roots to tread the boards at the **Williamstown Theatre Festival,** which made its reputation in the 1950s and 1960s by showcasing new plays by young playwrights. Today it blends classic and newer drama for its main stage at the Adams Memorial Theatre on the Williams campus and tries out experimental work on a second stage. *1000 Main Street; 413-597-3400.*

Throughout the year, however, the **Sterling and Francine Clark Art Institute** remains Williamstown's main attraction. Situated on a gentle, manicured rise at the west edge of town, this small museum is particularly known for its extensive Renoir collection and its French impressionist and American paintings, including works by Homer, Sargent, Cassatt, and Remington.

"Do not mention the opening of the Institute to anyone," its founder Robert Sterling Clark wrote to a friend in 1955, "as you will treat me to a cloud of newspapermen to the detriment of my health." One of the heirs to the Singer sewing machine fortune, Clark was an art collector and racehorse owner who opened his collection to the public in 1955, the year after his chestnut colt, Never Say Die, won the Epsom Derby. Relying on their own taste rather than expert advice, Clark and his French wife, Francine Clary, accumulated distinctly "Clarkian" works. Their taste is recognizably florid, but there are some delicate surprises in these airy galleries: the Italian Renaissance and 16th-century Dutch portraits, for instance; van Gogh's 1886 *Terrace in the Luxembourg Gardens,* which looks like a Renoir; the Renoir landscapes that look like J. M. W. Turner's. Turner himself is superbly represented by *Rockets and Blue Lights to Warn Steamboats off Shoal Water. 22 South Street; 413-458-9545.*

The chapel at Williams College stands tall in this early 1900s postcard. (Williams College)

There are also earthier pleasures. You can picnic on the beautiful grounds or take a half-hour walk up **Stone Hill** to Stone Hill Road, an 18th-century road traveled by George Washington in 1790, for fine views of Williamstown and the surrounding hills of the Taconic Ridge. The trail begins at the Clark Institute's west parking lot, passes through oak forest, crosses a gravel road, climbs through the hemlock, and turns right to reach a stone bench. Follow the path across Stone Hill Road and through an open field back to the Clark, for a total stroll of 1.5 miles.

Heading south from Williamstown along either Route 43 or Route 7 on a spring evening is like driving—or better still, bicycling—through one of the Clark Institute's French landscape paintings. Lush, tree-ringed fields border the curving road and cattle wade in the Green River. Locals call the intersection of the two highways **Five Corners,** where an 18th-century building has served as a stagecoach stop, a feed store, a general store, and a tavern of slightly notorious repute among Williams undergrads. In keeping with changing times, **The Store at Five Corners** (junction of Routes 7 and 43; 413-458-3176) is now a gourmet shop, with a good deli counter and a fine selection of wines.

Route 7 is the traditional connector between the northern and southern Berkshires. Even this main road south to Pittsfield is bucolic, however, and opportunities to wander into the pastoral scene occur at every minor intersection. For all the gentrification of summer visitors, year-round farm life endures. In Lanesborough, for example, a turn west onto Brodie Mountain Road, or east onto Summer Street and then Old Cheshire Road, will take you past maple sugar houses and farmstands where successive harvests, from June strawberries to October pumpkins, are sold at the side of the road.

■ PITTSFIELD *map page 254, A-2*

The largest city and shire town of the Berkshires seems a peculiarly landlocked place for Herman Melville to have finished *Moby-Dick,* but the author supplied in imagination what he lacked in shoreline. "I have a sort of sea-feeling here in the country . . . I look out of my window in the morning when I rise as I would out of a porthole of a ship in the Atlantic," he wrote of the view from **Arrowhead,** his 18th-century farmhouse south of Pittsfield. Here Melville also wrote *Pierre* and *The Confidence Man* and developed a deep friendship with Nathaniel Hawthorne. As scholar James C. Wilson has noted, the two writers in their literary prime "exchanged cigars, whiskey, and what Melville described as 'ontological heroics' during their visits. Hawthorne described their conversation as 'talk about time and eternity, things of this world and the next.'"

Whatever the critics might have said, especially in hindsight, neither man was making a good living from writing at the time. The market reaction to the publication of *Moby-Dick* in 1851 was lukewarm, and Melville was ultimately forced to sell Arrowhead to his brother in 1863. His death in 1891 went largely unnoticed, but today Arrowhead is a partially restored museum testifying to Pittsfield's pride in its Melville connection. *780 Holmes Road; 413-442-1793.*

The city library, the **Berkshire Athenaeum,** maintains a Herman Melville Memorial Room filled with books by, about, and owned by Melville—including the stunning Riverside edition of *Moby-Dick,* with Rockwell Kent illustrations, which signaled the resurgence of Melville's literary stock in the 1930s. The library also owns many Melville artifacts, including the Turkish slippers and tomahawk pipe that once hung over the fireplace at Arrowhead, and the bread box in which the author's widow, Elizabeth Shaw Melville, stashed his manuscripts after his death.

The prize is the beautiful mahogany desk where Melville penned *Billy Budd* at his 26th Street home in Manhattan. A curious motto that could almost have been Ahab's is inscribed in the cubbyhole at the back of Mrs. Melville's smaller desk: "To Know All is to Forgive All." *1 Wendell Avenue; 413-499-9486.*

The nearby **Berkshire Museum** shares much of Melville's operatic response to landscape, especially in the galleries of large mid- and late-19th-century paintings on the second floor. Painters of the Hudson River School were active around Pittsfield, and many of their minor works envision the Housatonic Valley as a Wagnerian frontier landscape. An 1849 oil, *Great Barrington,* by Henry Antonio Wenzler Jr., depicts the village—complete with church steeple and mill building on the river—squatting beneath a hilltop farm. The landscape rolls back in successive stages all the way to the Taconic Range. Several Albert Bierstadt paintings of the Rocky Mountains and California redwoods carry the Romantic impulse ever westward to its ultimate, if overblown conclusion. On the ground level, the museum's old-fashioned natural history exhibits range far and wide—the miniature dioramas of the Arctic tundra and the Serengeti plains, for example. But they also stay intimately close to home, with cases of stuffed and mounted local birds and mammals, and encyclopedic displays of butterflies and insects. *39 South Street; 413-443-7171.*

■ HANCOCK SHAKER VILLAGE *map page 254, A-2*

Unlike many other utopian groups, the United Society of Believers in Christ's Second Appearing, as the Shakers called themselves, embraced profitable innovation. This celibate sect was, after all, one of the nation's most successful separatist communities, accumulating thousands of acres of farmland, pioneering mail-order seed catalogues, and inventing numerous agricultural and domestic appliances. The mystics also knew good land when they saw it. Hancock Shaker Village, a museum since the last Shakers left in 1960, is set on 1,200 acres of rich pasture and lush forest west of Pittsfield. The village preserves 20 Shaker buildings, including the 1793 Meetinghouse, the Round Stone Barn built in 1826, the massive Brick Dwelling from 1830, and a modest privy, as well as a working farm and herb garden that emphasize heirloom varieties and historic animal breeds. Even without the Shaker inhabitants, the cycle of the agricultural year still rules the land, and the museum celebrates the seasons with special events from ice harvesting to spring plowing to autumn reaping.

(top) Shakers could speak with members of the opposite gender in this meeting room.
(left) A Shaker apothecary, with bowls for mixing medicinal remedies.

The Shakers were founded by dissenting English Quakers who reached America in 1774, led by Mother Ann Lee, whose followers believed that she represented the spirit of Christ. The sect eventually numbered about 6,000 in 19 communities throughout New York, New England, Indiana, Kentucky, and Ohio. Hancock was established in 1790, and at its peak in the 1830s the village supported 300 celibate, pacifist members, who professed equality but separation of the sexes, held property in common, confessed their sins to each other, and revived themselves with the ecstatic, trembling worship that led outsiders to dub them "shaking Quakers." The group, which originally called itself the United Society of Believers in Christ's Second Appearing, eventually adopted the name Shakers.

The village claims to have the "largest and most representative collection of Shaker artifacts available to the public at an original Shaker site." On display here are furniture, tools, household objects, textiles, manuscripts, and inspirational art. *Route 20 at Route 41; 413-443-0188.*

■ TANGLEWOOD *map page 254, A-3*

Route 41 heading south from Hancock Shaker Village traverses the swampy bottomlands east of the Taconic Range to the erstwhile iron-smelting village of Richmond. Here Lenox Road departs east to cross a series of hills before spilling down to the broad green lawns of Tanglewood, the summer home of the Boston Symphony Orchestra since 1937. Nathaniel Hawthorne rented a small red farmhouse on the estate from the Tappan family in 1851 and—with characteristic

On the lawn at Tanglewood in 1947. (Boston Symphony Orchestra)

Seiji Ozawa conducting the Boston Symphony Orchestra at Tanglewood in the 1990s.

humor—complained about the beauty of the surroundings. "I often find myself gazing at Monument Mountain," he wrote, ". . . instead of at the infernal sheet of paper under my hand." He did, however, complete *The House of the Seven Gables* and *A Wonder Book for Boys and Girls* here.

Visitors to Tanglewood for the summer concert series are less prone to complaint. The 1937 concerts were plagued by rain, so the following year, the BSO constructed the open auditorium with an overhead roof known as "The Shed," which seats 5,000. Yet many concert goers prefer to brave the elements, purchasing lawn tickets and spreading out blankets (or even Persian carpets) to enjoy picnics as they wait for the music to begin. The picnics, like many things in the Berkshires, often have an air of ostentation. Silver bowls of iced caviar may not be as common as Tupperware containers of potato salad, but they do appear on occasion. Recitals and chamber music performances, including many by the students at the Tanglewood Summer Institute, take place in the Seiji Ozawa Hall, named for the former BSO maestro whose American career began as a Leonard Bernstein protégé at the summer institute. *Route 183; 413-637-5165 or 800-274-8499.*

■ LENOX *map page 254, A-3*

Over the decades, Tanglewood's programs have made Lenox the cultural hub of the Berkshires. **Shakespeare & Company,** recently relocated to a new campus within walking distance of downtown, stands as the other artistic pillar of the summer season. Under the direction of Tina Packer, the company has forged an international reputation for its galvanizing productions of Shakespeare's major and minor works—the very antithesis of frothy summer stock. *70 Kemble Street; 413-637-3353.*

From 1880 to 1900, during America's self-styled Gilded Age, the new rich—Vanderbilts, Carnegies, and Westinghouses—discovered Lenox and transformed it, building immense summer "cottages" with names like Blantyre and Cranwell that stand today as monuments to Europhilia. The original owners of Bellfontaine would never have called their estate Canyon Ranch. They might, however, have enjoyed the pampering that the modern spa offers on the site of their old mansion. Lenox remains a fashionable retreat for New Yorkers, in particular, who inhabit such 19th-century mansions as Blantyre and Wheatleigh as inn guests today.

The **Museum of the Gilded Age at Ventfort Hall** typifies the country houses

built by wealthy New Yorkers at the turn of the 19th century. The Elizabethan Revival manse of brick and Longmeadow red stone is filled with period decoration—stained glass, elaborate plaster ceilings, complex wood paneling, and carved architectural details. *104 Walker Street; 413-637-3206.*

Novelist Edith Wharton had, perhaps, more taste than her fellow rusticators. Born Edith Jones to the family for whom the phrase "keeping up with the Joneses" was coined, she published her first book in 1897 at age 25, *The Decoration of Houses.* She put her theories into practice five years later when she commissioned

Edith Wharton. (Beinecke Library)

MATTERS OF TASTE

Before beginning to decorate a room it is essential to consider for what purpose the room is to be used. It is not enough to ticket it with some general designation as "library," "drawing-room," or "den." The individual tastes and habits of the people who are to occupy it must be taken into account; it must be not "a library," or "a drawing-room," but the library or the drawing-room best suited to the master or mistress of the house which is being decorated. Individuality in house-furnishing has seldom been more harped upon than at the present time. That cheap originality which finds expression in putting things to uses for which they were not intended is often confounded with individuality; whereas the latter consists not in an attempt to be different from other people at the cost of comfort, but in the desire to be comfortable in one's own way, even though it be the way of a monotonously large majority. It seems easier to most people to arrange a room like some one else's than to analyze and express their own needs. Men, in these matters, are less exacting than women, because their demands, besides being simpler, are uncomplicated by the feminine tendency to want things because other people have them, rather than to have things because they are wanted.

—Edith Wharton and Ogden Codman Jr., *The Decoration of Houses,* 1897

The Mount, modeled on an English country estate with bits and pieces of French and Italian detail that amused her. Although she was the first female novelist to win the Pulitzer Prize (for *The Age of Innocence*), she was more proud of her work on the house and its gardens. In a letter to her lover Morton Fullerton, she wrote, "I am amazed at the success of my efforts. Decidedly, I'm a better landscape gardener than novelist, and this place, every line of which is my own work, far surpasses *The House of Mirth*." Nonetheless, she left The Mount in 1911 to move permanently to Paris. The house and gardens were restored to Wharton's heyday in time for the property's 2002 centennial and are open for tours June through early November. *2 Plunkett Street; 413-637-1899.*

The grand "cottage" style was so entrenched in the Berkshires that a *Town & Country* headline proclaimed "Mutiny in the Berkshires" when artists George L. K. Morris and Suzy Frelinghuysen constructed their home on 46 acres adjacent to Tanglewood on the eve of World War II. Blending aspects of Southwest adobe with the International Bauhaus style, the **Frelinghuysen-Morris House** reflects

Edith Wharton's library at The Mount. (The Mount)

staunchly Modernist positions about both art and life. Yet the home seems very personal, with the couple's own abstract paintings hanging on the white walls next to works by their friends and contemporaries, including Picasso, Braque, Leger, and Gris. Morris and Frelinghuysen studied fresco technique at the Art Students League in New York to create the frescoes that appear over the living room fireplace and in the dining room. *Tours July 4–Columbus Day; 84 Hawthorne Street; 413-637-0166.*

Despite the town's concentration of wealth, the leafy center of Lenox is surprisingly quiet and modest. It's an easy place to spend a pleasant afternoon browsing the upscale boutiques. Of all the Berkshire villages, Lenox has the greatest concentration of serious galleries showing fine art, folk art, and art in craft media. When you need a break, there are coffee and ice-cream shops and a few restaurants with flower-decked patios. One of the village's older structures, elegant **Lenox Academy** houses the **Lenox Historical Society Museum** (65 Main Street; 413-637-1824). Displays include a sled similar to the one that figured in the pivotal accident scene of Edith Wharton's novel *Ethan Frome.*

■ STOCKBRIDGE *map page 254, A-3*

"In Lenox you are estimated, in Stockbridge you are esteemed," a Stockbridge aristocrat once informed a Lenox parvenu. Ironically, "old money" Stockbridge was immortalized for most Americans in 1967 by Norman Rockwell, the country's most populist artist, when he depicted its Main Street at Christmas. And on the first Sunday in December, when the town stages a live re-creation of Rockwell's painting, even the obliging late afternoon sky seems to turn just the right shade of pink.

The magic moments might continue when you repair to the **Red Lion Inn** after the festivities. Opened in 1773, destroyed by fire and rebuilt in 1896, this rambling establishment, crammed with antiques and oddball memorabilia, has had the good sense to disregard fashion. The smell of roast beef rather than potpourri greets you when you wander in off the enormous porch, and the waiters are busy serving, not reciting ludicrous specials. *30 Main Street; 413-298-5545.*

The Red Lion has also seen action. When 100 rebels involved in Shays's Rebellion looted Stockbridge in 1787, they occupied the inn while the sheriff hid in a wardrobe. After a night of plotting and revelry, they marched the next morning to their defeat at Great Barrington. The guest list has also included Presidents Cleveland, McKinley, Coolidge, and both Roosevelts; as well as Nathaniel Hawthorne, Henry Wadsworth Longfellow, John Wayne, and Bob Dylan—all of whom, no doubt, the Red Lion took in its generous stride.

The restored **Mission House** on Main Street was built in 1739 for Rev. John Sergeant, the first missionary to the Mukhekanews, or Stockbridge Indians. He is buried alongside his Christianized flock in the adjacent Village Cemetery. Provided with 6 square miles of town land and elected to town office, the Mukhekanews served as scouts during the Revolution, when their chief was killed in action. But this counted for little in subsequent transactions with the double-dealing settlers. The disillusioned tribe migrated to New York in 1785 and finally to Wisconsin. The Mission House has a collection of period furnishings, including a bookcase and chairs that belonged to Sergeant. The Colonial garden surrounding the house features herbs and bright perennials popular in the 18th century. *Tours Memorial Day–Columbus Day; 19 Main Street; 413-298-3239.*

Two other houses illustrate Stockbridge's development from missionary outpost to playground. The **Merwin House** (14 Main Street; 413-298-4703), a Federal-style jewel built around 1825 and doubled in size around 1900, reveals the cultural and decorative tastes of the town's 19th-century aristocrats, while

Naumkeag (5 Prospect Hill Road; 413-298-3239), a 23-room mansion and formal estate outside town, reflects the Choate family's appetite for novelty. Completed in 1886 for New York lawyer Joseph Hodges Choate, Naumkeag houses an extensive Chinese porcelain collection and a 16th-century Flemish tapestry. Its gardens, laid out by Fletcher Steele, feature a birch-lined stairway that you might call art deco Oriental. It is open for tours Memorial Day to Columbus Day. Naumkeag was designed by Stanford White, architect to the New York elite; he also created the main playhouse of the **Berkshire Theatre Festival** (6 Main Street; 413-298-5536), one of the oldest summer theaters in the nation.

Stockbridge has proved as salutary for artists as for millionaires. Sculptor Daniel Chester French described his estate, **Chesterwood,** as "six months in heaven," and drew inspiration from the landscape for his often inspiring sculpture. French's name is perhaps less well known than Norman Rockwell's, but some of his art is just as familiar, including the *Seated Lincoln* at the Lincoln Memorial in Washington D.C. and *The Minute Man* in Concord, one of his earliest commissions. French built his Stockbridge studio in 1898, incorporating railroad tracks through the barn doors so he could periodically roll immense marble statues out-

Stockbridge Main Street at Christmas *(1967), by Norman Rockwell.*
(Norman Rockwell Family Agency)

STARSTRUCK

Naturally, the arrival of someone like Duke Wayne or Frank Sinatra caused a flurry of excitement in Stockbridge. Having Norman Rockwell and his guests around was more fun than a three-ring circus and great for the town's tourist industry. If it wasn't a movie star showing up for a portrait sitting, it might be someone like the fried-chicken tycoon Colonel Sanders, a big-wheel politico, or just some run-of-the-mill Texas oil multimillionaire or Wall Street mogul.

—Donald Walton, *A Rockwell Portrait,* 1978

doors to study them by natural light. The studio is displayed almost as if French were next door on the porch of the farmhouse, sipping iced tea and enjoying the mountain view. As you explore the lawns and trails, you can also enjoy the outdoor installations of Chesterwood's annual contemporary sculpture exhibition. *Tours May–Oct.; 4 Williamsville Road; 413-298-3579.*

Closer to the center of Stockbridge, the **Norman Rockwell Museum** occupies one of the most beautiful hillsides in the area. On a spring afternoon, if you sit outside Rockwell's small studio (moved here from his South Street home) and watch the Housatonic River execute a graceful bend, you could suspect that the wall of birdsong is a recorded broadcast—until you notice the red-winged black-birds, mockingbirds, thrushes, and warblers darting between the trees. Picnickers are welcome and it seems a shame to go inside. But it is worth it.

Rockwell spent 25 years in Stockbridge before his death in 1978 and called the place "the best of America, the best of New England." His comforting and com-passionate vision of small-town life was most famously captured in 321 cover paintings for the *Saturday Evening Post.* They not only struck a popular chord, but also earned him some surprisingly high-tone admirers. John Updike once wrote that Rockwell's commercial art "always stood out by virtue of an extra intensity, a need . . . to provide a little more than the occasion strictly demanded."

Other fans include Robert A. M. Stern, the architect of the elegant museum, and filmmaker Steven Spielberg, a major donor to the campaign that resulted in the Rockwell holdings moving here from cramped quarters in the Old Corner

The summer studio of sculptor Daniel Chester French.

Baldwin's Vanilla Shop has been a Stockbridge fixture for more than a century.

House in Stockbridge. The museum owns the world's largest collection of Rockwell paintings, including the original oils used for magazine covers. Peter, the artist's youngest son, says Rockwell was fascinated with oil painting: "My father painted way beyond what he knew could be reproduced. Underneath it all, he adored the act of painting—look at how much fun he's having." *Route 183; 413-298-4100.*

■ LEE *map page 254, A-3*

Rockwell often painted the people and places of Stockbridge, but one of his most memorable images depicts a kindhearted policeman counseling a runaway as they sit on stools in Joe's Diner, on Main Street in neighboring Lee. Joe's is still here, as is Steve's Barber Shop downtown, with its spinning striped pole. Lee even manages to hold tight to its old-fashioned dime store, H. A. Johanson 5 & 10, which is also the bus terminal. The neighboring communities of Lenox and Stockbridge may have gone silk-stocking, but Lee has remained resolutely white-socked. It is also home to one of the last dairies to deliver milk to its customers in glass bottles: **High Lawn Farm.** Alas, if you stop in to purchase milk or cream, you'll get it in plastic jugs. *535 Summer Street; 413-243-0672.*

Not everything about Lee springs quite so directly from a Rockwell canvas, however. East of town, Route 20 begins to climb into the Berkshire Hills, a path known to drovers as Jacob's Ladder. Slightly less than 6 miles east of Lee center, just over the **Becket** town line, the pioneer modern dancer and choreographer Ted Shawn created a summer dance festival at a hilltop farm (during the 19th century a stop on the Underground Railroad) that he called **Jacob's Pillow.** Eclectic programming that blends urban and folk dance, mime, and ballet in a vigorous cross-fertilization has been a hallmark of Jacob's Pillow since its founding in 1933. The festival, which has been lauded by the likes of Mikhail Baryshnikov and Mark Morris, consists of dance concerts, free outdoor performances, lectures, demonstrations, and master classes. *358 George Carter Road, Becket; 413-243-0745 (box office) or 413-637-1322 (out of season).*

You Can Get Anything You Want

"I want tell you about the town of Stockbridge, Massachusetts," says Arlo Guthrie in his 1966 tale of a Thanksgiving trip to the dump gone awry. "They got three stop signs, two police officers, and one police car . . . ."

Some things haven't changed much since the 1960s, and Alice's Restaurant, immortalized in Guthrie's song of the same name, is still "around the back" in spirit, if not in name, at Theresa's Stockbridge Café, where the menu is a mélange of vegetarian and what can only be called Massachusetts Mexican.

Whatever indignities he might have suffered at the hands of Officer Obie, Guthrie seems to bear no grudges and has made his home quietly in the Berkshires since his dump-going days. His song "Massachusetts" was adopted by the Legislature as the official folk song of Massachusetts in July 1981.

Trinity Church, on the north end of Great Barrington, is the landmark property known in hippie lore as the home of Ray and Alice Brock, who allowed their garbage to pile up but also served a "Thanksgiving dinner that couldn't be beat."

Today the building, best known as Arlo's Church, is the interfaith Guthrie Center, with drop-in spiritual programs on weekdays and, during the summer, folksinger and singer-songwriter performances Thursday through Saturday nights. During concerts, the center serves food from Theresa's Café. Attendees are asked to bring canned goods for the food program.

Theresa's Stockbridge Café, 30 Main Street (rear), Stockbridge; 413-298-5465. Guthrie Center, 4 Van Deusenville Road, Great Barrington; 413-528-1955.

Ted Shawn and his Men Dancers perform Dance of the Ages *in the 1930s, the decade Shawn started the Jacob's Pillow festival. (Jacob's Pillow)*

Fall at Butternut Basin, a family-owned ski resort near Great Barrington.

■ **GREAT BARRINGTON AREA** *map page 254, A-4*

South of Stockbridge, Route 183 plays tag with the Housatonic River and skirts **Monument Mountain,** where David Dudley Jr. introduced Nathaniel Hawthorne to Herman Melville during a hike in August 1850. Not to be upstaged by this literary conjunction, nature staged a violent thunderstorm, and the group was forced to hunker down and drink Heidsieck champagne from a single silver mug. Lightning snapped, verses flew, and Melville teetered on a ledge, demonstrating how mariners haul in their sheets. Both of the trails leading to the summit—the 1.25-mile Indian Monument Trail and the steeper 0.75-mile Hickey Trail—take about an hour to climb.

Even if you don't make the ascent, nature is still an exhibitionist here, staging pyrotechnic extravaganzas during summer thunderstorms and rolling out shameless views of farmland and forested hillside. The pretty town of Great Barrington has been the site of two historic military engagements. In 1676, during King Philip's War, English troops slaughtered a band of fleeing Narragansetts as they tried to ford the Housatonic River. And in 1787, the Housatonic Valley branch of

Shays's Rebellion ended in Great Barrington with two fatalities on each side when the Sheffield militia defeated the 100 rebels who had spent the preceding night in Stockbridge. And the town has other claims to fame. It was the birthplace (in 1798) of Anson Jones, the last president of the Republic of Texas, and (in 1868) of W. E. B. Du Bois, the writer, educator, and civil rights pioneer. In 1886, the inventor William Stanley demonstrated the practical use of alternating current for street lights and made Great Barrington one of the first towns anywhere with electricity in its homes.

Great Barrington is the unofficial capital of the rural area south of Stockbridge that welcomed the counterculture of the 1960s with relatively open arms. Downtown Great Barrington has largely shed its hippie glad rags, thanks to an influx of permanent (or semipermanent) residents from Manhattan. Craft and folk art galleries compete with antiques shops and upscale home decor emporia. A preppy men's clothier dating from 1947 also rents tuxedos for special occasions. Several restaurants aspire to last year's hottest dishes from New York's TriBeCa. But not all the change is forced. Some truly inspired restaurants (Verdura comes to mind) celebrate the local agricultural bounty with inventive menus, and **Barrington Coffee Roasters** (955 South Main Street; 413-528-0998) has finally made it possible to get a decent cup of coffee.

Great Barrington also harbors the fine arts. The **Aston Magna Festival** (413-528-3595), based in St. James Church on Route 7, is the oldest American summer festival of baroque, classical, and early romantic music performed on period instruments. The **Berkshire Opera Company** (413-644-9988) presents three operas per summer in a 700-seat vaudeville house built in 1905, the Mahaiwe Theatre. The next town south, Sheffield, is home to the **Barrington Stage Company** (413-528-8888), which produces a dual summer season of mainstream theater and experimental new works to much acclaim.

Honestly, culture is less of a draw in **Sheffield** than antiques. It is the oldest town in the Berkshires, settled in 1725, and its main drag, Route 7, both north and south of the village, is lined with antiques dealers whose goods range from cheap Depression glass to extremely pricey 18th-century American furniture. Even more upscale dealers are located southwest of Great Barrington in **South Egremont,** where the **Splendid Peasant** (Route 23 at Sheffield Road; 413-528-5755) sets a museum-level standard—and auction-gallery prices—for the American folk art it sells.

South of Sheffield in Ashley Falls is **Bartholomew's Cobble,** a nature preserve along 2 miles of the Housatonic River that shyly reveals its treasures to the attentive walker. There are 53 species of fern, 500 different wildflowers, and 240 recorded species of birds in these fields and riverbanks. But the allure is not merely a matter of statistics. On a summer morning, the stillness and beauty settles in on you as you walk past yellow poplars and giant cottonwoods rarely found in this region. Even the turkey vulture above you, patrolling the sky, seems benevolent. *Weatogue Road, off Route 7A, Ashley Falls; 413-229-8600.*

Bash Bish Falls, the most dramatic waterfall in southern New England, lies within Mount Washington State Forest. It is most accessible from the parking lot on the New York side of the state line, along Route 344. As you stroll the woodland path to the 80-foot cataract, you can contemplate the delightfully sentimental tale of Bash Bish, an Indian maiden who, legend says, paddled her canoe over the falls to escape the clutches of pursuing white trappers. Her apparition is said to appear in the pool on moonlit nights. *Falls Road, Mount Washington; 413-528-0330.*

The hill towns east of Great Barrington are dotted with quirky surprises. The Turner & Cook company made buggy whips in **Southfield** from 1792 to 1977. The rather decrepit-looking factory on Norfolk Road has since been transformed into the **Buggy Whip Factory Antique Market Place,** where 20th-century collectibles are sold. A video documentary that runs continuously shows old-timers discussing and demonstrating their anachronistic craft. *Norfolk Road, Southfield; 413-229-3576.*

Route 23 heading eastward from Great Barrington is a particularly mild and scenic way to cross the Berkshire Hills to the Connecticut River Valley. If you are passing through the town of Monterey around 5 P.M., stop by the **Rawson Brook Farm** (New Marlborough Road; 413-528-2138), where you can watch the goats being milked to produce Monterey Chevre. In Otis, detour briefly north on Route 8 to visit the country store at **Otis Poultry Farm** (1570 North Main Road; 413-269-4438), the "home of the custom laid egg."

Stopovers such as these are gentle reminders that western Massachusetts, for all the wealth and urban airs of its summertime visitors, remains essentially an agricultural world.

The southern Berkshires.

■ TRAVEL BASICS

Getting Around: Enter the Berkshires in the north on Route 2 or in the south from the Massachusetts Turnpike. Route 7 runs the north-south length of the Berkshire Valley, linking the towns along the Housatonic River in the south with the Hoosic River Valley in the north at Williamstown. Follow any side road, numbered or not, that runs beside a brook and you will swiftly enter the land of Yankee farm country.

Climate: Mount Greylock is the barometer of season in the Berkshires, forecasting winter when its upper reaches whiten, promising spring as its southern slopes green. Berkshire Valley weather is moderate—reaching the mid-80s Fahrenheit in the summer, single digits in the winter. Hill towns are invariably cooler, often dropping below zero in mid-winter and remaining breezy and cool during August's dog days.

PRACTICAL INFORMATION

■ AREA CODES AND TIME ZONE

The state's area codes are 413 for the west; 978 and 351 for the northeast and north central portion; 617 and 857 for Boston; 781 and 339 for the areas near Boston; and 508 and 774 for the southern central portion as well as Cape Cod and the islands. Massachusetts is in the Eastern time zone.

■ METRIC CONVERSIONS

1 foot = .305 meters   1 mile = 1.6 kilometers   1 pound = .45 kilograms
Centigrade = Fahrenheit temperature minus 32, divided by 1.8

■ CLIMATE

Fall is the ideal time to visit Massachusetts, as temperatures are mild and there is little precipitation. Fall foliage schedules change each year, but from late September through the end of October, the state's trees are ablaze with color. Winter throughout the state is cold, with temperatures often dipping into the 20s Fahrenheit. Spring can be moist and windy, and summer is hot and humid, with temperatures in the upper 80s throughout July and August. Coastal areas and hill towns remain cool.

■ GETTING THERE AND AROUND

■ BY AIR

Logan International Airport (BOS) receives flights from many domestic and international carriers. *I-93 North, Exit 20; 617-561-1800 or 800-235-6426; www.massport.com/logan.*

T. F. Green State Airport (PVD), 10 miles south of Providence, Rhode Island, is convenient to eastern Massachusetts. *U.S. 1, Warwick; 401-737-4000; www.pvdairport.com.*

Bradley International Airport (BDL), in Windsor, Connecticut, is served by several U.S. carriers and is convenient to destinations in Massachusetts. *Schoephoster Road off I-91, Exit 40, Windsor Locks; 860-292-2000; www.bradleyairport.com.*

■ By Car

The Massachusetts Turnpike (I-90, or "Mass Pike," as locals call it) heads into Boston from the west; take I-93 from the north or south. U.S. 1 heads north from Boston to the North Shore. Route 128, I-95, and I-93 connect to form a loop around Boston, traveling south to Braintree, west to Newton and north to Burlington. Route 128 continues north from this loop toward Salem and the tip of Gloucester and Rockport; I-95 proceeds north to Newburyport and beyond. To get to Cape Cod, choose either U.S. 3 or I-495; on a summer Friday, expect delays.

The Massachusetts Turnpike links the state's western and central regions to Boston. A far more scenic, if also more clogged, highway runs east-west along the northern tier of the state: Route 2, known as the Mohawk Trail in the Berkshires and Connecticut River Valley. This same road continues east through northern Worcester County along the Johnny Appleseed Trail, passes through Concord, and penetrates metropolitan Boston on the western edge of Cambridge.

In the Berkshires, the principal north-south road is Route 7, which more or less follows the contours of the Berkshire Valley on the west side of Mount Greylock. The Connecticut River Valley has two main roads that parallel the north-south course of the river. The older road is U.S. 5 (known as Route 5), which plays tag with Routes 10 and 116 for much of the distance. Intense traffic along this road led to the creation of I-91, the fast route designed to let New Yorkers skip over Massachusetts in their rush to Vermont. Getting south to north in Central Massachusetts is no simple task, though the I-190/I-290/I-395 chain of highways, still under partial construction, does link Route 2 to the Massachusetts Turnpike.

■ By Train

Amtrak serves Boston with Northeast Corridor trains from New York, Washington, D.C., and other East Coast cities. Other lines service Worcester, Framingham, Springfield, and the Berkshires. *800-872-7245; www.amtrak.com.*

■ By Bus

Bonanza Bus Lines (800-556-3815; *www.bonanzabus.com*) and **Peter Pan Lines** (800-237-8747; *www.peterpanbus.com*) serve Massachusetts from East Coast cities. **Greyhound** (800-231-2222; *www.greyhound.com*) and its affiliates provide service from many destinations across the country. The **MBTA** *(800-392-6100; www.mbta.com)* serves the Boston area with subways, buses, and commuter rail.

A woman prepares fried dough, a speciality at the Portuguese Bakery in Provincetown.

■ FOOD

Known for centuries for fish, chowder, and standards like Yankee pot roast, in recent years Boston has developed a more diverse culinary scene. You'll find everything from Thai to Turkish in restaurants these days. Look to the North End for authentic Italian, Chinatown for tasty dim sum, and downtown for gourmet cuisine. In warm months, venture to the beach for lobsters and clams.

Small family farms figure significantly in the local cuisine of Central Massachusetts, the Connecticut River Valley, and the Berkshires. These areas produce most of the state's tree fruits, maple syrup, poultry, and dairy products. Yankee cooking predominates, though many spots in the Connecticut River Valley treat soybeans as food rather than fodder.

Some of the best places in the state to eat are the vintage diners of Central Massachusetts, and the pleasures of New American cooking can be found in the arts havens of the Berkshires.

■ LODGING

Chain hotels dominate Boston's lodging scene, though there are historic establishments, such as the Omni Parker House. Luxury standouts include the Boston Harbor Hotel, properties operated by Four Seasons and Ritz-Carlton, and the boutique hotel Nine Zero. The scale is reduced on the North Shore, South Shore, and Cape Cod, with many inns, motels, and B&Bs from which to choose.

In the Berkshires, tiny tourist-court motels still dot the countryside, and country inns provide a feeling of distinct continuity with tradition. Within the environs of Lenox and Stockbridge, some "cottages" have become exclusive resorts, and in retro hip North Adams there is Porches, where workers' tenements have been transformed into luxury accommodations. A few business hotels and a sprinkling of chain motels provide most of the rooms in the Connecticut River Valley, though it's worth seeking out one of the many Victorian B&Bs. Both Berkshires and Connecticut Valley lodgings tend to be expensive. In Central Massachusetts, chain motels provide the lion's share of the lodging.

■ RESERVATION SERVICES

Berkshires. *413-268-7244; www.berkshirebnbhomes.com.*
Boston. *617-720-3540; www.boston-bnbagency.com.*
Cape Cod. *508-255-3824; www.bedandbreakfastcapecod.com.*
Nantucket. *508-257-9559; www.nantucketaccommodation.com.*

■ HOTEL AND MOTEL CHAINS

Best Western. *800-528-1234; www.bestwestern.com.*
Days Inn. *800-325-2525; www.daysinn.com.*
Doubletree. *800-222-8733; www.doubletree.com.*
Hilton Hotels. *800-445-8667; www.hilton.com.*
Holiday Inn. *800-465-4329; www.6c.com.*
Hyatt Hotels. *800-233-1234; www.hyatt.com.*
Marriott Hotels. *800-228-9290; www.marriott.com.*
Radisson. *800-333-3333; www.radisson.com.*
Ramada Inns. *800-272-6232; www.ramada.com.*
Ritz-Carlton. *800-241-3333; www.ritzcarlton.com.*
Sheraton. *800-325-3535; www.sheraton.com.*
Westin Hotels. *800-228-3000; www.westin.com.*

■ CAMPING

Massachusetts Campground Owners Assoc. *781-544-3475; www.campmass.com.*
Massachusetts State Parks. *877-422-6762; www.massparks.com.*
National Recreation Reservation Service. *877-444-6777; www.reserveusa.com.*

■ OFFICIAL TOURISM INFORMATION

State Office of Tourism. *617-973-8500; www.massvacation.com.*

Amherst Area. *413-253-0700; www.amherstchamber.com.*
Berkshires. *413-443-9186; www.berkshires.org.*
Cape Cod. *508-862-0700; www.capecodchamber.org.*
Concord. *978-369-3120; www.concordchamber.org.*
Franklin County. *413-773-9393; www.co.franklin.ma.us.*
Greater Boston. *www.bostonusa.com.*
Martha's Vineyard. *508-693-4486; www.mvy.com.*
Nantucket. *508-228-0925; www.nantucketchamber.org.*
New Bedford. *508-979-1745; www.ci.new-bedford.ma.us.*
Northampton. *413-587-0969; www.northamptonuncommon.com.*
North Berkshires. *413-663-3735; www.nberkshirechamber.com.*
Plymouth. *508-747-7525; www.visit-plymouth.com.*
Shelburne Falls. *413-625-2544; www.shelburnefalls.com.*
Worcester. *508-755-7400; www.worcester.org.*

■ USEFUL WEB SITES

Boston Globe. E-version of region's biggest daily newspaper. *www.boston.com/globe.*
Boston Phoenix. Arts weekly with extensive listings. *www.bostonphoenix.com.*
City of Cambridge. Local services, tourist information. *www.ci.cambridge.ma.*
Fodors.com. Massachusetts hotel, restaurant, and other listings. *www.fodors.com.*
Massachusetts Maple Producers. Pancake breakfasts and more. *www.massmaple.org.*
National Park Service. Freedom Trail, Cape Cod, and other NPS areas. *www.nps.gov.*
Society for the Preservation of New England Antiquities. *www.spnea.com.*
Valley Advocate. Connecticut River Valley coverage. *www.valleyadvocate.com.*
Vineyard Gazette. Resources for Martha's Vineyard. *www.vineyardgazette.com.*
Weather. WCVB-TV forecasts. *www.thebostonchannel.com/weather.*
Yankee Publishing. Tips, history, culture, and resources. *www.newengland.com.*

■ Festivals and Events

■ January
Boston Cooks. Three-week culinary event. *617-439-7700; www.bostoncooks.com.*

■ February
Opening of Sugarhouses. Pancakes and waffles with fresh maple syrup. *413-628-3912; www.massmaple.org.*

Railroad Hobby Show, West Springfield. Large, entertaining show. *413-737-2443.*

■ March
St. Patrick's Day Parades: The one in Boston (617-268-8525) is huge and raucous; in Holyoke (413-533-1700) it's also large, but more kid-friendly.

■ April
Annual Daffodil Festival, Nantucket. Indoor and outdoor events. *508-228-1700.*

Boston Marathon. America's oldest. *617-236-4505; www.bostonmarathon.org.*

Reenactment of the Battles of Lexington and Concord. *781-862-1703.*

■ May
Maritime Days, Cape Cod. Lighthouse tours and other events. *508-362-3828.*

Rhododendron Festival, Sandwich. Peak bloom time. *508-888-3300.*

■ June
Old Deerfield Craft Fair, Deerfield. Traditional crafts. *413-774-7476.*

Portuguese Festival, Blessing of Fleet, Provincetown. *www.capecodtravel.com.*

■ July
Boston Harborfest. Activities, cruises. *617-227-1886; www.bostonharborfest.com.*

Lowell Folk Festival. Great performers. *978-970-5000; www.lowellfolkfestival.org.*

Vineyard Artisans Fair, West Tisbury. Art, crafts, furniture making. *508-693-8989.*

■ **AUGUST**

Berkshire Music Festival, Great Barrington. Edgy new music. *www.berkfest.com.*

Boston Chamber Music Festival. International virtuosos perform. *617-349-0086.*

Feast of the Blessed Sacrament, New Bedford. Portuguese festival. *508-999-5200.*

Gloucester Waterfront Festival. Lobster bake, whale-watching. *978-283-1601.*

■ **SEPTEMBER**

The Big E, West Springfield. Agricultural fair. *413-737-2443; www.thebige.com.*

Boston Blues Week. Weeklong citywide celebration. *www.bluestrust.com.*

Boston Folk Festival. Musicians, barbecue, beer, and crafts. *617-287-6911.*

Bourne Scallop Fest, Buzzards Bay. *508-759-6000; www.capecodcanalchamber.org.*

Essex Clam Fest. Clams, any way you like them. *978-283-1601.*

Fall Foliage Fair, North Adams. *413-663-3735; www.nberkshirechamber.com.*

Franklin County Fair, Greenfield. *413-774-4282; www.fcas.com.*

Three Apples Storytelling Festival, Harvard. Yarn-spinners' confab. *617-499-9529.*

■ **OCTOBER**

Haunted Happenings, Salem. Costume parade and contest. *www.salem.org.*

Lowell Celebrates Kerouac. Tours of the writer's hometown. *877-537-6822.*

■ **NOVEMBER**

America's Hometown Thanksgiving Celebration, Plymouth. *508-747-7525.*

Annual Nantucket Noel. Tree lighting, caroling, and concerts. *508-228-1700.*

Festival of Trees, Pittsfield. More than 200 decorated trees. *413-443-7171.*

■ **DECEMBER**

First Night. Two of the best New Year's Eve celebrations are the one in Boston (www.firstnight.org) and the one in Northampton (413-584-7327).

I N D E X

COMPASS AMERICAN GUIDES

Alaska	Kentucky	Pennsylvania
American Southwest	Las Vegas	San Francisco
Arizona	Maine	Santa Fe
Boston	Manhattan	South Carolina
Chicago	Michigan	South Dakota
Coastal California	Minnesota	Southern New England
Colorado	Montana	Tennessee
Connecticut & Rhode Island	Nevada	Texas
Florida	New Hampshire	Utah
Georgia	New Mexico	Vermont
Gulf South: Louisiana, Alabama, Mississippi	New Orleans	Virginia
	North Carolina	Wine Country
Hawaii	Oregon	Wisconsin
Idaho	Pacific Northwest	Wyoming

Compass American Guides are available at special discounts for bulk purchases for sales promotions or premiums. Special editions, including personalized covers, excerpts of existing guides, and corporate imprints, can be created in large quantities for special needs. For more information, contact your local bookseller or write to Special Markets, Fodor's Travel Publications, 1745 Broadway, New York, NY 10019. Inquiries from Canada should be directed to your local Canadian bookseller or sent to Random House of Canada, Ltd., Marketing Department, 2775 Matheson Boulevard East, Mississauga, Ontario L4W 4P7. Inquiries from the United Kingdom should be sent to Fodor's Travel Publications, 20 Vauxhall Bridge Road, London, England SW1V 2SA.

ACKNOWLEDGMENTS

Compass American Guides would like to thank Chris Culwell and Kristin Moehlmann for their editorial contributions, Rachel Elson for copyediting the manuscript, and Ellen Klages for proofreading it. All photographs are by James Marshall unless otherwise credited below. Compass American Guides would like to thank the following institutions and individuals for the use of their photographs, illustrations, or both:

American Antiquarian Society, p. 25; **Battleship Cove,** p. 144; **Beinecke Library/Yale University, New Haven, Connecticut,** p. 268; **Boston Public Library,** p. 64; **Boston Symphony Orchestra,** p. 42 (Michael Lutch), 266 (Howard S. Babbitt Jr.); **Bowdoin College Museum of Art, Brunswick, Maine,** p. 124; **Concord Free Public Library,** p. 30; **Concord Museum,** p. 96; **Connecticut Valley Historical Museum,** p. 215; **Dr. Seuss National Memorial,** p. 214 (Jim Gambaro); **Eric Carle Museum of Picture Book Art,** p. 227; **Fall River Historical Society,** p. 145; **Joseph Garland,** p. 137; **Hancock Shaker Village,** p. 185; **Higgins Armory Museum,** p. 195; **Isabella Stewart Gardner Museum,** pp. 37, 78; **Jacob's Pillow,** p. 277 (Shapiro Studio); **Markham Johnson,** pp. 170, 171; **John Fitzgerald Kennedy Library,** p. 39; **James Lemass,** pp. 44, 53, 75, 76, 84, 91; **Library of Congress,** p. 50; **Library of Congress Congressional Portrait Collection,** p. 41 (LC-USZ62-98059); **Library of Congress Daguerreotype Collection,** p. 34 (LC-USZC4-7396); **Library of Congress Prints and Photographs Division,** pp. 35 (LC-USZ61-361), 36 (LC-USZ62-53518); **Library of Congress, Rare Book and Special Collections Division,** p. 22 (LC-USZC4-538); **Marblehead Historical Society,** p. 109; **MASS MoCA,** p. 257 (both by Arthur Evans); **Massachusetts Audubon Society, Ipswich River Wildlife Sanctuary,** p. 120 (Kay George); **Massachusetts Historical Society,** p. 26 (#667); **Massachusetts Office of Travel and Tourism** (Kindra Clineff), p. 118; **Jim McElholm,** p. 11, 243; **The Mount,** p. 270; **Museum of Fine Arts, Boston,** pp. 79 (gift of Landon T. Clay), 114; **Museum of Modern Art/Art Resource NY,** p. 161; **Museum of Science,** p. 80; **Naismith Memorial Basketball Hall of Fame,** p. 43; **National Archives,** pp. 29 (NWDNS-148-GW-811), 31 (NWDNS-148-CD-4); **National Oceanic & Atmospheric Administration,** pp. 111, 168; **National Park Service, Lowell National Historical Park,** p. 33, 130; **New Bedford Whaling Museum,** pp. 147, 148–149; **Norman Rockwell Family Agency,** pp. 272–273; **Peabody Essex Museum, Salem,** pp. 99, 104; **Pilgrim Hall Museum, Plymouth,** p. 134; **Shelburne Museum, Shelburne, Vermont,** p. 101; **Thomas P. O'Neill Papers, John J. Burns Library, Boston College,** p. 38; **Williams College,** p. 261; **Worcester Historical Museum,** p. 192.

■ ABOUT THE AUTHORS

Cambridge residents Patricia Harris and David Lyon write extensively about art, travel, and food. They are frequent contributors to *Yankee Magazine's Travel Guide to New England*, and their articles have been published in *American Craft*, the *Boston Globe, Food Arts*, and other publications. Patricia and David are the authors of the upcoming *Compass Cape Cod*.

A native of Ireland and a resident of New Salem, Anna Mundow is a correspondent for the *Irish Times* and a book critic for the *Boston Globe*. A regular contributor to *Newsday*, she has provided commentary on BBC Radio, Monitor Radio, and WGBH television. The author of *Compass Southern New England*, from which this book was adapted, Anna has also written for the *Los Angeles Times, Mirabella, Boston Magazine*, the *Manchester Guardian*, and many other publications.

Medway resident Lisa Oppenheimer is the author of *Around the City with Kids: Boston* and *Around the City with Kids: Los Angeles*, both for Fodor's, and is the family travel columnist of the Fodors.com Web site. Lisa also contributes regularly to *Disney, Family Life*, and *Parents* magazines.

■ ABOUT THE PHOTOGRAPHER

James Marshall began making photographs as a teenager in his basement darkroom. Since 1978 he has traveled extensively throughout Asia, North America, and Europe, covering events and documenting cultures. Along the way, he produced and edited *Hong Kong: Here Be Dragons; A Day in the Life of Thailand;* and *Planet Vegas: A Portrait of Las Vegas*. James's photographs appear in *Compass Southern New England* and *Compass Connecticut & Rhode Island*.